Contracting-out Welf

Broadening Perspectives on Social Policy
Series Editor: Bent Greve

The object of this series, in this age of re-thinking on social welfare, is to bring fresh points of view and to attract fresh audiences to the mainstream of social policy debate.

The choice of themes is designed to feature issues of major interest and concern, such as are already stretching the boundaries of social policy.

This is the eighteenth collection of papers in the series. Previous volumes include:

Contracting-out Welfare Services

Comparing National Policy Designs for Unemployment Assistance

Edited by

Mark Considine and Siobhan O'Sullivan

WILEY Blackwell

This edition first published 2015
Originally published as Volume 48, Issue 2 of *Social Policy & Administration*
Book compilation © 2015 John Wiley & Sons, Ltd

Registered Office
John Wiley & Sons, Ltd, The Atrium, Southern Gate, Chichester, West Sussex,
PO19 8SQ, UK

Editorial Offices
350 Main Street, Malden, MA 02148-5020, USA
9600 Garsington Road, Oxford, OX4 2DQ, UK
The Atrium, Southern Gate, Chichester, West Sussex, PO19 8SQ, UK

For details of our global editorial offices, for customer services, and for
information about how to apply for permission to reuse the copyright material in
this book please see our website at www.wiley.com/wiley-blackwell.

The rights of Mark Considine and Siobhan O'Sullivan to be identified as the
authors of the editorial material in this work have been asserted in accordance
with the UK Copyright, Designs and Patents Act 1988.

Library of Congress Cataloging-in-Publication data is available for this book.

ISBN 9781119016496 (paperback)

A catalogue record for this book is available from the British Library.

Cover image: ©wakila/iStock

Set in 10.5/11pt New Baskerville by SPi Publisher Services, Pondicherry, India
Printed and bound in Malaysia by Vivar Printing Sdn Bhd

1   2015

CONTENTS

Contents

List of Contributors

Patrizia Aurich, Institute for Work, Skills and Training, University of Duisburg-Essen, Duisburg, Germany

Avishai Benish, Paul Baerwald School of Social Work and Social Welfare, the Hebrew University of Jerusalem, Jerusalem, Israel

Rik van Berkel, Utrecht School of Governance, Utrecht University, Utrecht, the Netherlands

Elle Carter, Department of Geography, University of Sheffield, Sheffield, UK

Mark Considine, Faculty of Arts, University of Melbourne, Melbourne, Australia

Vanesa Fuertes, Employment Research Institute, Business School, Edinburgh Napier University, Edinburgh, UK

Paolo R. Graziano, Department of Institutional Analysis and Public Management, Bocconi University, Milan, Italy

Matthias Knuth, Institute for Work, Skills and Training, University of Duisburg-Essen, Essen, Germany

Phuc Nguyen, School of Social and Political Sciences, University of Melbourne, Melbourne, Australia

Siobhan O'Sullivan, School of Social and Political Sciences, University of Melbourne, Melbourne, Australia

James Rees, Third Sector Research Centre, University of Birmingham, Birmingham, UK

Isabel Shutes, Department of Social Policy, London School of Economics, London, UK

Ludo Struyven, Faculty of Social Sciences and Research Institute for Work and Society, University of Leuven, Leuven, Belgium

Rebecca Taylor, Third Sector Research Centre, University of Birmingham, Birmingham, UK

Adam Whitworth, Department of Geography, University of Sheffield, Sheffield, UK

Katharina Zimmermann, Department of Social Services, CvO University of Oldenburg, Oldenburg, Germany

Introduction: Contracting-out Welfare Services: Comparing National Policy Designs for Unemployment Assistance

Mark Considine and Siobhan O'Sullivan

With welfare reformers in almost every country experimenting with forms of privatization and what its advocates have called 'supervisory approaches to poverty' or 'a new behaviouralism', it is timely to present this book. Dedicating a book to the governance of quasi-markets in welfare services attests to the momentous nature of the radical redesign the welfare state has undergone over the past two decades. A similar reinvention has occurred across numerous policy fields and has affected most social services. Yet nowhere have the changes been more radical, and the results more pronounced, than in the realm of welfare-to-work, employment services privatization and jobseeker activation. All too often, social policy commentators are forced to lament that reforms were 'oversold' by policy makers, things at the local level did not change all that much or major parts of the reform agenda of governments were effectively subverted by system inertia. Not in the case of employment services.

In 1992, Lawrence Mead argued that:

> dependency politics is growing in importance not only in the United States, but in the West as a whole. In Europe, disputes over the social behavior of low income groups, often immigrant communities, have become more contentious than traditional conflicts between organized labour and capitalism (Mead 1992: 3–4).

Deep concern for the large number of citizens who had become permanently dependent on unemployment benefits or related forms of social security such as single-parent payments or disability pensions profoundly undermined whatever trust remained in large, bureaucratic, inflexible responses to poverty. By the 1990s, a spirited debate had surfaced on both the political left and the right, concerning the extent to which welfare entitlements had helped generate perverse effects, including the twin problems of state paternalism and dependency.

No government responded to this challenge with greater enthusiasm than Tony Blair's New Labour. They took to public service reform with a zeal not seen since Gladstone and with obvious gestures to the US and the heyday of welfare reform under Roosevelt. Political devolution, strategic partnerships at local level, the various 'New Deals' for those on benefits and a new enthusiasm for engaging the private sector created a powerful momentum throughout the public sector. Blair and Bill Clinton had also forged a temporary consensus around new centre-left policies which aimed to 'square the circle' by adopting part of the right's critique of welfare and of the effect of passive welfare, but joining it to a better funded program for increasing opportunity in both education and work.

These new principles of obligation and activation were hybridized and adapted to become a new regime of innovations across the Organisation for Economic Co-operation and Development (OECD), involving the strengthening of obligations for welfare recipients to earn their income support, the contracting-out of services and the reform of pension systems themselves to link them to workforce participation wherever possible.

Central to the response identified by many policy makers was the idea of New Public Management (NPM). According to the logic of NPM, traditional bureaucratic instruments based upon norms of standardized treatment and universal service are best replaced by outcome targets, quasi-market contracting and efforts to engage employers and other users in service delivery. Welfare and employment ministries in many OECD countries are now more likely to purchase services than to deliver them, more concerned with regulating contracts than managing public servants and are increasingly concerned with managing an economy of incentives and opportunistic manoeuvres than with traditional forms of bureaucratic organization. Yet this spread of service outsourcing only tells part of the contemporary welfare-to-work story. Described elsewhere as 'a decisive turn away from universal state services and standardized responses to social problems' (Considine 2001: 2), in order to appreciate the vastly different conception of jobseeker assistance today, compared to just 15 years ago, one must also take account of the impact of a new notion of 'activation' which began to influence policy makers in the 1990s and challenged thinking about welfare entitlement.

California's Greater Avenues to Independence (GAIN) program had been the largest program of public assistance to the unemployed in the largest state in the US. In 1994, the Manpower Demonstration Research Corporation (MDRC), an influential non-profit evaluation agency, published the results of a three-year study of GAIN (Riccio et al. 1994). The evaluation drew 33,000 welfare recipients from the California welfare rolls and randomly assigned them to a study group and a control group. The conclusion was that the GAIN program itself was successful and that Riverside was the most successful county. The measures of success were the gains in earnings for those who undertook the program and the savings in welfare payments.

The Riverside model included a range of important differences compared to models trialed elsewhere. But despite multiple variables, the narrative that has developed around the Riverside case highlights a set of program features that have now achieved the status of accepted wisdom among policy makers. The first thing that evaluators noted about Riverside was that its managers made less commitment to education and training and certainly less to longer term educational deficits such as sending clients back to school to improve literacy and numeracy. Instead the local strategy was to focus upon job search and immediate placement into available job vacancies. Even where the job was not what a client was looking for or very happy about, the philosophy was to take this job now and then apply for a better one from the stronger position of being employed. Efforts were also made to reduce the capacity of clients to defer their job search obligations because of part-time work, training or childcare responsibilities. In all these cases, the program still required the client to participate in job search activities for up to 15 hours per week.

The staff in the program closely monitored their clients to see that they were active and motivated to take jobs that were offered and that they could resolve any issues that might make a successful job start more difficult. Having the right clothes, sorting out transportation and childcare, and having a clear understanding of the employers' expectations all played a part in this local strategy. The motivational message was strongly focused upon family values.

This commitment to what would later be called a 'work first' approach was complemented by very active engagement with local employers. Specialist staff with marketing skills were hired to manage these critical relationships with local employers. The key to success was the job agency's ability to offer employers immediate service so they would come to rely upon them for filling temporary vacancies and managing the stress of sudden departures. The promise was to send a suitable applicant the same day the employer lodged the request, to follow-up the placement and to see that he or she was happy with the resulting placement. The manager of the Riverside program also spent time promoting this pro-employer image in the local media and through existing employer networks. He further promoted a strong culture of performance among staff of the agency through his own motivational messaging and through the rapid dissemination of data about finding and filling vacancies.

While we might be unsure about what in particular made the Riverside model more successful than others, evidently it was an approach to employment assistance whose time had come. Critics of welfare were tired of hearing that clients lacked motivation, tended to avoid programs if they could and refused jobs if they felt something better would soon be available. Nor did the high cost of providing the educational skills missed at high school seem to these critics to be justified by the modest employment outcomes they appeared to produce. And most of all the growing coalition of welfare critics expressed dismay that local employers could have vacancies on their books, find it hard to get applicants or committed workers, while around the corner were welfare recipients sitting in an expensive public agency discussing other preferences they might have for work. Riverside became the poster child for program design throughout the OECD. What was needed was a program that was 'work first' but with tough requirements for participation and hard time limits for the receipt of benefits.

A new language of 'tough love' began to replace the liberal canon of entitlement. Where welfare programs worked best, they appeared to contain a good deal of pushing and prodding, and even stronger tactics to force claimants to take jobs. Plainly the new science of welfare had become an administrative discipline, a science of governance in which those delivering programs and those receiving them each had to be carefully activated through a new regime of exhortations and incentives, honed to achieve an explicit and exemplary change in behaviour. The tidal wave of administrative reform that would follow this shift in outlook by policy makers would carry as its leitmotif the charismatic figure of the Riverside manager, throwing the rule book of public assistance out the window with one hand and pointing all clients to the first available local job with the other. The new administrative methodology aimed to be uncompromising – no excuses accepted, no exceptions allowed. With that the contemporary notion of 'activation' was born. It would forever change the case manager/jobseekers relationship. It would also have serious implication for the purchasers/provider relationship as governments sought ways to employ and then activate contracted agencies in order to eventually activate the end user.

The willingness of policy makers to take radical steps in relation to welfare-to-work may be indicative of the service users' status. In short, those in receipt of employment assistance are more often than not poor and disenfranchised. This is particularly so in the case of the long-term unemployed. Is the state emboldened when service recipients are predominantly marginalized? Or is the explanation for the depth of the reforms to be found in the relationship between welfare-to-work and its new economy? After all, innovative labour market management now has material consequences for welfare recipients, employers, and perhaps most importantly, for those private for-profit and not-for-profit agencies that have grown wealthy and politically powerful as a result of their new roles in delivering these public services.

While we can only speculate as to the reasons why welfare-to-work has been the locus of significant policy experimentation, what is not in doubt is the widespread nature of the phenomenon. As the book's title 'Contracting-out Welfare Services: Comparing National Policy Designs for Unemployment Assistance' suggests, the widespread willingness of policy actors around the world to design and then redesign their welfare-to-work system makes this an ideal field for comparative policy analysis. In the Australian case, the approach to the public management of employment services taken by federal governments on both the right and the left has earned Australia an international reputation as a bold social policy reformer. Yet despite being the first country to introduce a fully privatized delivery model, steered by a rigorous contract management system and operated in a relatively benign labour market, the reform impetus has not achieved equilibrium and the Australian government has become involved in continual restructuring of the system. It is for this reason that we refer to Australian employment services policy process as 'the reform that never ends' (Considine 2005). But while the Australian experience is one of ambitious employment service redesign, this is by no means a uniquely Australian story. As the diversity of scholars featured in this collection demonstrates, the trajectory of reform is widespread, as is academic interest in the study, analysis and critique of the changes.

This volume represents a new high water mark in the field of employment services scholarship, yet participants draw on a much longer intellectual legacy. In particular, our contributing authors have all been influenced by research into NPM, social policy, public policy, activation, the welfare state, the third sector, 'flexsecurity', mission drift and quasi-markets. This book confirms employment services delivery as a discrete field of research and uses employment services as a case study to advance academic understanding in relation to a host of broader principles and concepts.

This book began as a round table hosted by the University of Melbourne in February 2013. The round table attracted chapters from ten speakers spanning seven countries. The round table audience included employment services PhD students and our industry partners Jobs Australia (JA), the National Employment Services Association (NESA) and Westgate Community Initiatives Group (WCIG). All round table participants were invited to submit an article for consideration, but submissions were also accepted from those who were unable to make the long journey to Australia.

The international perspective brought to bear on the topic is evidenced by the first two chapters, both of which take an international comparative approach. In Chapter 1, Katharina Zimmermann, Patrizia Aurich, Paolo R. Graziano and Vanesa Fuertes from Germany, Italy and the UK compare those three countries in relation to activation policy. In particular, the authors wish to identify the impact of 'marketized integrated activation policies' on different types of activation arrangements. In their own words:

'marketization in the delivery of activation policies strongly emphasizes both individual responsibility and the need of a broader scope of actors to ensure targeted services. However, the way these activation principles are translated into practice strongly depends on their implementation at the local level, framed by the discretion local actors have with regard to the marketized services' (p. 12).

An exploration of activation via marketization is well facilitated by a comparison of Germany, Italy and the UK, because each country has undertaken marketization to different extents, via various levels of government and the use of a range of policy mechanisms. The authors find that the local context matters and that local discretion and the local policy history inform how activation policy is translated into actual service delivery practice. In Chapter 2, Ludo Struyven from the Netherlands adopts a comparative approach examining the way in which quasi-markets developed in Australia, the Netherlands and Belgium. He asks:

what brought the two reform countries Australia and the Netherlands to make a similar choice for the restructuring of their PESs [public employment services]? How is it that Australia evolved after just a few years from an open to a closed market, whereas this did not happen in the Netherlands? [And] why did Belgium (Flanders) not opt in the period studied for a new administrative structure with more scope for market competition, despite a far-reaching reform plan? (p. 34).

He argues that the move towards service privatization does not necessarily equate to system convergence and that 'the three countries studied each follow their own path regarding the direction in which the system is evolving' (p. 48). Struyven carefully paints a complex picture and outlines the way in which various stakeholders influence system reform and re-reform.

Many of the countries examined in the two comparative chapters were used as case study jurisdictions by other contributing authors. Our own contribution, Chapter 3, coauthored with Phuc Nguyen, is focused on Australia. In it we consider the relationship between NPM and mission drift, from a unique perspective. We track the evolution of an Australian third-sector employment services provider as it grew from a small kitchen table, church-based charity into a $15 million enterprise. We complement that case study with data collected from CEOs and Boards of other not-for-profit employment services providers in order to investigate the extent to which large-scale government contracting has altered Board membership, process and ambition. We conclude that service privatization has changed the very nature of those who set the direction of third-sector service agencies. Those we interviewed emphasized the importance of being professional, business-like and emulating the for-profit sector. This raises important questions about the broader impact of employment services privatization. Is it changing the very nature of the third sector? Are employment services the types of services not-for-profits should be delivering? Furthermore, if not-for-profits feel driven to emulate the for-profit sector, do they remain distinctive? If yes, in what ways? And finally, does it matter?

In Chapter 4, Rik Van Berkel from Utrecht University's School of Governance focuses on the Dutch system and does so from a front-line perspective. He explores the dynamics between activation, 'risk selection' and the administration burden placed on client-facing staff. Van Berkel's study suggests that the relationship between the three is not as straightforward as might be imagined. Using extensive interview data, Van Berkel argues that on the question of risk selection, the process is complex and can happen at a range of points along the service continuum. He concludes that 'when studying processes of risk selection, research needs to analyze the entire service provision chain and to look at decisions taken by providers and purchasers throughout the service provision process' (p. 87).

Many social policy scholars, in particular employment services specialists, have been closely monitoring developments in the UK over the last three to five years. Two chapters are centred around the UK's bold reform agenda. In Chapter 5, Isabel Shutes and Rebecca Taylor from the London School of Economics (LSE) and the University of Birmingham respectively concentrate their analysis on the impact of conditionality in funding which they argue 'commodifies those out of work by attaching financial value to placing them in work' (p. 92). Within the context of the Work Programme, the authors find that conditionality in funding informs the types of agencies willing and able to deliver services, the 'mission' of those that do deliver services, the capacity of agencies to specialize and the willingness of providers to invest extensively in job-seekers. They also argue that it encourages 'creaming and parking'.

James Rees, Adam Whitworth and Eleanor Carter, Chapter 6, are also concerned with 'creaming and parking' within the context of recent UK employment services reforms. In their chapter, they find that despite careful system design aimed at minimizing adverse incentives, practices such as creaming and parking "were not just endemic […] they could also be seen as a rational response to the current payment by results model and its misalignment with the actual support needs of individual claimants across and within the claimant groups". (p. 116). The authors argue that funding differentiation between cohorts was the primary tool used by the policy architects to achieve their objective of 'differentiated universalism'. However, that design has not been effective as evidenced by different placement rates between different classification groups. Rees, Whitworth and Carter conclude that 'the Work Programme at present seems…to be reinforcing, exacerbating and making systemic the negative impacts of employment disadvantages' (p. 124).

In Chapter 7, Matthias Knuth provides a German perspective. He examines a special program known as 'Perspective 50plus', implemented to assist jobseekers over the age of 50 receiving minimum income benefits. Knuth argues that the success associated with

Perspective 50plus cannot be attributed to particular processes used to assist older jobseekers. Rather, positive outcomes are linked to innovative governance arrangements. For example, program participation was voluntary at both the Jobcentre and client level. Moreover:

'targets were straightforward and clearly defined with regard to employment outcomes and their quality and duration ... sanctions in case of missing the targets were very soft, but underperforming did have consequences. All this created a sense of ownership different from standard operations compared to which the procedure was more bottom-up, more specifically targeted, and tied to locally specific action plans (p. 142).

The Perspective 50plus case study is used by Knuth to further answer the more abstract question: 'how [should] hierarchical rules and market transactions...be designed as to allow network relations to flourish and bear fruit' (p. 145)?

Finally, in Chapter 8, Avishai Benish makes a rather unique contribution by examining the purchaser/provider relationship in Israel. Much active labour market policy research is European or Australian focused. It is therefore particularly interesting to view the challenges presented by NPM from a relatively new jurisdictional perspective. Benish argues that:

the Israeli case, still understudied in activation scholarship, offers an excellent context for studying transformation in public accountability... As a radical case of privatization, in which significant discretionary powers were devolved to for-profit street-level activation agencies (including the power to sanction participants from receiving income support payments), it may help us to understand and critically evaluate how accountability changes under privatized service delivery systems (p. 152).

Benish concludes that a distinction between public and private accountability is a false dichotomy. Rather, there is a need to think in terms of a hybrid accountability model because 'decades of public sector welfare delivery, it seems, have created certain public expectations of how discretionary powers should be operated and how they should be accounted for, and these expectations remain when the functions are privatized' (p. 162).

While each of the chapters included in this book utilizes a national/ program case study, and each considers employment services policy in general, and activation practices in particular, they are nonetheless unique and stand-alone contributions to the literature. It is our hope that combined they make a significant contribution to scholarship, and practice, in this important field.

References

Considine, M. (2001), *Enterprising States: The Public Management of Welfare to Work*, Cambridge: Cambridge University Press.

Considine, M. (2005), The Reform that Never Ends: Quasi-Markets and Employment Services in Australia. In E. Sol and M. Westerveld (eds) *Contractualism in Employment Services: A New Form of Welfare State Governance*, The Hague: Kluwer Law International: Aspen Publishers.

Mead, L. (1992), *The New Politics of Poverty: The Nonworking Poor in America*, New York: Harper Collins Publishers.

Riccio, J. A., Friedlander, D. and Freedman, S. (1994), *GAIN: Benefits, Costs, and Three-Year Impacts of a Welfare-to-Work Program.* New York: Manpower Demonstration Research Corporation.

1

Local Worlds of Marketization[1] – Employment Policies in Germany, Italy and the UK Compared

Katharina Zimmermann, Patrizia Aurich, Paolo R. Graziano and Vanesa Fuertes

Introduction

Most western European welfare states have experienced a turn towards so-called activation policies during the last two decades. Different policy reforms have increasingly put the emphasis on activating individuals who are out of work by implementing various governance and programmatic changes, in different policy schemes, such as social assistance, unemployment protection and disability benefits.

From a broader perspective, these activation policies are often embedded in the context of broader reforms which imply changes beyond the simple introduction of new measures in existing systems. Already in the late 1970s/ early 1980s, the concept of New Public Management (NPM) (among others: Pollitt *et al.* 2007) came up and led to a shift in the perception of the role of the state in public discourses. In this framework, several countries have – especially since the late 1990s – adopted reforms tackling the relationship between the state, the individual and the providers of welfare services. On the one hand, most activation reforms strengthen individual choice and responsibility by the introduction of financial incentives or sanctions. On the other hand, the provision of a very broad range of labour market measures and social services exists in order to increase individual employability (Aurich 2011). In both dimensions, we often can observe a certain trend towards what has been called 'marketization' (among others: van Berkel *et al.* 2012b). Although marketization is not the only relevant governance aspect of activation reforms, it has nevertheless become an important part of policy delivery in most welfare states, often supported by the

Contracting-out Welfare Services: Comparing National Policy Designs for Unemployment Assistance,
First Edition. Edited by Mark Considine and Siobhan O'Sullivan.
© 2015 John Wiley & Sons, Ltd. Published 2015 by John Wiley & Sons, Ltd.

assumption that contestability increases the efficiency and effectiveness of provision. However, marketization is not a clear concept itself, and national reforms under this label show a variation on regulation characteristics, which hold the potential to crucially affect activation policies in practice. However, the outcome of activation significantly depends on the lower tiers of policy implementation, where legal changes are implemented and often adapted to a given local context. An important element in this regard, and the main focus of the article, is the level of discretion of local actors and its relation to activation interventions. The argument we make is that marketization in the delivery of activation policies strongly emphasizes both individual responsibility and the need of a broader scope of actors to ensure targeted services. However, the way these activation principles are translated into practice strongly depends on their implementation at the local level, framed by the discretion local actors have with regard to the marketized services. This discretion varies across different activation schemes according to different policy regulations and institutional setups. Therefore, this study is set out to describe and analyze the regulation and explore the implementation of marketized integrated activation policies in different types of activation schemes.

The analysis shows a clear link between the regulation of market-based interventions (i.e. type of marketization, outsourcing decisions and purchaser-provider split) and the level of local discretion for local policy-makers. With regard to the usage of this discretion, the explorative results show that it depends on the local contexts of policy-making and their suitability and willingness to become marketized. Therefore, notwithstanding a common marketization trend, its reach and its multilevel domestic adaptation varies in function of the embedded relationships (and its legacy) among levels of governments and stakeholders, rather than in function of the welfare regime type.

First, the article discusses governance reforms and marketization against the backdrop of activation policies in three different worlds of welfare and activation, namely Germany, Italy and the UK. We then develop a theoretical framework of regulating marketization in regard to activation, which we apply to three empirical cases, one in each country covered by this study. The national developments of the three countries are then checked against what is happening at the local level.

Activation Policies and Marketization

Activation policies aim at integrating broader parts of the population into the labour market. The approach developed in the 1990s is based on the assumption that long-term unemployment can have detrimental effects on individual employability thus manifesting structural unemployment (Jackman and Layard 1991), and, therefore, groups with significant barriers to labour market participation needed to be integrated into employment. Thus, in order to address the complex problems of unemployed and socially excluded people, individual responsibility (often expressed by compulsion and incentives) was complemented by the provision of client-centred counselling and multiple social services tailored to individual needs. The provision of such services requires new structures of policy implementation and new forms of governance. In this regard, among the aspects of governance most frequently discussed are decentralization, marketization, collaboration/network and NPM (van Berkel *et al.* 2012a; Considine and Lewis 2003). It can be assumed that decentralization and NPM allow for more leeway of action on lower levels of policy implementation. Marketization and collaboration, on the other hand, aim at broadening the set of actors from classical actors (e.g. public employment service [PES]) to other actors assumed to have more knowledge about needs of unemployed individuals (Considine 2001: 28), either because they are closer to the beneficiary group (e.g. non-governmental organizations [NGOs]) or due to external mechanisms (market actors).

However, as already outlined above, the introduction of marketization in employment policies goes beyond the aim to broaden the scope of actors involved in service delivery and has often taken place in the context of NPM discourses (Pollitt *et al.* 2007), often justified by the assumption that contestability will increase provision efficiency and effectiveness. By marketized services, we mean measures and instruments where the delivery is based on a competitive selection procedure. Marketization has become a common characteristic of service provision, albeit in different forms (van Berkel *et al.* 2012a) and to different degrees, across European countries. Diversity seems to exist across various dimensions, such as the relationship between purchaser and provider or between the provider and the client. Nevertheless, the question remains how these different forms of marketization are implemented. This can only be answered taking into account the scope of action which local actors have towards the provision of marketized services. As outlined below, different forms of regulating these services exist, as well as different scopes of local leeway to implement the marketized measures. In this article, based on the analytical framework developed below, we aim at analyzing both these dimensions (the regulation of the services itself and the level of local discretion they imply) in the UK, Germany and Italy. As we state, the analysis shows a clear link between the regulation of market-based interventions and the level of local discretion regarding their usage.

Marketization as a new form of governing the provision of labour market services

As outlined above, activation reforms increased the scope of labour market services provided to the unemployed. Marketization brings two new aspects into the governance of social policy: competition and tendering. The tasks to be outsourced can vary from simple job placements to more complex social services. Criteria for selecting a competitive provider include cost and quality (van Berkel *et al.*

2012a), and the performance is usually rewarded in form of financial payments (Considine and Lewis 2003), either based on strict (outcome) or soft performance measures (process-related) (van Berkel *et al.* 2012a). Contracts can be designed for short-term or long-term use and they can be targeted at different groups of unemployed.

The different characteristics of marketization of concern in this article are the level of control which national or sub-national public bodies exert over potential providers (requirements which need to be met by them); service delivery discretion (process specification: what is to be delivered?); and service users' choice over providers. Although marketization is not a standardized phenomenon or a static process (van Berkel *et al.* 2012a), it makes sense to assess marketization models as shown in table 1: ranging from no regulation to full regulation and hybrid types in between. These types of marketization, based on regulation characteristics, are related to the degree of discretion of local actors in implementing marketization, and to the purchaser-provider split as it is mentioned below.

According to van Berkel *et al.* (2012b), ideal-typical marketization involves a clear split between purchasers and providers of services, in order to encourage efficiency and responsiveness to citizens' preferences, although in most cases this split is not strictly implemented. Therefore, the governance of marketized activation measures is not only regulated regarding the characteristics of the measure (delivery, clients' choice and providers' control), but also regarding the discretion which core agencies in the field of activation have towards these services.

The regulation of the services, how strictly the purchaser-provider split is implemented, and also where the decision on outsourcing is

Table 1

Type of marketization

Marketized services regulation	Service users'/ clients' choice	Providers	Service delivery
Unregulated	Client choice	No controls (based primarily on cost)	No controls (only outcome performance)
Client regulation	No client choice	No controls (based primarily on cost)	No controls (only outcome performance)
Provider regulation	Client choice	Criteria imposed (e.g. cost and quality, etc.)	No controls (only outcome performance)
Service regulation	Client choice	No controls (based primarily on cost)	Process or type of service determined
Full regulation	No client choice	Criteria imposed (e.g. cost and quality, etc.)	Process or type of service determined

Source: own depiction, based on van Berkel *et al.* 2012a.

Figure 1

Regulation of marketization and discretion of local actors

	Low local discretion			**High local discretion**	
Marketized services	*Full regulation*	*Client regulation*	*Service regulation*	*Provider regulation*	*Unregulated*
Decision on outsourcing	*Centralized*		*Mixed*	*Decentralized*	
Purchaser-provider split	*Split*		*Mixed*	*No split*	

Source: own depiction.

taken (centralized or decentralized) are crucial for the implementation of marketized activation services, as they allow more or less local discretion. Figure 1 summarizes the link between the regulation of marketization, the level of local discretion, and the purchaser-provider split.

Studying the implementation of marketized activation policies, therefore, requires an analysis of existing regulation in this policy field in order to understand the room for manoeuvre implementing actors have. However, if we are interested in the translation of activation principles via marketization of service-delivery, we must also study the usage of the local discretion. Which local factors influence the adaption and implementation of market-based activation services by local actors? This question should be addressed in an explorative manner on the basis of three in-depth case studies.

Research Design

We chose our research design in a way to represent most different cases of welfare regimes and worlds of activation: one Anglo-Saxon, one Continental and one Southern European welfare state (Esping-Andersen 1996; Ferrera 1996). From the literature, it would be expected the Anglo-Saxon case (UK) to be more prone to marketization than the Continental (Germany) or the Southern European case (Italy). At the same time, the UK's traditionally highly centralized policy-making (Minas *et al.* 2012) stands out compared to the other two cases (Bonoli 2001). The theoretical reasoning – which follows historical neo-institutional premises (Pierson 2000) – supporting the hypothesis is that, in times of welfare state retrenchment (Ferrera and Hemerijck 2003), states with a less state-centred welfare regime will be more inclined to provide more opportunities for private actors or social enterprises to act as policy implementers.

Therefore, due to the relevant and traditional role of the family in the Southern European case and the highly relevant role of the social partners in the Continental case, we would expect the UK to have gone further in the direction of marketization, with Germany and Italy showing less marketized activation policies but higher levels of local discretion. The article aims at testing these hypotheses by analyzing the regulation of marketized interventions in each country in the context of activation reforms. Our study is based on an in-depth analysis of the legislative regulations of marketized active labour market policy (ALMP) instruments in each of the three countries. Here, we identify the different types of regulations of market-based interventions and the room for manoeuvre for implementing actors. The detailed analysis of national expenditure on market-based interventions, in the framework of ALMPs, shows the extent to which ALMPs are market-based. On the basis of Eurostat ALMP qualitative reports (European Commission 2013) and the Eurostat ALMP database, we provide data for both optional and obligatory marketized interventions in Italy, the UK and Germany. In addition, by going beyond the analysis of regulative aspects, the role of the usage of local discretion in the implementation of marketized interventions and its effects on service delivery is of crucial interest. Here, we aim at exploring local factors influencing the usage of the discretion.

The local cases which were chosen for this explorative analysis are Edinburgh (UK), Milan (Italy) and Oldenburg (Germany). From a methodological standpoint, the research was conducted via documentary analysis and, for the local case studies, 73 interviews with key stakeholders were conducted – 21 in Edinburgh,[2] 29 in Oldenburg[3] and 23 in Milan.[4] All interviewees hold senior roles, such as head of department, director or senior manager, within their organizations and are in charge of at least minor decisions regarding the usage of market-based interventions in their territorial unit. Interviews took place in the spring/summer of 2012. Questions focused on operational governance of activation policy development and implementation and on the relations between policy levels, fields and stakeholders. The selection of interviewees was done following the so-called positional method (Denzin and Lincoln 2005) and the interviews, which lasted an hour on average, were mostly recorded, and transcribed, and were analyzed using a method of qualitative content analysis (Mayring 2003).

Market-based Interventions in Activation Policies in the UK, Germany and Italy

UK

Marketization of labour market policies in the UK has taken place since at least the 1970s, with a progression since then towards contracting-out, competition and targets (Damm 2012; Hudson *et al.* 2010; Freud 2007;

DWP 2006). One of the main arguments for the use of marketization has been the claim of efficiency and effectiveness (Davies 2010), despite mixed evidence (Davies 2010; Hudson *et al.* 2010; Hasluck and Green 2007). Employment policy and income maintenance transfers are controlled centrally, while there is administrative decentralization via Jobcentre Plus (JCP). UK employment policy has therefore been characterized as 'centralised localism' (Lødemel 2001).

From the 1990s, ALMPs, usually consistent with work-first approaches (Lindsay *et al.* 2007), have increased in the UK. Current welfare policies are mostly generic in terms of groups targeted, access is generally determined by unemployment length and service users largely do not have a choice of provision or provider. There has been a net-widening of individuals mandate to participate on national welfare-to-work initiatives.

Client services are the dominant active labour market instruments in the UK, and marketization is highly specialized and well established in this field. Vocational training in the UK in many cases is not directly linked to ALMPs,[5] due perhaps to the fact that it is funded by central devolved governments through skills agencies.[6] We can identify a closer interaction between basic training aspects and client services, expanded now through the recently introduced skills conditionality in activation policies.[7] There are a number of national 'Get Britain Working' welfare-to-work programmes (Gov.UK n.d.), which the Department for Work and Pensions (DWP) contracts-out nationally, to private, public or third sector organizations. There is no discretion by local government or JCP in national initiatives, unless specified. The level of provider discretion depends on the nature of the programme and contract. The short-term unemployed and 'inactive' groups are the responsibility of JCP, which provides direct support and advice, and refers clients to external provision; in some cases it contracts-out other services (such as training and placements or specialist provision) although contracts are with the DWP (DWP 2007). JCP's role, function and service delivery are determined nationally by the DWP, although providers and partners may vary across the country. Local discretion is very limited, although more flexibility in service provision is being introduced by the current Coalition government (JCP 2011) through the Flexible Support Fund.

The current national welfare-to-work policy for the long-term unemployed is the Work Programme, which replaces a number of previous programmes. It is mandatory for up to two years for certain benefit claimants (DWP 2012a) and sanctions are imposed for non-participation. Providers have complete service discretion due to the black-box approach to service delivery. The approach aims to increase flexibility which should, it is claimed, allow individualization and effectiveness. There are a number of concerns on the capacity/ability of providers to meet complex needs of users, based on previous programmes' evidence, but there is not enough publicly available data at present to determine provision in the Work Programme. The level varied of in-house or outsourced services provided by the prime providers we interviewed. Similar to other national initiatives, payment is by results, although the criterion to draw full payment includes a longer sustainability require-ment. Differential payments depending on the benefit type the ser-vice user is claiming have also been introduced, attempting to tackle the 'creaming' and 'parking' effect of outcome-based activation pro-grammes (Casebourne *et al.* 2006, cited in Davies 2010). The tendering process has been novel to some extent due to the requirement for organizations to have no less than a £20 million annual turnover: as a result, many private, public and mainly third sector organizations were unable to compete (Damm 2012). The requirement to have supply chains could balance this exclusion, although there are no further requirements in their use. Longer contract lengths (up to seven years) aim to tackle criticism of short-contracts continuity difficulties.

Local councils have responsibility for local employability and eco-nomic strategy, but not for employment policy. Interviewees mentioned that local strategies are constrained by central government policy and budget allocation. Local government-funded employability services are mostly contracted-out through tendering (CEC 2011). In Edinburgh, outcome-based contracts are developed around the Hub Contract (an employability pipeline approach) which aims at making services seamless by wrapping around the individual. An interviewee tellingly recalls the reasoning behind the contract: '*you will get far more actual on-the-ground integration from a contractualised arrangement than from another 10 years' worth of encouraging collaboration*'.

In summary, marketization in national UK employment services has not implied client choice of service or provider and local discretion is very low or non-existent in most cases. This is the case for services directed to the short-term unemployed (provided via JCP) and for the long-term unemployed. Local government employability provision has, arguably, increased choice, although grant funding could have achieved similar results. Generally, bids are assessed in terms of cost/quality although there have been concerns that national contracting is heavily decided on cost.

Local discretion by JCP could allow individualization and localization of service-provision. It is difficult to assess if bigger contracts, such as the Work Programme, will bring individualization, although sustaina-bility and differential payments could encourage that. Nevertheless, if competitive contractualization promotes unrealistic targets set up by providers in order to win contracts (Damm 2012), due to funding deci-sions based on cost (Osborne *et al.* 2012; Simmonds 2011), the effect could be of inadequate support for those hardest to help. It is interesting nevertheless that in order to achieve multi-stakeholder coordination (horizontal coordination), the Work Programme at national level, and the Hub Contract at local level could rationalize the providers' land-scape through contracts acting as case-management 'centres'.

The most dominant marketization type to be identified in national activation policies in the UK is, therefore, client regulation. However, provider regulation through mainly cost and outcome targets can also be found, and in provision for the short-term unemployed service regulation is present, although it is currently declining. Furthermore, the UK is a country with a clear purchaser-provider split (van Berkel *et al.* 2012a).

Germany

German labour market policy is formulated at the national level and traditionally characterized by corporatism and hierarchical governance of the public employment service.[8] Vocational training was for a long time focused on the industrial model and delivered by social partners' related training institutions or public providers. Social assistance as well as social services such as counseling, housing, etc. are to a great extent under sub-national responsibility. Here, service delivery was and is highly dominated by – often large and well organized – third sector organizations, in co-operation with public actors.

Since the beginning of the 1990s, NPM reforms were introduced especially in local public administration, which affected also social services (Dahme *et al.* 2008). Although contracting-out of formerly public social services increased, this contracting-out is not always based on competitive tendering but on non-competitive commissioning. Nevertheless, competitive tendering can also be found in social services and the idea to open the market for new actors has also been implemented for the social sector. With regard to labour market policies, several reforms – the Hartz-reform package[9] being the most important – introduced market-based instruments and NPM structures step-by-step. In addition, the role of social partners in tripartite self-government was not abolished but significantly constrained. Marketization in ALMPs was limited to training and placement until 2012, when additional 'activation measures' targeted on increasing the opportunities for labour market integration were added to the scope of marketized services. These do not focus solely on quick labour market integration but can have the aim to reduce placement obstacles as a first step before taking up a job.

With regard to the organizational dimension of the currently existing instruments, we identify competitive contracting-out of service delivery and a voucher system. In the case of the voucher system, the dominant marketization type is provider regulation, while we identify full regulation in competitive contracting-out:

1. The voucher system has been introduced in placement (2002) and training (2003). Since very recently (2012), the 'activation and placement voucher' can also be used for additional activation measures. The use of vouchers is voluntary but the choice by the client is limited to accredited providers. In addition, clients' choices often seem to be dependent on case managers' information, as Bruttel (2005) states, for both types of vouchers the practice of consumers' choice might not always be applicable due to information asymmetries and personal restrictions.

19

2. There is competitive contracting-out in training (since 2005, partly also before), placement (since 2002) and 'activation measures' (since 2012). All tendering processes are organized by the regional directorates of the Federal Employment Agency (FEA), which act as purchase centres. However, the leeway of local Jobcenters and employment agencies to define which kind of measures they need is relatively high although they do not select the providers. The selection process is based both on cost and quality. There is no service users' choice with regard to these measures. Cost-efficiency and quality are mentioned as positive aspects, while a lack of suitable training providers in rural areas and the destruction of existing co-operation structures due to competition are complaints (Bernhard *et al.* 2008: 28). It has been criticized that social partners' related training providers have been favored before due to close relationships based on local tripartite structures (Kemmerling and Bruttel 2006). All private placement measures are judged as being easily subjected to 'creaming' practices.

With regard to regulation, we observe differences between training and placement/activation: while all training measures are obligatory and either contracted-out or voucher-based and, therefore, in no case provided by the PES, placement by private providers is optional. This means that there is no local discretion with regard to the decision whether training should be provided market-based or not, while the local PES can decide if they want to provide placement services in-house or outsourced. Therefore, both the decision on outsourcing and the purchaser-provider split depend on the service to be provided.

Concerning the local practice, interviews showed that this difference in local discretion is definitely relevant for implementation: from the perspective of the local PES in Oldenburg, placement is mostly seen as a task for the public employment service. Both the delivery rate and redemption rate of placement vouchers and the competitive contracting-out of placement services are quite low compared to the national average (Bundesagentur für Arbeit 2011). There are very few private placement providers in the region. However, when it comes to the new possibility of outsourcing activation measures, the usage of contracting-out has increased. Due to the quite high local discretion (' *a gumparagraph*' as one interview partner put it) with regard to service delivery, Jobcenter actors use this instrument to finance individualized and integrated measures (linking basic skills with psycho-social counselling, etc.). Vouchers are perceived as more or less an inadequate instrument for beneficiaries in need of activation measures since they are often overwhelmed with the required choice.

When it comes to training, we find a totally different picture: local discretion in terms of the content of training measures is quite high and training-planning is based on their own analysis of the regional labour market. Nevertheless, outsourcing of training is obligatory, be it voucher-based or via tendering. In Oldenburg, vouchers are the most relevant instrument in training both for the Jobcenter and the employment agency. According to the results of the local case study, clients' choice is not a problem in most of the cases. Although the introduction of the market-based training has broadened the scope of providers, the PES still seems to co-operate with the same local providers if possible. Competition among training providers is mentioned as a crucial hinderer for effective service delivery, since co-operation and alignment is reduced.

Both private placement (since 2012) and training providers (since 2003) offering voucher-based measures, or participating in tendering-processes need to be accredited. This accreditation was done until 2012 by *de facto* public certification institutions, while now the independent National Accreditation Body (DAkks, *Nationale Akkreditierungsstelle*) has taken over the responsibility. Results of the local case study emphasize what has been outlined in literature (Jantz and Klenk 2012): both accreditation and the complex tendering process privilege larger providers. Therefore, market entry relies on accreditation and tendering rules which have been dominated until recently by the *de facto* purchaser, the FEA. Nevertheless, although providers' selection is highly formalized and local discretion is that low, local PES actors seem to find ways to keep alive established co-operation with certain actors.

To sum up, local PES actors, therefore, have a relatively high leeway when it comes to service delivery, but local discretion is low with regard to providers' control. The results of the German local case study show that local PES actors do certainly use this discretion in service delivery, which has an impact on the scope of providers, the efficiency of service delivery and as well policy integration. Especially the recently installed possibility of contracting-out activation interventions and the high leeway in designing these measures lead to individualized and integrated services. Nevertheless, marketized instruments can be hinderers of co-operation since their high regulation strengthens the dominant position of the FEA.

Italy

In Italy, with respect to labour market policies, PES and education/vocational training, in 1997 a comprehensive reform was adopted at the national level aimed at setting the stage for a process of decentralization of administrative functions to regional and local levels, and marketization with respect to job counselling and temporary work. More specifically, the 1997 Law known as the 'Treu Package' ('Measures for the promotion of employment') innovated employment policy in a number of aspects. First, a gradual process of deregulation was undertaken through the provision of so called 'atypical', flexible contracts. The new legislation introduced 'temporary agency work' contracts and measures aimed at increasing part-time jobs. Second, the traditional predominance of passive policies was limited, moving towards a more 'equilibrated policy mix' (Graziano 2004) through the development of ALMP aimed at facilitating labour insertion, especially of young people and disadvantaged groups. Third, the public monopoly on placement services was ended by allowing private temporary work agencies to fully operate. This policy innovation represented a fundamental change in Italian employment policy, as it relied on the acknowledgment that private actors and market mechanisms could give a beneficial contribution to labour market performance (Jessoula and Alti 2010). The new marketization trend was further consolidated in 2003 with the so called Biagi Law, which provided further opportunities for private agencies to perform labour market policies beyond mere temporary work (Jessoula *et al.* 2010). Currently, about 70 private agencies perform employment services functions at the national level (CIETT 2012: 12), which include – beyond temporary work – job counselling, vocational training, career transition services, outsourcing and long term employment opportunities. Nevertheless, in Italy the overall number of 'agency workers' is still particularly low, also in comparative perspective (CIETT 2012: 27).

In general, in the case of employment policies, the central government via the Ministry of Labour and Social Affairs remains the key actor. Although central institutions via specific directories have also generally carried the main responsibility with respect to the other tasks which fall under its sub-section 'Social shock-absorbers and incentives for occupation', from the mid-1990s there have been clear signs of the creation of a new, open and multi-level governance model: since for several new policy programmes, regional levels of government including provinces, regions and municipalities have gained increased influence and responsibility in these services.

Social assistance has traditionally been covered primarily by local administrations, and over the past 20 years local public administrations have increasingly 'marketized' several services (as in Milan). The reforms adopted in the late 1990s tried to introduce a national scheme in order to close the gap with other EU countries where minimum income schemes had already been developed. In this respect, the 1998–2001 period witnessed the experiment of a nationally managed social assistance scheme in the form of minimum insertion income. This activation measure was meant for unemployed citizens living on an income below a certain threshold. The guidelines were set on a national level, to be further determined and implemented by the regions, in co-operation with the municipalities and local health centres. Furthermore, in the field of social assistance in the formulation of the Local Programming Plans, the reform called on local non-institutional actors (such as NGOs, trade unions and individual citizens) to participate in the local programming (and implementation) activities. This was an open door to subsidized private social assistance services, which were offered by NGOs or co-operatives in the various fields of social assistance policy. More specifically, private actors have been involved in local welfare via public administration contracting-out, accreditation and partnerships in the co-formulation of local welfare plans. Within the social assistance policy field, the main private actors have been non-profit actors, unlike those who have become increasingly relevant in employment policy. Given the fragmentation of Italian social assistance and the large differences across the country regarding both the levels of need and the availability of resources to meet these needs, it is impossible to provide a general picture concerning the activation services available for Italian social assistance recipients (Madama 2013).

Opening the provision of employment services to private actors has partly been a consequence of the flexibilization of the Italian labour market, which has been accompanied as mentioned previously by the establishment of (private) temporary work agencies for matching supply and demand where temporary work and work on fixed-term contracts is concerned. The dominant marketization types to be identified in Italy are full regulation (in training and social assistance) and client regulation (in employment services). With respect to activation, whether services are provided in-house or outsourced is decided by (local, i.e. provincial) public agencies. In fact, since there is the opportunity of outsourcing for all active labour market instruments, both traditional employment services and vocational training – which is the most relevant part of active labour market instruments in Italy (cf. figure 1) – have been 'marketized'. Therefore, we cannot identify a clear purchaser-provider split but a decentralized decision on outsourcing in employment policies.

Marketization has been even more evident in the case of social assistance policies. For example, in the case of Milan (one of the most important and populated Italian cities), by the end of 2000s the overall employment and social assistance policy[10] accounted for roughly 40 per cent of the local total expenditure on social assistance policies[11] (Suriano 2011: 14).

In summary, the intense period of reforms (1997–2012) has promoted a new governance architecture which allocates political-administrative responsibilities to the state, regions and municipalities on the principle of vertical subsidiarity, and at the same time increasing marketization with respect to both labour market and social assistance policies has occurred. The (possible) benefits of marketization are still to be fully assessed but some preliminary remarks can be put forward. First, marketization is much more developed in the social assistance sector than in the labour market policies. The latter set of policies have been only marginally touched by the marketization trend since the passive policies are still managed by (primarily national public bodies) and (decentralized) PES are the most important providers. Vocational training has been significantly reformed, both in terms of decentralization and marketization, and this has particularly empowered the regional level of regulation since in several regions vocational training agencies have to be 'accreditated' by regional public authorities. The former set of policies, being traditionally organized at the local level, have gone through quite an intense marketization process which has created new opportunities for private actors in social service provision: the above mentioned example of Milan shows how relevant outsourcing may be in local social assistance policies. Second, in terms of labour market policies, the main consequence of the new public-private mix has been greater targeting of employment services – although this covers only a very limited amount of workers, as highlighted above. Third, in the social assistance sector marketization has not only better targeted the services provided but also enables them to be better monitored by both private (or 'social private', as they are often labelled in Italian) companies and public institutions.

Comparative Discussion

As the country analyses outline, all our three cases have experienced marketization to some degree. Nevertheless, we observe differences in the extent to which labour market instruments are based on competitive contracting out in the three countries. Figure 2 illustrates these differences on the basis of those interventions which are included in the Eurostat ALMP-database: it shows the share of expenditure on market-based interventions with regard to the total active labour market expenditure, including 'labour market services' which are often contracted out.[12]

Here we observe that in the UK almost all active measures are market-based, while Italy and Germany show much lower figures. However, we

Figure 2

Market-based interventions as share of expenditure on active labour market policies (ALMP $_{2-7}$) and labour market services (ALMP $_1$)

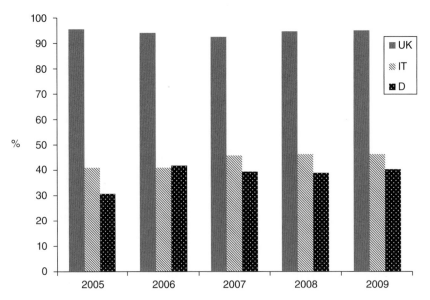

Source: Eurostat, own calculations.

observe increasing marketization in both countries between 2005 and 2009 (no current data available). All national programmes have experienced marketization, and attempts are visible to regulate these also in regard to their local implementation. Whereas in the UK most market-based interventions are highly regulated on the national level (with regard to clients, providers, and/or delivery), in Italy there are only few regulations, for example on providers. In Germany, marketization is most highly regulated, which might be the result of merging a national scheme (employment policy) with an inherently local scheme (social assistance).

At the same time, we find differences in the way in which market-based interventions are regulated, and in the degree of local level discretion. Therefore, what are the drivers of these different patterns of marketization? First of all, marketization seems to depend to some extent on the policy field in question: in Germany, training and labour market services (such as job brokerage, counselling, etc.) are both of relevance in contracting-out, in the UK, it is mostly client services and, in Italy, it is training which matters more, respectively.

Especially in Germany, marketization differs broadly between training and client services in terms of the marketization type, the purchaser-provider split, and the decision on outsourcing. In Italy, we find different marketization types for employment services and training but conformity regarding the decision on outsourcing and the purchaser-provider split. In UK, there is no such difference between the types of measures due to the fact that vocational training is less directly linked to ALMPs, however some variations are observed concerning services targeted to the short- or long-term unemployed.

Figure 3 shows the variance in the decision on outsourcing: here, all labour market interventions based on competitive contracting out were summed up and compared to the total expenditures for passive labour marked policies (LMP expenditures) (including passive benefits, which were excluded in figure 2).

In the UK, all market-based measures are contracted out; local actors have no choice in this question. In Italy, we find a totally different picture: here, the decision on outsourcing is decentralized and local actors have an increasing opportunity to decide autonomously. In Germany, this question depends on the type of measures. However, the degree of discretion is low as only about 2 per cent of these interventions (labour market services) are optional, while the others (vocational training) are necessarily to be outsourced.

However, local discretion does not only depend on the decision on outsourcing, but also is influenced by type of marketized services' regulation and the purchaser provider split. Table 2 summarizes the findings of the analysis of the regulation of market-based interventions in all three countries.

We observe a clear link between the regulation of market-based interventions and the level of discretion regarding their usage, which is significantly low in the UK, very high in Italy, and in Germany depends

Figure 3

Market-based interventions as share of total LMP-expenditure (2007)

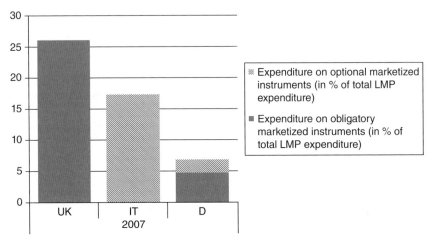

Source: Eurostat, own calculations.

Table 2

Varieties of regulation

UK		Germany	Italy
Regulation of marketized services	Client regulation or full regulation in some client services	Training: full regulation Client services: provider regulation	Training and social assistance: full regulation Client services: client regulation
Decision on outsourcing	Centralized	Mixed (depending on type of intervention)	Decentralized
Purchaser-provider split	Split	Mixed (depending on type of intervention)	No split
Local discretion	Low	Depending on type of measure	High

Source: own depiction.

26

on the type of measures. However, what do these results tell us about implementation of activation policies on the local level?

In Germany, we observe a contradictory constellation of institutional designs: an attempt of nationalization via regulating the use of market instruments is counteracted through local policy implementation, which is related to formerly local schemes based on strong relationships with the social partners. Marketization in this context is not necessarily seen as helping to achieve greater labour market integration, especially as it is so highly regulated and thus relatively inflexible. The higher the leeway of local actors, the lower seems to be the interest of outsourcing these interventions: local actors do not see a necessity to broaden the scope of actors to ensure targeted services, due to an already well-established broad landscape of service provision; marketization is not judged as an adequate measure to ensure individual responsibility which is perceived as relevant for some unemployed, but not as a general aim to be enforced. However, the argument of cost-efficiency has been made by several local actors.

In the UK there is a more centralized institutional context: on the one hand, the national-local link is secured through bypassing the local level through direct contracts of providers with the DWP; on the other hand, even where there are instances of local policy-making (employability programmes), these are evidently framed by a national context and use almost exclusively marketized approaches. There is a broad scope of actors on services provision, and horizontal coordination in seen as necessary in a mostly fragmentized landscape (e.g. the integrated Hub-Contract). Recent reforms maintain a high level of individual responsibility, could increase local discretion of PES, and could impact on the provider landscape by using marketization to rationalize it.

The relatively high degree of marketization on both levels in Italy might be due to the combination of rather unregulated and flexible national marketization programmes and a local level more akin to implementing interventions which favour private actors. On the one hand, the principle of subsidiarity prevalent in Southern European welfare states might be more conducive to the acknowledgement of individual actors rather than of collective efforts. On the other hand, marketization of the rather undeveloped social assistance scheme faced no opposition from weak networks of local stakeholders. Again, we see an influence of the policy field and its history. Whereas social assistance policy as a local programme experiences high degrees of marketization, employment policy experiences barriers to marketization since it is based on management of national bodies and public local providers. Despite this difference, it is interesting to note that marketized programmes in employment policy in Italy have seen greater involvement of private actors than marketized programmes in social assistance policy, which are based on the involvement of 'social' providers, such as NGOs, co-operatives and self-help groups.

Conclusion

This explorative study set out to describe and analyze both regulation and implementation in marketization of activation policies in different types of welfare states. Marketization certainly has become an important part of policy delivery in most welfare states. Despite minor national differences, in all of our cases we observe national reforms emphasizing marketization and regulating different aspects of it. Here, we observe a clear link between the regulation of market-based interventions and the level of discretion for local actors with regard to these measures. The type of marketization, the decision on outsourcing and the purchaser-provider split are highly relevant determinants of regulating market-based instruments. As the analysis showed, regulations often depend on the type of interventions, which also leads to different levels of discretion.

With regard to the usage of this discretion, the explorative results show that it depends on the local contexts of policy-making and their suitability and willingness to become marketized. For example, even though local discretion is relatively high both in Italy and Germany, we observe much lower degrees of marketization in Germany and more opposition to use of market-based interventions. The local context in this case is framed by long-established networks between public actors and social partners, thus inhibiting the involvement of a broader set of actors. In the UK, levels of local discretion are weak and the national level has secured the implementation of marketization via a centralized system which combines regulating access of clients and service providers. In Italy, national policy history has been partly supportive and partly inhibitive to marketization. On the local level, however, it seems that the marketized character of interventions was over-shadowed by the general changes in social assistance, which had only recently been introduced.

Activation principles such as individual responsibility and the need of a broader scope of actors to ensure targeted services are, therefore, only to a small extent translated into practice via marketization of service delivery. Although the objectives of an NPM paradigm are obviously inherent in marketized activation measures in all countries, they do not seem to affect local implementation effectively which is more dependent on local discretion and affected by local policy histories. In summary, notwithstanding a common marketization trend, its reach and its multilevel domestic adaptation varied in function of the embedded relationships (and its legacy) among levels of governments and stakeholders and not – as hypothesized – in function of the welfare regime type. Moreover, this study calls for a more in-depth analysis of the implementation of market-based interventions in more local entities in different types of countries, linking the level of local discretion defined by regulation of interventions with the local context.

Notes

1. The research leading to these results has received funding from the European Union Seventh Framework Programme (FP7-2013) under *grant agreement* n°266768. (LOCALISE, further information can be found at http://www.localise-research.eu [accessed 27 November 2013].)
2. Two interviews were conducted with national and local government officials, four with public agencies, 12 with service providers and three with local experts.
3. Seven interviews were conducted with the PES, six with public administration, two with municipal politicians, four with social partners, seven with service providers, and three with other organizations.
4. Six interviews were conducted with local government, ten with local bureaucrats, one with the public employment service, three with service providers and three with federations.
5. In some instances, training is directly mentioned within active policies, such as Sector-based Work Academies.
6. Skills Funding Agency in England and Wales (a partner organization of the Department for Business, Innovation and Skills), and Skills Development Scotland in Scotland (an executive non-departmental public body of the Scottish Government).
7. Introduced in England in August 2011 and in Scotland in June 2012. Claimants of Jobseekers' Allowance or Employment Support Allowance work-related activity group can be mandated to undertake skills activity (DWP 2012b).
8. The German public employment service is the Federal Employment Agency (FEA), a public body under tripartite self-government. Service delivery for the relative status maintaining, earnings-related and limited unemployment insurance (UB I, *Arbeitslosengeld* I) is implemented by the local employment agencies. Service delivery for the tax-financed, flat-rate and needs-tested so-called unemployment benefit II (UB II, *Arbeitslosengeld II*) is administered in the local Jobcenters, which are in the majority of the cases a co-operation between municipalities and the FEA.
9. The Hartz-reforms between 2003 and 2005 introduced highly relevant changes in governance structures, labour market instruments and the minimum income system of German labour market policies.
10. It included – beyond public institutions – 148 foundations, 220 social cooperatives, about 200 associations, 147 voluntary organizations and 206 self-help groups (Suriano 2011: 6).
11. Which accounted for an overall outsourcing value of €645 million.
12. This means that the expenditure of all single measures based on contracting-out were summed up and compared to the total expenditure, except passive benefits. Eurostat LMP category 1 includes labour market services such as counselling, PES administration, job brokerage, etc., while the categories 2–7 contain measures on training, employment incentives, job creation or start-up incentives (cf. Eurostat 2013).

References

Aurich, P. (2011), Activating the Unemployed – Directions and Divisions in Europe, *European Journal of Social Security*, 13: 294–316.

Bernhard, S., Hohmeyer, K., Jozwiak, E., Koch, S., Kruppe, T., Stephan, G. and Wolff, J. (2008), *Aktive Arbeitsmarktpolitik in Deutschland und ihre Wirkung*, IAB-Forschungsbericht 2/2008, Nürnberg.

Bonoli, G. (2001), Political Institutions, Veto Points, and the Process of Welfare State Adaptation. In P. Pierson (ed.), *The New Politics of the Welfare State*, Oxford and New York, NY: Oxford University Press.

Bonoli, G. (2010), The political economy of active labour market policy, *Politics & Society*, 38, 4: 435–57.

Bruttel, O. (2005), Delivering active labour market policy through vouchers: experiences with training vouchers in Germany, *International Review of Administrative Sciences*, 71: 391–404.

Bundesagentur für Arbeit (2011), *Statistik*, Eingliederungsbilanz nach §54 SGB II. Casebourne, J., Davis, S. and Page, R. (2006), *Review of Action Teams for Jobs. Research Report 328*, London: Department for Work and Pensions.

CIETT (2012), *The Agency Work Industry around the World*, Brussels: CIETT.

City of Edinburgh Council (CEC) (2011), *New Commissioning Strategy for Council Supported Employability Services*, 27 October, Item no 8.4, Report no CEC/52/11-12/CD.

Considine, M. (2001), *Enterprising States – The Public Management of Welfare-to-Work*, Cambridge: Cambridge University Press.

Considine, M. and Lewis, J. M. (2003), Bureaucracy, Network, or Enterprise? Comparing Models of Governance in Australia, Britain, the Netherlands, and New Zealand, *Public Administration Review*, 63, 2: S. 131–40.

Dahme, H.-J., Schüttert, S. and Wohlfahrt, N. (2008), *Lehrbuch Kommunale Sozialverwaltung und Soziale Dienste*, Weinheim: Juventa.

Damm, C. (2012), *The Third Sector Delivering Employment Services: An Evidence Review*, Working Paper, 70, London: Third Sector Research Centre.

Davies, S. (2010), Outsourcing and the Voluntary Sector: A Review of the Evolving Policy Landscape. In I. Cunningham and P. James (eds), *Voluntary Organizations and Public Service Delivery*, London: Routledge.

Denzin, N. K. and Lincoln, Y. S. (2005), *Handbook of Qualitative Research*, London: Sage.

Department for Work and Pensions (DWP) (2006), *A New Deal for Welfare: Empowering People to Work*, Green Paper, London: DWP.

Department for Work and Pensions (DWP) (2007), *Transfer of Responsibility for Contracted Employment Programmes*, London: DWP.

Department for Work and Pensions (DWP) (2012a), *The Work Programme*, http://www.dwp.gov.uk/supplying-dwp/what-we-buy/welfare-to-work-services/provider-guidance/work-programme-provider.shtml (accessed 10 April 2012).

Department for Work and Pensions (DWP) (2012b), *Mandatory Programmes Official Statistics*, 14 November, London: DWP.

Esping-Andersen, G. (1996), *Welfare States in Transition: National Adaptations in Global Economies*, London: Sage.

European Commission (2013), *Qualitative Labour Market Reports*, https://circabc.europa.eu/faces/jsp/extension/wai/navigation/container.jsp (accessed 23 September 2013).

Eurostat (2013), *Labour Market Policy Metadata*, http://epp.eurostat.ec.europa.eu/cache/ITY_SDDS/EN/lmp_esms.htm (accessed 15 August 2013).

Ferrera, M. (1996), The 'Southern' Model of Welfare in Social Europe, *Journal of European Social Policy*, 6: 17–37.

Ferrera, M. and Hemerijk, A. (2003), Recalibrating Europe's Welfare Regimes. In J. Zeitlin and D. M. Trubek (eds), *Governing Work and Welfare in a New*

Economy: European and American Experiments, Oxford, Oxford University Press, pp. S. 88–128.

Freud, D. (2007), *Reducing Dependency, Increasing Opportunity: Options for the Future of Welfare to Work*, Leeds: Department for Work and Pensions.

Gov.UK (n.d), *Moving from benefits to work*, https://www.gov.uk/moving-from-benefits-to-work/overview (accessed 12 January 2013).

Graziano, P. (2004), *Europeanisation and Italian unemployment policies in the '90s: more change than continuity?* working paper given at the Final COST A15 conference, Reforming Social Protection Systems in Europe: Co-ordination and Diversity, Nantes, France, 21–22 May.

Graziano, P. R. (2009), Choosing Welfare or Losing Social Citizenship? Citizens' Free Choice in Recent Italian Welfare State Reforms, *Social Policy & Administration*, 43, 6: 601–16.

Graziano, P. R. (2012), Converging Worlds of Activation? Activation policies and governance in Europe and the role of the EU, *International Journal of Sociology and Social Policy*, 32: 312–26.

Green, A. E. and Orton, M. (2012), Policy Innovation in a Fragmented and Complex Multilevel Governance Context: Worklessness and the City Strategy in Great Britain, *Regional Studies*, 46, 2: 153–64.

Hasluck, C. and Green, A. E. (2007), *What works for whom?: a review of evidence and meta-analysis for the Department for Work and Pensions* (No. 407), London: Department for Work and Pensions, Corporate Document Services.

Hudson, M., Philips, J., Ray, K., Vegeris, S. and Davidson, R. (2010), *The influence of outcome-based contracting on Provider-led Pathways to Work (Vol. 638)*, London: Department for Work and Pensions.

Jackman, R. and Layard, R. (1991), Does Long-term Unemployment Reduce a Person's Chance of a Job? A Time-series Test, *Economica*, 58: 93–107.

Jantz, B. and Klenk, T. (2012), *Coordination in a Fragmented Welfare Market*, paper given at the Integrated employment and activation policies in a multilevel welfare system conference, Milan, 30 August.

Jessoula, M. and Alti, T. (2010), Italy: an uncompleted departure from Bismarck. In B. Palier (ed.), *A Long Good-bye to Bismarck*, Amsterdam: Chicago University Press.

Jessoula, M., Graziano, P. and Madama, I. (2010), 'Selective flexicurity' in segmented labour markets: the case of Italian 'mid-siders', *Journal of Social Policy*, 49, 4: 561–83.

Jobcentre Plus (JCP) (2011), *Jobcentre Plus Delivery Plan 2011 to 2012*, Ref: JPDP1112, London: Department for Work and Pensions.

Kemmerling, A. and Bruttel, O. (2006), 'New politics' in German labour market policy? The implications of the recent Hartz reforms for the German welfare state, *West European Politics*, 29: 90–112.

Künzel, S. (2012), The local dimension of active inclusion policy, *Journal of European Social Policy*, 22, 1: 3–16.

Lindsay, C., McQuaid, R. W. and Dutton, M. (2007), New approaches to employability in the UK: combining 'Human Capital Development' and 'Work First' strategies? *Journal of Social Policy*, 36, 4: 539–60.

Lødemel, I. (2001), Discussion: workfare in the welfare state. In I. Lødemel and H. Trickey (eds), *An Offer You Can't Refuse: Workfare in International Perspective*, Bristol: Policy Press, pp. 295–345.

Madama, I. (2013), Beyond Continuity? Italian Social Assistance Policies between Institutional Opportunities and Agency, *International Journal of Social Welfare*, 22, 1: 58–68.

Mayring, P. (2003), *Qualitative Inhaltsanalyse – Grundlagen und Techniken*, Weinheim und Basel: Beltz Verlag.

Minas, R., Wright, S. and Van Berkel, R. (2012), Decentralization and centralization: Governing the activation of social assistance recipients in Europe, *International Journal of Sociology and Social Policy*, 32, 5/6: 286–98.

Newman, J. (2001), *Modernising Governance: New Labour, Policy and Society*, London: Sage.

Osborne, S., Bond, S., Dutton, M. and Honore, E. (2012), *The Opportunities and Challenges of the Changing Public Services Landscape for the Third Sector in Scotland: A Longitudinal Study Year Two Report*, Scottish Government Social Research Series, http://www.scotland.gov.uk/Resource/0040/00405019.pdf (accessed 3 December 2013).

Pierson, P. (2000), Increasing returns, path dependence, and the study of politics, *American Political Science Review*, 94: 251–67.

Pollitt, C., Thies, S. V. and Homburg, V. M. F. (2007), New public management in Europe, *Management Online Review:* 1–6.

Serrano Pascual, A. and Magnusson, L. (2007), *Reshaping Welfare States and Activation Regimes in Europe*, Brussels: Peter Lang.

Simmonds, D. (2011), *Work Programme Results: Perform or Bust*, Working Brief, May, London: Centre for Social and Economic Inclusion.

Suriano, P. (2011), *Numeri e azione dell'amministrazione comunale*, Milano.

van Berkel, R. and Borghi, V. (2008), New modes of governance in activation policies, *International Journal of Sociology and Social Policy*, 27, 7/8: 277–86.

van Berkel, R., de Graaf, W. and Sirovatka, T. (2012a), Governance of activation policies in Europe, *International Journal of Sociology and Social Policy*, 32, 5: 260–72.

van Berkel, R., Sager, F. and Ehrler, F. (2012b), The diversity of activation markets in Europe, *International Journal of Sociology and Social Policy*, 32, 5/6: 273–85.

2

Varieties of Market Competition in Public Employment Services – A Comparison of the Emergence and Evolution of the New System in Australia, the Netherlands and Belgium

Ludo Struyven

Introduction

The emergence of active labour market policies in the 1980s, to different extents, went hand in hand with a shift from the public employment service (PES) to private providers. Inherent to this new system of market competition are new steering models and instruments. The often suggested thesis is one of policy convergence between countries' quasi-market systems. The new market arrangements necessarily evolve from an open to a closed market and make way for new control instruments (Considine 2005b; Struyven 2007; Bredgaard and Larsen 2008; Weishaupt 2010; van Berkel et al. 2011). These reverse shifts are considered as a rational consequence of inefficient, unsuccessful and costly contracting-out mechanisms. In this article, we build on an alternative explanation that countries do not necessarily converge towards the same model. Our explanation builds further on Streeck's and Thelen's work on the notion of institutional evolution and change (Streeck and Thelen 2005; Mahoney and Thelen 2010). Unlike path dependence theory, small changes can equally well set in motion a process of gradual transformation. But in itself the process does not constitute the causal mechanism. In this article, we explain change due to an interaction of institutional, functional and actor-centric factors.

What is happening with PESs fits into the movement towards labour participation and privatization (Gilbert 2002). Moreover, this is also related to reforms in the benefits system. The relationship between

Contracting-out Welfare Services: Comparing National Policy Designs for Unemployment Assistance, First Edition. Edited by Mark Considine and Siobhan O'Sullivan.
© 2015 John Wiley & Sons, Ltd. Published 2015 by John Wiley & Sons, Ltd.

the two functions – benefits and job brokerage – is a fundamental and continually recurring area of tension in labour market policy. The activation goal again brings a certain rapprochement between the two. Introducing quasi-markets has formed part of the core of institutional reforms in the PES in several Organisation for Economic Co-operation and Development countries since the early 1990s. Considine calls this a change in the administration paradigm with respect to labour activation, to which he assigns the term 'enterprising states' (Considine 2001). This far-reaching institutional change entails a new institutional logic.

This research is concerned with the way in which three countries have implemented quasi-market arrangements in their PES system during the 1990s and the first decade of 2000s (until the financial crisis of 2008). Based on an in-depth analysis of the reform process, we arrive at the observation that Australia and the Netherlands, unlike Belgium, make comparable choices when restructuring this policy domain, although their context of a welfare state is different. Second, the new structures in those countries which have made the same choices are seen to evolve differently after only a short period of time. What brought the two reform countries Australia and the Netherlands to make a similar choice for the restructuring of their PESs? How is it that Australia evolved after just a few years from an open to a closed market, whereas this did not happen in the Netherlands? Why did Belgium (Flanders) not opt, in the period studied, for a new administrative structure with more scope for market competition, despite a far-reaching reform plan?

This qualitative comparative study is based on a comparison between three countries. The number of cases which are relevant for studying the phenomenon of market competition in PESs is by definition limited. Looking for the 'genuinely important cases' (Mahoney and Goertz 2006), Australia and the Netherlands can be regarded as the extreme values (Ragin 1987) which are the most relevant for a study of market competition. Belgium is a representative of the public system. For this study a mix of research methods was used: interviews, documents, statistical data and secondary sources (Struyven 2006).

The following sections present the findings on the origin and further development of the system. First, the origin and evolution of the system in the two 'reform countries', Australia and the Netherlands, is discussed; this is followed by a discussion of the evolution in Flanders. In what follows, we first explain our theoretical model.

A Model for Explaining Policy Change

According to the theory of path dependence, a system fosters its own continuity; change is only possible if the existing structure is impacted upon by an exogenous factor, which cannot be explained on the basis of the preceding event (Pierson 2000a; Mahoney 2000; Deeg 2005). The possible transition to a new path implies a crisis moment or 'critical juncture', which acts as the trigger for change. On the contrary, the theory of Thelen (Thelen 1999, 2003, 2004; Streeck and Thelen 2005: 9) identifies 'incremental change with transformative results' as a variant alongside abrupt change. With this study, we add several elements to the theory of gradual change and institutional evolution. These relate to the question of which factors – or, more accurately, mechanisms – cause change. Recent theories on path dependence attribute the cause of *non-change* to feedback mechanisms (Pierson 2000a, 2000b, 2001; Mahoney 2000) and to the internal logic or sequentiality of the path (Mahoney 2000: 530–1). Identifying the intervening processes in a sequence of events can reveal the causal mechanism. In itself, however, this does not constitute a sufficient condition to explain the evolution along a given path. Thelen/Streeck attribute the reasons for change to the forms in which change occurs, such as institutional layering (a new function is overlaid on an existing institution) or conversion (an existing institution acquires a completely new function). But, in itself, the process does not constitute the causal mechanism. For these authors, what ultimately explains change are the political actors. The evolution of the process can be seen as an arena, in which the actors continue to struggle and renegotiate to gain influence and power. Explaining changes on the basis of the political power factor alone is, however, too limited. In our view, change arises due to an interaction of institutional, functional and actor-centric factors.

First, there is the 'logic of action' (Deeg 2005) of the system. A system of market competition ushers in a complex concatenation of elements: a level playing field, management by results, functioning of the pricing mechanism, maximization of placements, definition of obligations which have to be met by jobseekers (Struyven 2005, 2007). Only when these conditions have been met does the system become operational. This new logic conflicts with the elements of the existing logic, which continue to be necessary even in a market arrangement: the position of the public player, process control, the role of quality and experience alongside price, quality control, the provision of training for jobseekers and the sustainability of placements. If both logics are present, they 'compete' with each other, so that one logic suppresses the other. The new system logic in itself does not constitute a sufficient condition for change to occur. The inherent system logic can thus be distinguished from mechanisms of change. Another institutional factor lies with the parallel processes in related policy domains (Thelen 1999, 2004). Interaction occurs between reforms in the benefits administration and reforms in the job brokerage system (Considine 2005a, 2005b). This can go in two directions: from the benefits system to the job brokerage system or vice versa. If no interaction occurs, this change mechanism is absent.

A further explanatory factor is the functionality of the existing system. Increasing institutional density (Pierson 2000a: 483) leads to unintended effects, which generate a need for new changes which, in turn, in order to keep the system coherent, generate yet more pressure for change. An important factor here is the impact of new control structures and instruments on the organization and implementation in the field. In this way, changes alternate with each other rapidly and the outcome of the original intentions varies. An essential element is the way in which the functioning is perceived. Perception of success or failure of the existing system is cultivated. If the (lack of) success of the new system is cultivated, the change mechanism is present.

The third category has to do with the actors. Following the line of Skocpol (1992), we distinguish the political/administrative actor from the field of service providers, including the interest groups. Two mechanisms for change can be distinguished here: the changed political-bureaucratic power situation and the anticipatory behaviour of actors.

To summarize, small changes in a process culminate in successive gradual changes if an interaction occurs between the inherent system logic on the one hand, and parallel reform processes, the cultivated success/failure of the new system, the changed power coalitions and the anticipatory behaviour of actors on the other hand. How these mechanisms exert their influence on the process is illustrated by the countries studied here.

The Origin of Market Competition in Australia and The Netherlands

The first step in analyzing the process in the three countries is what changes when. Formal criteria, such as new legislation, is not adequate for establishing dividing lines. The various stages in the process towards institutional innovation are related to the elements on which the new institutional logic is based (Deeg 2005). The analysis of the process of change in Australia and the Netherlands begins with the situation as at the end of the 1980s. The first stage continues up to the point of the full introduction of market competition, namely 1997 in Australia and 1999 for the Netherlands. We trace the path for each country in turn, followed by an explanation. The path change is illustrated in figures 1 and 2.

Australia

Stage t_o. The introduction of Job Network (1997) is often regarded as the beginning of the reform of the system. In reality, however, the reform was introduced earlier, under the Working Nation initiative (1994); this was a first version of a competitive system, which in turn built on the system of 'case management' under the Newstart strategy introduced in 1989 for the long-term unemployed. And even before then, there was a tradition of outsourcing job creation and training programmes, with the first initiatives introduced in the state of Victoria in the 1970s. The growing involvement of the private sector during this period took place with the Commonwealth Employment Service (CES) as commissioning principal. The outsourcing laid the basis for the later private market.

Figure 1

Forms of gradual change in the evolution of a market system in Australia

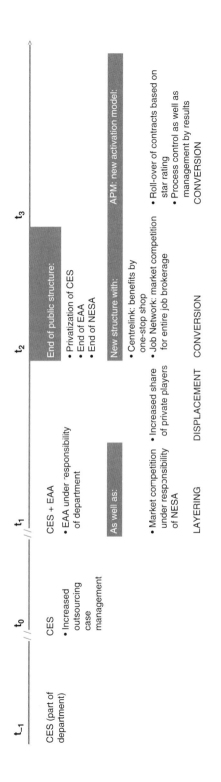

Figure 2

Forms of gradual change in the evolution of a market system in the Netherlands

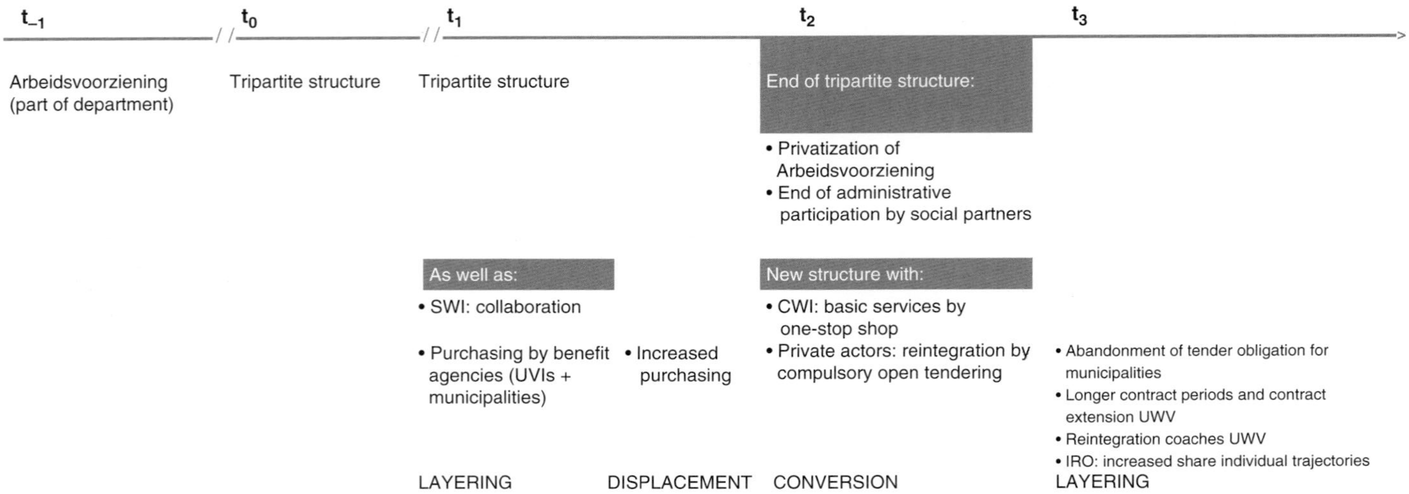

t_{-1}	t_0	t_1	t_2	t_3
Arbeidsvoorziening (part of department)	Tripartite structure	Tripartite structure	**End of tripartite structure:** • Privatization of Arbeidsvoorziening • End of administrative participation by social partners **New structure with:** • CWI: basic services by one-stop shop • Private actors: reintegration by compulsory open tendering	• Abandonment of tender obligation for municipalities • Longer contract periods and contract extension UWV • Reintegration coaches UWV • IRO: increased share individual trajectories LAYERING
			As well as: • SWI: collaboration • Purchasing by benefit agencies (UVIs + municipalities)	• Increased purchasing
			LAYERING	DISPLACEMENT	CONVERSION

Note: SWI = Cooperation Structure for Work and Income; CWI = Centre for Work and Income; UVI = social insurance implementing body; UWV = Implementing Body for Employee Insurance; IRO = individual reintegration contracts.

The introduction of the new labour market strategy for the long-term unemployed was accompanied by changes to the conditions of eligibility for income support. The principle of 'reciprocal obligation', later 'mutual obligation', was explicitly embedded in the Australian benefits system for the first time under Newstart. All these elements formed the basis for the later Job Network.

From t_o to t_1. The second step in a gradual change to a new path took place in 1994 when the Labor government published the White Paper, *Working Nation*, a broad programme which incorporated case management for the reintegration of jobseekers and a job guarantee, called 'Job Compact', for the long-term unemployed (18 months) and for all those who were at risk of long-term unemployment (Commonwealth of Australia 1994b). Working Nation foresaw a gradual increase in the share taken by commercial and non-commercial players.[1] The statutory framework for the competitive system was given form in the Employment Services Act 1994. The reforms in 1994 followed a dual track: on the one hand, a broadening of the playing field, on the other, strengthening of the CES.

A characteristic of the new structure under Working Nation is that it was based on two logics:

1. a new market competition logic through the contracting of case management for the long-term unemployed to the private sector, headed not by the public player but by a new regulator, the Employment Services Regulatory Authority (ESRA);
2. continuation of the existing logic by placing the government case management player created by the CES – Employment Assistance Australia (EAA) – within the ministerial department, outside the sphere of influence of ESRA.

Yet ESRA was not the only commissioning body; the government player EAA operated outside the authority of ESRA, was allocated a guaranteed market share and, as a spin-off from the CES, came under the Department, as did the CES itself.

With the introduction of the Job Compact, the government was generalizing the principle of 'reciprocal obligation' (DEWRSB 2000). The case manager was required to monitor his or her clients and inform the CES, including where the client failed to co-operate. This was linked to the start-up fee paid to the provider (Considine 2005b).

From t_1 to t_2. A next step in the process towards a new path was the introduction of the Job Network system by the Conservative Coalition government elected in 1996. A fully competitive market was introduced, while the EAA became an autonomous government agency without any guaranteed market share.[2] This decision led to a considerable saving over the coming three years (DEWRSB 2000). The new principle of 'mutual obligation' strengthened the obligations for jobseekers to do something in return for society.

39

When Job Network was introduced, the activities of ESRA were suspended and the CES was wound up. The department took over the task of principal from ESRA. The other tasks of the CES were assumed by the department and Centrelink which served as a one-stop shop for a large number of services provided to the public.

Heavy emphasis was placed on outcomes. Accordingly, the share of outcome financing increased. Price competition was introduced for certain elements of the tender. The reform of 1997 forms the crystallization of the figure which emerged under Working Nation, one not even rubber-stamped by new legislation in Australia (Considine 2005b).

The gradual transformation into a full market model explained. The partial change in the existing system brought elements of institutional renewal to the fore: the separation of principal and agent (at least for the ESRA portion); the use of financial incentives through the introduction of outcome fees; and the greater importance of placement. At the same time, the protected status of the CES and the guaranteed share allocated to the public player EAA were left intact. In other words, this phase of institutional change was a form of what Streeck and Thelen (2005) call *layering*: the existing system is left intact, but is layered with elements of a new system. At the same time, the elements of a new institutional logic forced the partially reformed structure in the direction of full market competition. The continued existence of the public system alongside the market system created an ambiguity in the existing structure which led to conflict due to the aversion of market players to the CES. In this transition from t_1 to t_2 the process took on two forms: *displacement* and *conversion*; displacement because the public logic gradually had to make way for the market logic, and conversion because the existing structure was converted in accordance with the new logic.

As stated in the theoretical section, we can identify four change mechanisms which help to explain the process of the nature of a full market model in the following way:

– *Interaction with reforms in the benefits system.* The great emphasis on compliance with obligations, first introduced in the Newstart programme, was continued under Working Nation. The creation of Centrelink under the Coalition government in 1996 brought a solution for the intake and referral of job seekers, the selection of candidates in advance and the imposition of sanctions. Candidates who could not be referred to Job Network (because they did not possess the 'capacity to benefit'), had no choice ('mutual obligation') but to accept a work experience offer such as 'Work for the Dole'. This created an interaction between the process of tightening up the benefits regime and the process of market competition in job brokerage.

- *Cultivation of the failings of the existing system.* In the 1990s, there had been unrelenting negative criticism of the results of existing programmes and of the CES as a system, which was losing the support of employers and jobseekers. The failings of the existing structure were cultivated by an official evaluation by the department (DEWRSB 2000).
- *Strengthening the grip of the department on the system.* During the first reforms, the department retained control over the CES, while the beginning market came under the control of an independent regulator (ESRA). The CES ultimately also lost the support of the department. During the reforms of 1997 the CES was hived off, so that the department was able to assume the full role of principal and ESRA could be rendered redundant.
- *Anticipatory behaviour by actors.* In 1994 the Labor government wanted to reform the CES structure in such a way that the reforms went far enough to be left intact if a government of a different colour should come to power. The reformers were, in other words, anticipating a subsequent reform. A growth scenario was projected for the beginning market, which was overtaken by developments in the market. Non-profit and profit actors, who saw their share of the playing field expanding, anticipated a further enlargement of the quasi-market.

The Netherlands

Stage t_o. The Dutch PESs landscape was relatively calm until 1980, when preparations began for a new tripartite structure, introduced in the Manpower Services Act 1990, which marked the end of the government monopoly on job brokerage. In the first half of the 1990s, the practice of sub-contracting for *Arbeidsvoorziening* increased as more scope was created for training programmes. In parallel with this, a quest was under way for a new institutional structure for the administration and implementation of the social insurance system. In the 1990s, virtually all aspects of the social security system were subjected to major or minor reforms (van der Veen and Trommel 1999).

From t_o to t_1. A first gradual change occurred in 1994, when certain tasks were configured according to a new logic. The new Coalition, a combination of right and left, conducted a dual change:

1. on the one hand, the basis was laid for the purchasing model, in which *Arbeidsvoorziening* began performing services on commission from the social insurance implementing bodies (UVIs) and local authorities;
2. on the other hand, a process was initiated of bottom-up co-operation between the public employment agencies, the municipal social services and the UVIs for intake and referral (the Cooperation Structure for Work and Income [SWI], which later gave birth to

41

the Centres for Work and Income and the new Implementation Structure [SUWI]). This double renewal was effected without altering the underlying structure of *Arbeidsvoorziening*.

From t_1 to t_2. A third process took place in 1999, with the introduction of compulsory open tenders and the abandoning of *Arbeidsvoorziening* under the new SUWI structure. The new market logic was generalized and clarity gradually emerged in the position of the public service *within* the new market rather than *alongside* the market. There was an end to the co-administration by the social partners, which were given a purely advisory role, while the former *Arbeidsvoorziening* became a public provider in a position which was fully in line with the market.

The public employment agencies and benefits agencies which previously existed disappeared, to be replaced by two new national organizations:

1. for benefits, a single Implementing Body for Employee Insurance (UWV) was created instead of the five existing UVIs[3] and the umbrella National Social Insurance Institute (LISV);
2. in the field of job brokerage, a number of tasks in the area of 'basic services' which were previously covered by *Arbeidsvoorziening*, the UVIs and the municipalities, became the responsibility of the Organization for Work and Income, which managed a nationwide network of 131 Centres for Work and Income (CWI) in 110 municipalities (approximately one in five municipalities).

Both organizations were fully within the public domain. For the reintegration of jobseekers, subsistence benefit claimants and the disabled, the choice was made for a fully privatized market. The reintegration activities of the existing *Arbeidsvoorziening* were privatized in the form of a reintegration company, the state-owned company NV Kliq, bidding on an equal basis with other providers.

Since unemployment insurance benefits are limited in duration, many long-term unemployed people end up on subsistence benefit (usually 'Stream 4' clients). The municipalities are responsible for the implementation of social assistance benefits and also for subsidized work. The municipalities have a direct financial interest in outflow from subsistence benefit.[4]

The gradual transformation into a full market model explained. As in Australia under Working Nation, the reforms in 1994 contained the ambiguity of a double system logic. The new logic was introduced while the logic of the public system remained intact – this is the process of *layering*. Gradually, the system of purchasing by benefits agencies (UWV and municipalities) came to dominate the existing structure – a process that can be characterized as *displacement*. In 1999, the structure was converted to bring it into line with new political objectives and – for the reintegration task – a new market logic; this process is characterized as *functional conversion.*

The four factors which influenced the process can be identified in the following way:

- *The embedding in the new implementation structure for social insurance.* After the second tripartite Manpower Services Act came into force in 1996, it became clear that the future would be determined by the process of reform of the implementation structure for social insurance as a whole. An inherent element of the Coalition Agreement was that a balance needed to be found between the distribution of tasks in the public and private sectors. For which tasks ('reintegration') and in what form ('compulsory purchasing', 'compulsory tenders') market competition could form an alternative became clear only gradually.
- *The functioning of the public system.* Right from the start of the introduction of the tripartite structure, *Arbeidsvoorziening* remained confronted with disappointing results. Despite the slight improvement in the results after the introduction of the new Act in 1996, political support for the public system evaporated entirely. The political masters reacted to the persistent financial impasse[5] with a combination of financial compensation mechanisms and political risk-aversion.
- *The loss of political support to the tripartite structure.* Many observers saw the tripartite experiment for *Arbeidsvoorziening* in the mid-1990s as doomed to failure. Neither the government nor the social partners regarded themselves as the owners of the organization. *Arbeidsvoorziening* no longer belonged to anyone, according to one of the respondents. But it was not clear what could replace it.
- *The anticipatory behaviour of the actors involved.* The various actors in the field began repositioning themselves strategically, and thus responding to anticipated developments. Both the UVIs and *Arbeidsvoorziening* anticipated developments and reinforced each other in their new roles. This created a coordination effect. *Arbeidsvoorziening* began projecting itself more as an attractive market player for the growing volume of activities via purchasing. The spending cuts also drove *Arbeidsvoorziening* in this direction. The UVIs, as principals, in turn anticipated the situation by purchasing services where they saw fit, even though this was not yet permitted. In order to position itself better in the growing 'market', *Arbeidsvoorziening* decided on its own initiative to split up the internal organization into separate units within a single concern. At that time the management did not yet realize that the next step would be external splitting up. The decision for this external splitting came relatively late, and was speeded up after the definitive SUWI became known.

The Evolution of Market Competition in Australia and The Netherlands

Australia

The basic mechanism of market competition which Australia has showcased to the world is the competitive tender procedure (OECD 2001; Productivity Commission 2002). However, for the third contract period 2003–06, the Australian government partially removed the tender mechanism (roll-over). Whereas, in the past, the tender procedure occupied a central position, management by results via the star ratings now forms the heart of the system. Moreover, only fixed prices are now used and providers are paid after each completed interview with a jobseeker in accordance with a strictly regulated frequency. Direct intervention in the market share of the provider has replaced indirect management based on price competition and outcome financing. These interventions mean that the public-hierarchical logic has come to dominate. The break lies between the second and third contract periods, which according to respondents was a more radical transition than the transition in 1997 from Working Nation to the first edition of Job Network. This phase is marked by *functional conversion* in the process of Job Network. The transition between the two points in time (from t_2 to t_3) is represented schematically in figure 1.

The new activation model, the Active Participation Model (APM), introduced a service continuum consisting of Job Search Support and Intensive Support, with in between periods of compulsory activity under the mutual obligation principle.

The star rating instrument clashed with the logic of market competition because the star ratings functioned purely as part of a public hierarchical logic and played no part in the transactions on the quasi-market in the individual choice from different providers. The dominant influence of the star ratings was reinforced by the linking of this mechanism to the contracts and the six-monthly review of the share of referred jobseekers. This made the quasi-market transparent, but it was a transparency which was unilaterally useful to the government.

Based on our analysis, the evolution can be attributed to the following four mechanisms:

– *Interaction with the new model for the Australian welfare state.* The permanent job search model of APM implies a close link between the Department of Employment and Workplace Relations and Centrelink. But the increasing activation pressure exposed a cultural difference between the two organizations: the department was in favour of a firmer approach to jobseekers, while Centrelink favoured a milder approach. At Centrelink, there was a tendency to broaden the service provided to jobseekers in order to increase its added value. In the view of the department, however, this went beyond Centrelink's role. The department wanted to prevent the former CES rising from the ashes.

- *The functioning of the new system.* In the third contract period, the transition problems were worse than ever, the service became further standardized, problems such as 'parking' and limited freedom of choice were still apparent. The new information technology (IT)-driven model imposed a heavy administrative burden on providers, as well as a heavier caseload and constant uncertainty regarding the intake volumes and income. To help the system run more smoothly, the government introduced a number of financial compensation measures. Together with the announcement of steadily improving results, these measures served to compensate for the institutional incongruence in the system.

- *The influential position of the department.* Characteristic of the configuration of the quasi-market in Australia is the position of the central department in Canberra as the sole principal. The department can adopt an omnipotent stance and can unilaterally change the rules of the game. It can also mean that the prices are in reality too low. This undermines the trust between the parties involved. The new IT system further exacerbates the centralization trend. The department is not willing to discuss changes and sticks rigidly to the stipulations of the tender and the contract.

- *The behaviour of market players.* Throughout the successive rounds, there has been an increasing concentration of the market. The market concentration is strongly influenced by the automatic contract extension, the elimination of the pricing mechanism and the growing importance of past results. The providers only gradually realized what indications the new choices – flow continuum, IT system, enlargement of the target group – would have for the functioning of the system.[6]

The Netherlands

The further development in the Netherlands is marked by a period of increasing market competition between 2000 and 2003, followed by a period of new elements with resultant limited shifts in 2004–08. This transition from t_2 to t_3 is represented schematically in figure 2. In the municipalities, the tender regime under SUWI and the outsourcing obligation lapsed.[7] At the UWV there is the introduction of longer contracts, contract extensions and case management by reintegration coaches. Then there is the rapidly growing practice of devising individual trajectories in the context of the individual reintegration contracts (IRO). This phase can be identified as a form of *layering*. The effect is that market competition is strengthened because of the fairly unrestrictive conditions for companies and the open-ended budgeting for IROs.

The following four mechanisms can be identified:

- *Interaction with parallel processes.* A first development was the creation of the IRO, which was motivated by the political desire for a more client-centric focus of the SUWI structure. From their launch in 2004, the number of individual trajectories rapidly overtook the number of tendered trajectories. In this way freedom of choice was given a more central position in the system. A second development was the introduction of the Work and Social Assistance Act. At municipal level, a contradiction was perceived between the 100 per cent responsibility for social assistance spending and the additional requirement imposed by central government to engage in tendering. The reasoning was that giving municipalities full financial responsibility would not require the imposition of any additional obligations.

– *The functioning of market competition in the context of SUWI.* In the period from 2002 there was growing criticism of the lack of figures on the results of the reintegration market. This explains the greater process control by the UWV, using performance indicators, satisfaction surveys, classification and profiling of jobseekers.

– *Building of a strong bureaucratic position.* The existence of government organizations such as the UWV and CWI alongside the municipal services meant that power was more widely spread. As a result, the minister/ministry cannot simply push through plans unilaterally. Initially, the UWV (and a number of municipalities) had the intention of cutting the preferential ties with the government-allied provider. This made the autonomously operating UWV a major proponent of a fully transparent tender procedure.

– *Anticipatory behaviour by actors.* Lastly, the evolution of the Dutch system has been influenced by the behaviour of key market players: the providers, united in the sector federation, and the social partners who (together with the municipalities) were assigned a consultative and advisory role. Both organizations anticipated the need for transparency and benchmarking of the market. It is an example of how the Dutch consensus-based 'polder model' still survives in the system of market competition.

Explanation in Comparative Perspective: The Netherlands/Australia

The Dutch evolution is much less pronounced than the Australian development towards more stable market relations, greater weight assigned to past results and greater process control. How can this be explained? The differing development in Australia and the Netherlands is related first and foremost to differences in institutional structure. Then there are differences in the form in which the tender mechanism is cast. Third, there are also differences in the control instruments.

First, the presence of several different principals created a very different starting point for the institutional structure in the Netherlands from that in Australia. It gave rise to a market with many principals (UWV, 480 municipalities, private employers[8]) and different, partially overlapping markets (for the disabled and jobseekers, social assistance benefit clients, sick employees). The pluralistic tendering system is attractive from the perspective of providers because it helps to spread the risk better and avoids dependence on a single principal. In Australia, there is only one principal for the entire continent, which is moreover strongly centralized in Canberra. In Australia, the launch of a new tender round has a greater impact, because of its size (a single mastodon for all contracts) and duration (every three years). In the Netherlands, changes can be implemented more continuously and in the short term through the many national and municipal tenders, both successive and simultaneous. As a result, the evolution in the Netherlands is less abrupt than in Australia. Third, the instruments used to control the market refer to the forms of intervention which direct and streamline the day-to-day processes between principal, provider and jobseeker. They help establish the 'logic of action' of the system. As in the Australian quasi-market, quality control, performance measurement and benchmarking are becoming increasingly important in the Dutch quasi-market owing to the growing focus on quality and placement. Since these instruments have been developed and are currently administered by the providers' sector, they also function more as elements of a market logic than if they were in the hands of the government.

Explanation in Comparative Perspective: The Netherlands/Belgium

Like Australia and the Netherlands, at the end of the 1990s a new Coalition government in the Flemish region launched a large-scale reform of the PES system. This plan was based on a new steering role with regard to the labour market. The aim was to split the existing PES structure into separate institutions for the control, *casu quo* purchasing tasks and implementing tasks. The plan exercised minds for four years, before ultimately being reaffirmed by decree as the existing Flemish PES, including its name.[9] The question arises why Flanders did not opt, in the period studied, for a new administrative structure with more scope for market competition.[10] This question is answered by exploring the different institutional configurations in Flanders and the Netherlands.

First, at the end of the 1990s, there were striking differences in the form of control: job brokerage in Flanders started from a rich tradition of joint management by social partners, and the Flemish public service became acquainted relatively early on with management by results via performance contracts, which guaranteed a contractually laid down budgetary framework (Struyven and Verhoest 2005). The position of the local administration in Belgium is, moreover, limited due to the unlimited duration of unemployment benefits and, as a consequence, the residual nature of the locally governed social assistance system. There was also another important explanatory factor behind the expansion drive of the Flemish PES: the desire to make the most of the Flemish competence and throw off the old national shackles. After the state reform of 1988, unemployment insurance schemes remained a federal responsibility of the National Employment Service,[11] while the responsibility for job brokerage and reintegration of jobseekers became a responsibility of the *Vlaamse Dienst voor Arbeidsbemiddeling en Beroepsopleiding* (VDAB). To some extent unintentionally, this also fuelled a monopolist attitude on the part of the VDAB towards other players in the market.[12] Second, there was no general climate in Flanders in favour of market competition and privatization in the sphere of social security and PESs. Temporary agency work was less widespread in Belgium.[13] Another difference relates to the position of trade unions and employers' organizations in the social insurance system. Historically, corporatism was deeply rooted in both countries in the organization of the social security system. The job brokerage domain in the Netherlands formed an exception to this. In Belgium, there was no general discussion about the position of the social partners in the management of the social security system. In particular, the trade unions in Belgium have acquired much greater support and legitimacy, with the result that their veto power is also greater when it comes to political reforms.[14] The strong position of the social partners in the policy and management of labour market institutions can be explained by the high organizational density of employers' organizations and the trade union density among both workers and the unemployed (Ebbinghaus and Visser 2000).[15]

Conclusion

This study shows that countries, which developed new market arrangements in their PES systems, do not necessarily converge towards the same model. The three countries studied each follow their own path regarding the direction in which the system is evolving. This direction cannot be anticipated in advance by the dynamics concealed within the change process.

Important events for change were the effective entrance of private commercial organizations to the market of publicly funded services, the separate positioning of the role of principal relative to the players' market and the autonomy or privatization of the former public service. Defined in this way, the turning point for Australia came not in 1997 but in 1994. In the Netherlands, the turning point lies not in 1999, but in 1995, when the purchasing scheme for reintegration by municipal social services and benefits agencies was introduced. In turn, this was able to happen because of the process of smaller changes which preceded it. These earlier points in time characterize the gradual nature of the processes of change.

In each country, change arises due to an interaction of institutional, functional and actor-centric factors. An initial change mechanism is interaction with parallel processes. In both Australia and the Netherlands, the field of job brokerage via the activation policy is once again more closely tied to the area of benefits. Through links to reforms in the broader social security system, a strong influence is exerted on the institutional route for job brokerage. In the period of the further development of market competition, the interaction with parallel processes explains the differences in the process. In Australia, another link is made to a reform of benefits (APM), but not in the Netherlands. In Flanders, the intended reform at the end of the nineties did not mesh with a reform in the area of benefits. The absence of interaction with parallel processes is facilitated by the constitutional allocation of areas of competence between the federal state (competent for benefits) and the regions (competent for job brokerage). Second, in Australia and in the Netherlands, the faulty operation of the existing public structure facilitated the steps of reform in the mid- to late 1990s. The negative perception placed high effectiveness pressure on the new system. In the Flemish political and bureaucratic context, no room was left for a sceptical attitude towards the public structure. The recently acquired constitutional autonomy in employment placement absolutely had to succeed.

The following two mechanisms relate to the coalition and the behaviour of actors. A change of course took place in the 1990s in Australia and the Netherlands with the help of political and bureaucratic power among the advocates of the reform. A coalition of public agency and government department was initially able to keep the public service outside the market. At the same time, actors and players on the market seemed to anticipate the arrival of a fully competitive market system. In Flanders, no broad reform-oriented coalition could be formed for the reform plan of 1999 because influential actors in the existing public structure for job brokerage were against reform and were supported in their views by the trade unions. From the further evolution of market competition in Australia in 2003, it appears that the government department responsible for the tender has such bureaucratic power that a change of course could be pushed through against the wishes of actors in the field. In the Netherlands, power is distributed more widely among different actors and, initially, subordinate actors could strengthen their position through anticipatory behaviour.

Here, we have given a primarily institutional explanation. Yet the question can also be asked as to the decisive role of political parties. In both Australia and the Netherlands, the path for market competition was smoothed by progressive coalitions led by social-democratic politicians. In Australia, it was a Labor government which introduced an early form of market competition in 1994, in the Netherlands, it was the two successive 'purple' coalitions of 'red' social democrats and 'blue' liberals in the period 1994–2002 which stood at the helm of the reforms. In Flanders, too, it was a social-democratic minister who, in 1994, introduced management by results for the Flemish PES and launched the reform plan of the PES in 1999, albeit without success. But in Australia, the second, more radical phase was introduced under the subsequent conservative administration involving a coalition of Liberals and Nationals. The Conservative governments which followed the 'purple' coalitions in the Netherlands continued the trend of market competition and privatization of the former public service. Further removed from the cases studied here, in Denmark, market competition was introduced in early 2003 under a Conservative government (cf. Bredgaard and Larsen 2008). The choice

49

for the introduction of market competition can thus not be traced back to the position of social-democratic parties in the government.

Market arrangements also entail a new logic of performance management. The Australian case shows how this can inhibit the process of market competition. The new set of instruments penetrates all phases in the implementation of the service: it plays a leading role in the selection of providers, in the matching of clients to a certain service, in the measurement of performance, in the financing of the outcome, in the registration and in the quality control. New instruments generate solutions for specific problems, but also give rise to new problems which in turn generate new solutions. The result is a multiplication of unintended effects and interaction effects. With a greater focus on short-term placements, authorities have less direct control of the quality of the process. There is a risk that the service will be reduced (e.g. by providing less training) or that the difficult groups will be excluded from intensive assistance because they are less profitable for the provider (the phenomenon of parking) (Considine 2005a; Struyven and Steurs 2005). Purchasing authorities have to rely on self-regulation by the market or they have to fall back on more process control. For the jobseeker, freedom of choice continues to receive scant attention, while the pressure for activation is increasing. Market competition makes high demands on government steering capacities and on the responsibility and self-motivation of jobseekers. This is the greatest challenge compared with the public system.

Acknowledgements

This research has received funding from the European Community's Seventh Framework Programme under grant agreement No. 320121 (Project INSPIRES). It is mainly based on my own PhD work, for which I would like to thank my then supervisors Romke van der Veen and Jan Bundervoet, as well as David Thompson, Mark Considine, Jos Mevissen and Els Sol. I would also like to thank my informants, the reviewers and editors for valuable comments on the article.

Notes

1. The government anticipated that around 10 per cent of cases eligible for case management would be contracted out in 1994–95, 'It is planned that this figure will increase to around 20 per cent in 1995–96 and to 30–40 per cent in subsequent years' (Commonwealth of Australia 1994a: 131). In 1996–97, the share of case management taken by the private (profit and non-profit) sectors had increased to 50 per cent.
2. Employment National steadily lost market share, and the organization was wound up on 1 July 2003.
3. The merger of UVIs is regarded as the biggest nationalization operation since the Second World War. The largest implementing body is GAK. The others are Cadans, GUO, SfB and USZO.
4. In the past, municipalities were able to claim 90 per cent of the funds needed for subsistence benefit from the central government. Since 1 January 2001, this 90:10 distribution has been converted to a 75:25 distribution. From

2002 onwards, the 25 per cent budget is distributed partly on the basis of objective and partly on the basis of historical distribution measures. All the funds are brought together in a single Work and Income Fund (FWI) at the municipality level. The Work and Social Assistance Act (2004) made municipalities 100 per cent financially responsible.

5. In May 1999, irregularities came to light and fraud was suspected involving European Social Fund (ESF) monies in the public employment agencies. It turned out that *Arbeidsvoorziening* did not have a separate project administration and also did not maintain the mandatory separate bank account for its ESF income. The financial embarrassment of *Arbeidsvoorziening* was increased significantly by the ESF scandal.

6. It should be noted that, recently, there has been more consultation with the sector than in the past on the implementation of the new model.

7. Early and ahead of the SUWI evaluation in 2006; the more limited European tender rules and experience and expertise functioned as a dam in a number of municipalities.

8. Due to the privatization of the risks of illness and incapacity for work (van der Veen and Trommel 1999), employers provide additional purchasing power on the reintegration market.

9. *Vlaamse Dienst voor Arbeidsbemiddeling en Beroepsopleiding* (VDAB).

10. Instead of adopting a quasi-market system, the VDAB experimented with small tenders of reintegration trajectories for the long-term unemployed.

11. Rijksdienst voor Arbeidsvoorziening (RVA).

12. In Flanders, the government monopoly remained in force until 1999, after publication of the ILO Convention concerning Private Employment Agencies, 1997 (No 181).

13. Figures for 1999 show a penetration rate of temporary employment in the Netherlands and Belgium of 4 per cent and 1.9 per cent, respectively, of total employment (CIETT 2000).

14. Following Visser and Hemerijck 1997, the failure of corporatism in the Netherlands broke the dam of institutional stability and the social security system was laid open for thorough restructuring.

15. Between 1970 and 2003, the trade union density in Belgium increased, against the European trend, from 42.1 per cent (1970) to 54.1 per cent (1980) and from 53.9 per cent (1990) to 55.4 per cent (2002), whereas in the Netherlands the trade union density fell from 36.5 per cent (1970) to 34.8 per cent (1980) and from 24.3 per cent (1990) to 22.3 per cent (2003). Together with three other small European economies (Finland, Sweden and Denmark), Belgium succeeded in maintaining the trade union density that had been built up in the 1970s. By way of comparison: the sharp fall in trade union density also occurred in Australia, from 50.2 per cent (1976) to 22.9 per cent (2003), a fall of 27.3 percentage points (Visser 2006). The parallel dwindling impact of the trade unions in Australia and the Netherlands suggests that this may have played a role in the market-based reforms of the public job brokerage service.

References

Bredgaard, T. and Larsen, F. (2008), Quasi-markets in employment policy: Do they deliver on promises? *Social Policy and Society*, 7, 3: 341–52.

CIETT (2000), *Orchestrating the Evolution of Private Employment Agencies Towards a Stronger Society*, Brussels: CIETT.

Commonwealth of Australia (1994a), *Working Nation: Policies and Programs, Government White Paper*, Canberra: Australian Government Publishing Service.

Commonwealth of Australia (1994b), *Working Nation. The White Paper on Employment and Growth*, Canberra: Australian Government Publishing Service.

Considine, M. (2001), *Enterprising States. The Public Management of Welfare-to-Work*, Cambridge: Cambridge University Press.

Considine, M. (2005a), Steering, Efficiency and Partnership: The Australian Quasi-market for Public Employment Services. In T. Bredgaard and F. Larsen (eds), *Employment Policy from Different Angles*, Copenhagen: DJØF-publishers.

Considine, M. (2005b), The reform that never ends: Quasi-Markets and Employment Services in Australia. In E. Sol and M. Westerveld (eds), *Contractualism in Employment Services: A New Form of Welfare State Governance*, The Hague: Kluwer Law International and Aspen Publishers, pp. 41–72.

Deeg, R. (2005), Change from Within: German and Italian Finance in the 1990s. In W. Streeck and K. Thelen (eds), *Beyond Continuity. Institutional Change in Advanced Political Economies*, Oxford: Oxford University Press.

Department of Employment, Workplace Relations and Small Business (DEWRSB) (2000), *Labour Market Review of Australia, Background Paper for the OECD Review Team*, Canberra: DEWRSB.

Ebbinghaus, B. and Visser, J. (2000), *Trade Unions in Western Europe since 1945*, London: Macmillan.

Gilbert, N. (2002), *Transformation of the Welfare State. The Silent Surrender of Public Responsibility*, Oxford: Oxford University Press.

Mahoney, J. (2000), Path Dependence in Historical Sociology, *Theory and Society*, 29: 507–48.

Mahoney, J. and Goertz, G. (2006), *A Tale of Two Cultures: Contrasting Quantitative and Qualitative Research*, Department of Political Science and Sociology, Evanston, IL: Northwestern University.

Mahoney, J. and Thelen, K. (2010), A Theory of Gradual Institutional Change. In J. Mahoney and K. Thelen (eds), *Explaining Institutional Change. Ambiguity, Agency and Power*, Cambridge: Cambridge University Press, pp. 1–37.

Organisation for Economic Co-operation and Development (OECD) (2001), *Innovations in Labour Market Policies. The Australian Way*, Paris: OECD.

Pierson, P. (2000a), The Limits of Design: Explaining Institutional Origins and Change, *Governance*, 13, 4: 475–99.

Pierson, P. (2000b), Increasing Returns, Path Dependency and the Study of Politics, *American Political Science Review*, 94, 2: 251–67.

Pierson, P. (ed.) (2001), *The New Politics of the Welfare State*, Oxford: Oxford University Press.

Productivity Commission (2002), *Independent Review of the Job Network: Inquiry Report*, Canberra: Commonwealth of Australia.

Ragin, Ch. (1987), *The Comparative Method. Moving Beyond Qualitative and Quantitative Strategies*, Berkeley and Los Angeles, CA: University of California Press.

Skocpol, T. (1992), *Protecting Soldiers and Mothers: The Political Origins of Social Policy in the United States*, Cambridge, MA: Belknap Press of Harvard University Press.

Streeck, W. and Thelen, K. (eds) (2005), *Beyond Continuity. Institutional Change in Advanced Political Economies*, Oxford: Oxford University Press.

Struyven, L. (2005), The New Institutional Logic of Public Employment Services. In T. Bredgaard and F. Larsen (eds), *Employment Policy from Different Angles*, Copenhagen: DJØF Publishing Copenhagen, pp. 175–91.

Struyven, L. (2006), *Hervormingen tussen drang en dwang. Marktwerking bij arbeids-bemiddeling*, Leuven: Acco.

Struyven, L. (2007), Between Efficiency and Equality: New Public–Private Arrangements in Employment Assistance for the Unemployment. In J. de Koning (ed.) (2007), *The Evaluation of Active Labour Market Policies. Measures, Public Private Partnerships and Benchmarking*, Cheltenham: Edward Elgar Publishing, pp. 193–220.

Struyven, L. and Steurs, G. (2005), Design and redesign of a quasi-market for the reintegration of jobseekers: empirical evidence from Australia and the Netherlands, *Journal of European social Policy*, 15, 3: 211–29.

Struyven, L. and Verhoest, K. (2005), The Problem of Agency at Organisational Level and Street Level: The Case of the Flemish Public Employment Service. In E. Sol and M. Westerveld (eds), *Contractualism in Employment Services: A New Form of Welfare State Governance*, The Hague: Kluwer Law International and Aspen Publishers.

Thelen, K. (1999), Historical Institutionalism in Comparative Politics, *Annual Review of Political Science*, 2: 369–404.

Thelen, K. (2003), How Institutions Evolve: Insights From Comparative Historical Analysis. In J. Mahoney and D. Rueschemeyer (eds), *Comparative Historical Analysis in the Social Sciences*, Cambridge: Cambridge University Press.

Thelen, K. (2004), *How Institutions Evolve. The Political Economy of Skills in Germany, Britain, the United States, and Japan*, Cambridge: Cambridge University Press.

van Berkel, R., de Graaf, W. and Sirovatka, T. (eds) (2011), *The Governance of Active Welfare States in Europe*, Basingstoke: Palgrave.

van der Veen, R. and Trommel, W. (1999), Managed Liberalization of the Dutch Welfare State: A Review and Analysis of the Dutch Social Security System, 1985–1998, *Governance*, 12, 3: 289–310.

Visser, J. (2006), Union membership statistics in 24 countries, *Monthly Labor Review*, January: 38–49.

Visser, J. and Hemerijck, A. (1997), '*A Dutch Miracle': Job Growth, Welfare Reform and Corporatism in the Netherlands*, Amsterdam: Amsterdam University Press.

Weishaupt, J. T. (2010), A silent revolution? New management ideas and the reinvention of European public employment services, *Socio-Economic Review*, 8, 3: 461–86.

3

Governance, Boards of Directors and the Impact of Contracting on Not-for-profits Organizations – An Australian Study

Mark Considine, Siobhan O'Sullivan and Phuc Nguyen

Introduction

Since the 1990s, the Australian employment services sector has undergone several waves of significant institutional reform: Working Nation (1994–96), three Job Network (JN) contracts (1996–2009) and the introduction of Job Services Australia (JSA) (2009–present). Arguably, not-for-profit (NFP) providers are among those most significantly impacted by this new contracting regime. Previously, NFP agencies worked in partnership with government on a grant-for-service basis. Under these reforms, they have had to adapt first to a limited competitive framework of contracted case management under Working Nation and then to full-scale competition with both private sector and corporatized public agencies, and with each other, under JN and JSA (Eardley 2002).

Various researchers have investigated the impacts of the reform on NFPs from different perspectives. For instance, Considine (1999) tested the effect of changes upon actual service delivery and concluded that frontline staff behaviour did not meet all the expectations of a post-Fordist welfare state and new public management (NPM), although some signs of specialization, flexibility and networking were evident. Cooper (2005) explored the challenges which NFP boards faced in maintaining accountability towards aged clients through effective governance of NFP aged care facilities. Rogers (2007) found that the requirements of JN had significantly influenced, and even distorted the values and behaviours of many church-based NFPs. Ramina and Carney (2003), on the other hand, were interested in strategy formation within NFPs operating within JN and how that has been influenced by NPM. In a study of the first JN contract in

Contracting-out Welfare Services: Comparing National Policy Designs for Unemployment Assistance,
First Edition. Edited by Mark Considine and Siobhan O'Sullivan.
© 2015 John Wiley & Sons, Ltd. Published 2015 by John Wiley & Sons, Ltd.

2001, Eardley *et al.* (2001) found evidence that competition had changed the way community-based employment agencies shared information and co-operated. For example, they demonstrated some resistance to sanctioning jobseekers and their advocacy role was also arguably undermined (Eardley 2002). However, little is known about the impact of these various waves of reform on the governance of NFPs and of their boards. One could expect that major changes in the funding of these organizations and in the competitive environment in which they operate would impact their internal structure (Pfeffer and Salancik 1978). However, the structural and behavioural changes which boards of directors have undertaken in response to the increasing competitive environment remain an under-researched field. This article aims to address that knowledge gap.

In this study, we examine how the reforms associated with contracted employment services in Australia have impacted the NFP boards of directors. We find that to effectively govern NFPs in a competitive market, NFP boards – the 'apex of the firm's decision control system' (Fama and Jensen 1983: 311) – have seen themselves as having little choice but to make changes to the way they perform their roles. Such changes are then reflected in boards' demographic and behavioral characteristics. Moreover, NFP boards face dilemmas, for example, in handling conflicts between organizational values and requirements imposed by the new management regime, which is described as the 'potential tension between governing nonprofit organisations as agents of community and operating them as agents of government' (Smith and Lipsky 1993: 72). We find that these tensions are significant and have a demonstrable impact on NFP governance.

Method

An inductive and qualitative method was employed to examine current practice in this NFP cohort. Ideally, all NFPs would be investigated for optimum validity of the findings. Unfortunately, this is not a feasible approach. There are too many agencies and they are widely dispersed across the country. Consequently, we opted to focus on a sub-set of providers which are broadly representative of NFP agencies delivering employment services in Australia. Two focus groups were held, one in Sydney and the other in Melbourne. Participants included board chairs, board members and chief executive officers (CEOs) from NFP organizations of various sizes in the employment services sector. Sixteen additional semi-structured interviews were undertaken with former and current board chairs, directors, CEOs and staff from a medium size NFP delivering the same kinds of contracted social services to those in the focus groups. Interviewees were chosen for their extensive experience and understanding of the organization at both board and operational level, as well as their institutional memory.

As a starting point, the focus groups and interviews were designed to ascertain the basic features and decision making processes of the boards in relation to the ongoing government reform process, values and decision-making. The focus groups also addressed the question of how to evaluate the board evaluation and the board's role in organizational governance and management. In order to encourage respondents to provide as much context as possible, open-ended questions were also adopted and a non-attribution method was used.

The focus groups and interviews were recorded and transcribed. The data analysis was conducted using NVivo (a software supporting qualitative data analysis). Methods employed during the analysis process included identifying patterns and themes, making contrasts and comparisons, cross-case synthesis, pattern matching and content analysis.

Employment Services Reform in Australia

Since the 1990s, the Australian government has implemented a series of radical reforms in the employment services sector in order to deal with the country's high rate of long-term unemployment (Considine 2001). The subsequent reforms have been numerous, with each later reform having been introduced for the purpose of addressing problems identified in previous regimes. These reforms include some complex and demanding alterations in the way services are delivered, as well as new pressures on the entitlement to income support (Considine 2001). The core element of Australia's employment services reform involves gradual privatization of the delivery of employment services. More specifically, employment services delivery has been put in the hands of numerous contractors. With each new tender process the pool of employment services agencies active in Australia's quasi-employment services market has reduced. At the start of JN in 1998, around 300 agencies acted as contracted service providers. At the time of writing, fewer than 100 agencies hold contracts. Downward pressure on agency numbers continues, and under Australia's unique 'Star Ratings' system, under-performing agencies may lose their service contract even between tender rounds.

Under Australia's contracted employment services system, for-profit (FP) and NFP agencies have to compete for the right to provide basic services to the unemployed (Considine 2005). The inclusion of FP and NFP agencies in Australia's employment services contracting regime is no coincidence. In designing Working Nation, Prime Minister Paul Keating pledged that he would engage 'community and private sector agencies' (Keating 1994). The Coalition government, responsible for implementing the world's first fully contracted employment services system, also saw value in dividing the sector between FP and NFP providers.

Former Minister for Employment Tony Abbott argued in relation to 'faith based' NFPs that, 'There is something extra about people with faith in their hearts, and the love of God on their lips, that gives them that extra commitment to job seekers' (cited in Mendes 2009: 107). Yet despite the professed desirability of a mix of agency types delivering services, Australia's procurement process affords NFP agencies no special status. Australia has a single purchaser model and tender speci-fications do not solicit information which might favour NFPs, such as links to community or commitment to mission. While commercial-in-confidence requirements make it difficult to form a reliable picture of either the market share, or profitability, of the private agencies which deliver Australia's employment services, industry insiders we talked to on occasions such as conferences tend to agree that the Australian mar-ket is fairly evenly split between FP and NFP agencies.

Arguably, NFP providers are among those who have been most sig-nificantly impacted by the new management regime in the Australian employment services industry. The dual processes of privatization and corporatization have created multiple challenges for NFPs, for example, 'being pushed towards corporate governance systems that may be at odds with their mission statement and/or ethos' (Cooper 2005: 71) or being forced to make changes which threaten the attributes which make them different from FPs (Ryan 1999). Various researchers have empir-ically investigated the impact of the reform on NFPs from different perspectives. Eardley *et al.* (2001) found evidence that competition had changed the way community-based employment agencies shared infor-mation and co-operated. Instead of traditional collaborative approaches (Abello and MacDonald 2002), NFPs now have to guard their market knowledge and power in competition for funding resources (Eardley *et al.* 2001). Many were found to be resistant to sanctioning jobseekers (Laragy 1999; Eardley 2002) at the expenses of their competitiveness (Abello and MacDonald 2002). Some faced greater difficulty in pursuing their advocacy role because they could not maintain a critical distance from the government (Laragy 1999; Eardley 2002). The impacts included the vanishing of those which could not accommodate these challenges (Abello and MacDonald 2002).

Rogers (2007) studied the impact of JN on church-based NFPs. She found evidence of both direct and in-direct impacts: the former were seen through providers' dependence on JN revenue and 'their conformance to the clearly articulated accountability and performance measurement requirements of the contract', while the latter occurred when 'the gov-ernment extends its reach to influence the defining values of the NFP provider, and the morale and composition of its staff' (Rogers 2007: 395). Having investigated how NPM influenced the way NFPs operating within the JN formulated their strategies, Ramina and Carney (2003) urged NFP managers to significantly broaden their strategic mindset. Cooper (2005), on the other hand, discussed the challenges board directors faced in maintaining accountability to aged clients through effective governance of NFP aged care facilities.

Being interested in how NFP and FP agencies behaved under JN, Lyons and Chan (1999) found some convergence emerging between the two sectors in their operations. NFPs became more commercial-like, while some private firms were 'displaying the kind of social concern about clients and their needs generally associated with the community sector' (Eardley 2002: 302). The convergence between NFP and FP sectors was also identified in the delivery of frontline social services by Considine (2001) and Considine *et al.* (2011). However, little is known about the impact of these various waves of reform in the Australian employment services sector on NFP boards *per se*. More specifically, structural and behavioural changes which boards of directors have undertaken in response to the increasing competitive environment remain an under-researched field.

The Role of Boards of Directors

Boards of directors are thought to have two distinct roles: control and direction (Aguilera 2005; Forbes and Milliken 1999; Nicholson and Kiel 2004; Petrovic 2008). Control refers to a board's legal duty to monitor management on behalf of the firm's shareholders and to carry out this duty with loyalty and care (Monks and Ninow 2011). Direction involves 'boards' strategic guidance of the company' (Petrovic 2008: 1374). Underlying these two roles are agency and resource dependency theories respectively. As stipulated in agency theory, when organizational ownership is separated from control – that is, owners (also called principals) hire other people (agents) to manage the organization instead of exercising direct control themselves – principal-agent problems arise (Jensen and Meckling 1976). More specifically, principals' welfare is at risk when agents engage in opportunistic behaviours which maximize their own personal interests and expend insufficient effort towards achieving agreed-upon objectives (Jensen and Meckling 1976). Boards of directors, the representative of principals (Mizruchi 1983; Walsh and Seward 1990), are established as an endogenous response to such agency problems (Dey 2008). They are responsible for 'monitoring of the management for the benefit of principals to ensure that strategic objectives are achieved' (Petrovic 2008: 1374). Examples of their activities as listed by Petrovic (2008) include hiring, compensation and replacement of the CEO and senior managers, approval of major initiatives proposed by management, reporting to the shareholders/stakeholders, and ensuring compliance with the law.

Viewed from a resource dependence perspective, organizational success is measured by an organization's ability to maximize its power in its operating environment (Pfeffer 1981). An organization can maximize its power by:

1. minimizing its dependence on external organizations by having access to, and control over, resources (e.g. knowledge, capital and venture partnering arrangements) (Ruigrok *et al.* 2007) which are essential to its survival; and
2. maximizing other organizations' dependence on it by having access to, and control over, resources which other organizations need (Medcof 2001; Tillquist *et al.* 2002; Ulrich and Barney 1984).

Put simply, an organization's ability to acquire important resources plays a critical role in its success. Boards of directors, with their human capital (that is, experience, expertise, reputation) and relational capital (that is, network of ties to other firms and external contingencies), are seen to help organizations secure provision of valued resources (Hillman and Dalziel 2003) which would otherwise be beyond their reach (Brown 2006; Dalton *et al.* 1998; Pfeffer and Salancik 1978). Their services include advice and counsel to the CEO and other top managers, and to participate actively in the formulation of strategy (Forbes and Milliken 1999).

Compared to public and FP agencies, those governing NFPs arguably face challenges which are rarely found within the other two sectors. Such challenges, according to Lyons (2001), are generated by the six distinctive characteristics of the NFP sector. They are: first, centrality of values. In NFPs, values play a central role and are not easily compromised. Values are of such high importance in NFPs that it can be difficult for them, for example, to resolve disagreements or make changes in response to new circumstances (Lyons 2001). Second, the fact that NFPs usually have multiple sources of operating revenue, for example, membership dues; donations; bequests; sale of core services; profits from unrelated business ventures; government grants or contracts; grants from trusts or foundations; sponsorship; other forms of partnership arrangement with business; and interest on capital reserves, complicates the governance accountability and management of the organizations (Lyons 2001).

Third, most NFPs rely on volunteers to some extent and ensuring the most effective combination of volunteers and paid staff is no easy task (Lyons 2001). Fourth, boards and managers of NFPs generally have difficulty judging the organization's performance because many of the services NFPs provide, such as childcare and environmental advocacy, are 'intrinsically difficult to judge' or there is 'a lack of relevant data for the purpose of performance evaluation' (Lyons 2001: 24). Fifth, stakeholders of an NFP organization are usually multiple, including owners (that is, its members); funding bodies; clients; staff; partner organizations; Indigenous organizations; governments; consultants; suppliers; researchers; customers; members of the association; professional bodies; and the general public (Cooper 2005). It is, therefore, not at all clear to whom ultimately these organizations should be accountable, which poses a great challenge for boards in the decision-making process. A final challenge, 'a perennial challenge for those NFP that employ staff', is tension, often conflict, between senior staff and the board or management committee (Lyons 2001: 26). These tensions arise from a lack of clarity about the role of boards, a difficulty made worse by lack of clear performance measures (Lyons 2001).

Not surprisingly, then, boards of directors are thought to have a significant potential impact on organizational performance. Positive contributions are expected when they perform effectively and vice versa. Therefore, researchers and practitioners alike have sought to better understand demographic attributes of boards and the processes and behaviours involved in effective board performance (Forbes and Milliken 1999). Examples of board demographic characteristics which have been subjected to various studies are as follows:

1. Board size (Forbes and Milliken 1999; Golden and Zajac 2001; Hardwick *et al.* 2011; Shan and Xu 2012; Van-Ness *et al.* 2010).
2. Board tenure (Van-Ness *et al.* 2010; Forbes and Milliken 1999; Golden and Zajac 2001).
3. Average age of members of a board (Golden and Zajac 2001; Van-Ness *et al.* 2010).
4. Board diversity – for example, age, occupation, education, experience, gender, minorities, nationality (Forbes and Milliken 1999; Guzzo and Dickson 1996; Golden and Zajac 2001; Hardwick *et al.* 2011; Hartarska and Nadolnyak 2012; Jackson 1992; Van-Ness *et al.* 2010).
5. Board composition – for example, the proportion of outsiders to insiders (Forbes and Milliken 1999; Hardwick *et al.* 2011; Hermalin and Weisbach 1991; Johnson *et al.* 1993; Shan and Xu 2012; Van-Ness *et al.* 2010).
6. Full board meeting frequency (Forbes and Milliken 1999; Shan and Xu 2012).
7. Board structure – for example, committees (Hardwick *et al.* 2011).
8. CEO duality (Hardwick *et al.* 2011; Van-Ness *et al.* 2010).
9. Boards' incentives (Hillman and Dalziel 2003).
10. Board dependence and director compensation (Dey 2008; Hermalin and Weisbach 1991).
11. Board faultline – that is, board sub-grouping based on multiple attributes (Bezrukova *et al.* 2009; Lau and Murnighan 2005).
12. Board capital – that is, human and relational capital (Forbes and Milliken 1999; Hillman and Dalziel 2003).
13. Board dynamics – that is, how board directors engage with and work with each other in shaping the future of a company (Mellahi 2005; Petrovic 2008).

Board processes which have been argued to have profound implications on boards' decision-making (Mellahi 2005) include the following:

1. Board attention – that is, 'types of issues that capture boards' attention and the degree of attention they devote to particular issues' (Golden and Zajac 2001: 1093).
2. Boards' evaluation – for example, CEO evaluation (Golden and Zajac 2001).
3. Effort norms – that is, boards' shared beliefs regarding the level of effort each individual is expected to put toward a task (Wageman 1995).
4. Cognitive conflict – that is, 'task-oriented differences in judgment among group members' (Forbes and Milliken 1999: 494).

61

5.   Board cohesiveness – that is, 'the affective dimension of members' inclusion on the Board and the ability of the board to continue working together' (Forbes and Milliken 1999: 493).
6.   The board's use of its knowledge and skills – including:
     a.   the knowledge and skills present on the board; and
     b.   the way in which those resources are used by the board (Forbes and Milliken 1999).
7.   Board power (Golden and Zajac 2001).

Researchers have also sought evidence of links between multiple board characteristics and processes and the different organizational performance criteria, for example:

1.   board effectiveness (Petrovic 2008);
2.   boards' involvement in restructuring (Johnson *et al.* 1993);
3.   organizational fraud (Wang *et al.* 2010);
4.   inclination to strategic change (Golden and Zajac 2001);
5.   profit efficiency (Hardwick *et al.* 2011);
6.   agency conflicts (Dey 2008); and
7.   firm performance (Hermalin and Weisbach 1991; Hillman and Dalziel 2003; Kaczmarek *et al.* 2012; Shan and Xu 2012; Van-Ness *et al.* 2010).

Results of those empirical studies, however, are mixed. In short, what is required to ensure an effective board remains open to a number of possible explanations and is certainly related to the character of initiatives adopted by boards themselves.

Australian Not-for-Profit Boards' Response to Service Contracting

As noted, the billion dollar per year Australian employment services industry has seen a major transformation since the inception of the reform in the early 1990s, or *'a long journey from that day to JSA'* as one interviewee described the process. Key to such a transformation is the emergence of the role of competition which, according to interviewees, has exercised a great influence on NFP organizations. Previously, NFPs used to be *'small organisations that were working in their community'*. They co-operated and shared information with each other in order to achieve their social values. There was not *'a sense of competition'* between them. However, such neighbourly and friendly practices are no longer common. With the implementation of Working Nation, then JN and, lastly, JSA, NFPs have been *'under increasing pressures on having to compete and to achieve outcomes'* and they have to be guarded about what contributes to their competitive advantage. Their relationships with the government have also been subjected to changes. Initially, NFP organizations *'might have just been funded by donations'* and then *'they started getting subsidies from government'* and came to have *'contractual relations with governments'*.

The newly introduced competitive nature of the employment services market had also challenged NFPs' existence and longevity. Legally, NFPs are 'bound by a nondistribution constraint which prohibits the distribution of the organisation's earnings or assets' (Hansmann 2010: 60). On the one hand, non-distribution constraint makes NFPs favourable in some situations where the information flow between service providers and customers is severely asymmetric (Hansmann 2010). For instance, when people make donations to charities, they are in fact customers who purchase services to be delivered to unrelated third parties. They, however, have virtually no control of the quantity and quality of the service especially when service receivers are in remote areas. They may, therefore, feel safer when the organization receiving their donation is an NFP (Hansmann 2010). On the other hand, non-distribution constraint is argued by Hansmann (2010) to potentially disadvantage NFPs in competition with FP providers. According to Hansmann (2010), non-distribution constraint's prohibition on owners essentially exposes NFPs to higher managerial costs than FP providers in the form of a failure to minimize costs; a bias toward excessive quality and/or quantity; and inflexibility in response to changes in market demand (Hansmann 2010). It also prevents NFPs from raising much needed capital by selling equity shares, as is practiced by their FP counter-partners. That might be one reason why the employment services market has seen *'a significant reduction in the number of service providers'* since privatization commenced. According to those inside the industry, there were providers which could not cope with such challenges and disappeared. Only those which *'picked up the challenges and took on the diversity and recognised the right time to change the skill set'* have survived and become larger. As illustrated by one interviewee, his/her organization has survived the reforms and grown from *'a very small operation'* to a *'$30 million business'* over the last 19 years.

Importantly, in the research participants' view, the market has become 'pretty tight' in terms of competition. While this can be explained by an escalation of the scale of competition, the growth of the surviving providers is also thought to play a role. Despite the increasingly aggressive introduction of the quasi-market regime in the industry, respondents agreed that in the early stages of JN, government contracts were a major funding source or *'a cash cow'*, as one interviewee put it, for NFPs. Many organizations could build their reserves and grew bigger and have become *'a little bit more business-like or commercial in the way in which you operate'* accordingly.

Interestingly, NFPs, once having grown bigger, have faced further pressures to grow even larger. Internally, while they needed to *'become self-sustaining'* and *'maintain their current service provision'*, they now had to serve a bigger organization which required, without doubt, more resources. Externally, as perceived by interviewees, they were locked into growth. Otherwise, they believe they would be discriminated against and lose government contracts. They, therefore, claimed they had no choice other than *'keep doing that work and grow'* their businesses further, which in turn has imposed greater need for them to become *'more professional'* in their operations. Understandably, with larger and increasingly professional players in the market, more intense and exacting forms of competition appear inevitable.

In brief, there exists an interactive relationship between competition, organizational growth and professionalization. More specifically, competition filters out players with more limited reach; successful survivors enjoy extra resources and grow and subsequently face greater need for professionalization; and fewer, bigger and more professional competitors in the market in turn intensifies this form of competitiveness. On the purchasing side, increased professionalism by agencies probably increases pressure on the purchaser to choose agents who exhibit recognizable forms of professionalism in both their bids and their track records.

In other words, the Australian policy reform has played no small a part in this trajectory by directly or indirectly inducing competitiveness and organizational growth. As previously mentioned, the competition concept was first introduced as a key reform agenda and its scale has been escalating since. Furthermore, reform has also fuelled the scaling-up process inside agencies by providing them with substantial financial reserves in the early stages of JN and the perception that small players will be vulnerable. Therefore, without any speculation on its absolute magnitude, a causal relationship between the policy reform and organizational growth, and subsequent professionalization, can be observed with reasonable confidence.

In charge of governing growing NFPs with ever greater pressures for these organizations to become more professional, boards of directors, according to those we interviewed, have evolved and *'lifted standards'* to accommodate these challenges. There was a general agreement among interviewees that NFP boards have become *'more responsible'* and *'provided a professional approach to the nature of work'*. In other words, they have embarked on a process for improving their own professional-managerial skills.

In light of the much contested literature on what constitutes a profession, a brief discussion on this issue is needed before going further into the empirical findings. The most widely accepted perspective among sociologists in the professionalism field is that 'profession' is a prestigious occupation with special characteristics and attributes (Watson 2002; Williams *et al.* 2009; Yee 2001). A profession holds an important and distinguished status in the society and thus becoming 'professional' is desirable. 'Professionalization' is subsequently defined as a process of an occupation attempting to obtain the status and recognition of a profession (Freidson 1988).

However, this approach has been subjected to operational problems and criticisms from various authors. For instance, while many occupations are aiming to achieve the position of a 'profession', saying exactly what attributes constitute a profession is still a matter of debate, and each competing theory has a different perspective (Yee 2001). Profession or professionalization is also criticized as a market strategy adopted by occupations seeking monopoly control over an area of activity which would guarantee them an advantaged position within the class structure (Larson 1977) or a 'vehicle used to further or defend particular occupational interests' in certain ways (Watson 2002: 94). Becker (1970: 92) even claims that 'professions' are 'simply those occupations which have been fortunate enough in the politics of today's work world to gain and maintain possession of that honorific title'. Alternatively, Yee (2001) proposes that 'profession' is a changing concept and what really matters are the dynamics underlying the professionalization of a particular organization. Watson (2002) on the other hand suggests that 'profession' and 'professionalism' are interpreted in accordance with the way people in society generally, and spokespersons for occupational groupings in particular, use such notions to achieve particular purposes.

For the purpose of the research at hand, observations by Garratt (2003) on professionalization in the context of organizational boards of directors are useful. For him, professionalization of the boards of directors (which is extremely important if improvements in shareholder value are to be sustained) is achieved when 'directors are selected, trained, developed, appraised, and sacked, in an open and systematic way' (Garratt 2003: 530). Importantly in this context, the standard against which such decisions are made is commercial performance, not the capacity to represent non-commercial interests. As we show, this focus upon commercial performance is what has been happening in the professionalization process at the board level in Australian NFPs engaged in contracted social service delivery.

With these commercial imperatives and increased competitiveness, boards have come to adopt a more business-oriented view of NFP organizations. It was made clear by interviewees that *'not-for-profit didn't mean it was for a loss'*. They were there to *'make it longevity and make it business based'*, *'so that they can be there in the long term'*. They no longer accepted the point of view that poor performance could be tolerated just because organizations they were governing were NFP. Importantly, they clearly confirmed that turning an NFP into a commercial organization did not mean that they ceased to be an NFP. Instead, it was seen as necessary to generate a profit because, like any other organizations, NFPs need resources in order to achieve their social values and mission.

Boards also recognized that director skills are critical to organizational performance in light of the new challenges of the competitive market. They suspected that they could not *'sustain and give an organisation any leadership without those skills and experience'* and thus they should move towards recruitment of directors based on these skills, *'We don't have the skills, well let's get more skills, let's get more attitude, let's take more risk and they're the sort of cultures you need to move towards'*. In reality, some NFPs have implemented commercial skill-based recruitment practices. Specifically, they first define a skill set required of the board based on the needs of the organizations and then address whatever skills shortfall

65

may remain by either board training or recruiting new directors with the desired skills:

'It is fortunate that we can, we ... had a drive to bring in people like – some fine candidates ... to lead the organisation in that next phase of growth that we had and we found that we had a short fall in skill sets and we needed to replenish our board membership in order to fit the ... to satisfy the needs of the organisation.'

Interestingly, the interviewees had a very dynamic view of these responsibilities. They pointed out that the skill set required of the board was not static. Rather it would change to accommodate a particular development stage of the organization, *'The timing for getting the right skills, in this particular sector, has got to be balanced with where the organisation is, so that you get that right ...'.* *'It wasn't until it got to that stage that the organisation was starting to say "Well, hang on, now we can do that for you" but now they needed another skill set, that's where I came onto that board'.* Therefore, many respondents considered it their responsibility to continuously improve their skills in accordance with the new organizational require-ments, *'As you're growing, you need the skilled based boards as a board – as a director with a commitment to the organisation, you have to identify where you're short on skills and target them and chase them'.* They were also open to board training opportunities, both formal and informal, in their pursuit of these skills. Some members had even voluntarily resigned when they found their skills had apparently passed their 'use by date' and they could no longer make meaningful contributions, which is quite a radical approach, especially when it seems to have come directly from the board members themselves.

Associated with this new mind-set regarding board responsibilities was increased utilization of more strategic and aggressive recruitment practices in NFPs. Before, directors used to *'step up and put my hand up'* or be *'hand-picked'*, *'identified and tapped on the shoulder'*, *'asked'*, *'suggested'* or joined the board by *'invitation'*, *'word of mouth'* and *'network'*. Now the practices of using *'advertisement'*, *'head hunter[s]'*, *'executive recruitment firm[s]'* or *'a recruitment agency'* have become more popular. Organizations have grown much larger and so have the requirements for boards. It was, therefore, not easy to acquire a director with the required skills using the traditional volunteering methods.

According to one interviewee, *'finding the right skill set sometimes requires a recruitment agency to go out there'.* Consequently, in order to be able to recruit individuals with the required skill sets, some NFPs have moved towards paying board members. Most of the interviewees strongly objected to the idea of paying boards in NFPs by clearly stating that they would not look for payments as an NFP director and would not accept payments even if offered. However, they had to admit that while *'the high profile not-for-profits will always manage to attract people to their boards without pay'*, the situation would be much more difficult for small and medium NFP boards. Payments were, therefore, necessary:

'It's growing, in my opinion. I believe it has to, if you're going to be serious about a large organisation, you need to – and you want serious commitment from the board and you want them to spend the time, the effort. It's far too difficult to find the people that are – or at least in my experience, it's becoming more and more difficult to find people with the commitment to sit on a board like that without charge.'

However, this paid-board tendency could undermine NFP boards' distinguished status as 'embodiment and representation of community interests' (Smith and Lipsky 1993: 74). According to Smith and Lipsky (1993), that status of NFP boards is sustained via two practices. First, directors volunteer (that is, give unremunerated time and effort to the organization) and thereby commit to fight the problems of the community (Smith and Lipsky 1993). Second, 'they are selected, and are understood to be selected, on the basis of their allegiance to the ideas and values embodied in the organisation's character, history and current purposes' (Smith and Lipsky 1993: 74). With a move towards a paid board model, the unique status of NFP boards may be at risk. Also, the introduction of paid boards may result in boards themselves being less committed to the community and its problems and consequently less inclined to assume an advocacy role, which traditionally has been 'one of the most important roles played by NFPs' (Kimberlin 2010: 166).

To accommodate organizational growth, NFP boards have also grown in size and been structured into specialized committees accordingly. For example, we now see boards with audit committees, finance committees, risk committees and governance committees:

'With that we have become very professional I'd like to think in the last couple of years where we've broken into committees the audit finance risk committee and also a governance committee and that does I guess take a lot of pressure off the chair because they do a lot of work those two chairs; the one on the governance and the audit finance and risk committee.'

While the influence of board size on board effectiveness is not always linear (Golden and Zajac 2001), growth and structuring of boards into multiple committees was viewed by respondents as a sign of becoming more professional.

Other developments that were reported by interviewees to have been linked to the professionalization process include new forms of board induction, board training and board evaluation. Traditionally, there used to be no or very limited induction for directors when they joined NFP boards. As organizations have grown, directors are increasingly having to complete a formal induction process with a full induction manual provided to them with information about the organization and their roles and responsibilities, for example, *'the operation of the board and responsibilities'*, *'overview of government policy (for example, how the funding contracts operate)'* and *'work of organisation'*. Other forms of director induction also include induction time with the board, the chair, management (e.g. CEO, chief financial officer) and *'introduction across the sorts of work (for example, employment work, crisis support work, youth work …)'*.

Directors reported that they also had more training opportunities than before. They could attend conferences where there were specific sessions for board members or be sent away for courses. Some interviewees even recommended that induction and training process should be made mandatory and *'there should be some sort of basic certification for people coming onto committees'*.

Last but not least, some NFP boards have now had regular evaluations usually once a year for internal evaluation and once every two years externally. Directors are evaluated against a defined skills matrix and those who do not show the required skills may be asked to leave their board. Although considered tough by directors themselves, they all agreed that such processes are necessary to ensure the full presence of the required skill set on the board:

> *'We, every year, look at skills matrix, we evaluate the board, the chairman evaluates the directors each year, each two years we get a full either external evaluation or probably a really intense evaluation. We've – some directors have left our board in the last year or so because the skill sets were seen not to be there, so if you're going to do that you have to then take this next approach otherwise you don't get the value.'*

The Challenges to Not-for-Profit Boards Posed by Competitive Tendering

According to our respondents, NFP boards have faced further challenges or side-effects of the professionalization process. Directors made clear in interviews that they joined NFP boards for reasons which can be divided into three categories: cause-related, skill-related and political. The first and foremost motive for directors to join an NFP board is their desire to give back to the community. Skill-related reasons are various, for example:

1. Directors had skills and professional experiences which organizations need and they *'can help that organization by bringing those skills to the table'*.
2. It was seen as an opportunity for them to *'sharpen their swords'* and *'expand [their] professional development'*.
3. They were intellectually stimulated by involvement in board activities.
4. It provided them with personal satisfaction, including making a contribution to an organizational transformation.
5. The organizations which they joined were tolerant of new members.

Political reasons are present when some directors considered their responsibility to boost the presence of a particular sector at the national level. However, to obtain the required skill set on the board, many NFPs have taken on board directors who have skills but *'might not share the values of the organisation and might just be there for the dollar value'.* While most of our interviewees agreed that an NFP director did not have to be passionate about organizational values and only a certain alignment between directors' values and organizations was required, a director who did not have a real empathy towards organizational values could be problematic.

For example, some NFP boards were reported to suffer from serious board tensions and conflicts due to the presence of some individuals who did not have real empathy towards the organization's missions or focus. This ultimately negatively impacted on the organization as a whole. Furthermore, this practice effectively undermines the second cornerstone supporting the previously discussed status of NFPs' boards as embodiments and representatives of community interest, as argued by Smith and Lipsky (1993), which again calls for caution among directors in NFPs in the sector concerning how far they should go in the direction of professionalization.

While becoming more business-like and professional is said to be the objective of this process, it was also a challenge for the boards to correctly position their organizations in the new operating environment, especially with regard to achieving financial performance without losing identities and changing their organizational mission and values, *'So I think it changes the nature of – it's always concerned me that organisation, that charities are becoming more an agent of government and that is now swamping or diluting or changing their values'.*

Another problem facing NFP boards is the handling of directors who did not pass board evaluations and were, therefore, either under-contributing or had become a liability. While this task would be easier for boards which pay directors, in the view of those we interviewed, it was a very sensitive process for non-paying boards. As previously mentioned, political and job-related motives aside, most directors joined NFP boards, especially in cases where there is no pay, because they want to help. It, therefore, would be natural for them to think that they are making a contribution. That said, a director's view of his or her own performance might be different from others' evaluations and as a result self-perception about a suitable time to leave a board might be impaired. In addition, because most NFP board members voluntarily devote their time and effort without expecting payment, the task of dismissal is made even more difficult.

In short, under pressure to professionalize with more managerial skills and experience, NFP boards have been found to embark on a very fundamental transformation process. More specifically, NFP boards have adopted a more business-like view of their organizations in general and lifted their board skill sets and responsibilities accordingly. They reportedly made radical changes, for example, utilizing strategic recruitment strategies (e.g. skill-based, paid boards), board restructures and the introduction of more comprehensive induction, training and evaluation processes. However, some practices which were deployed during the professionalizing process, such as paid board membership and recruitment of non-value-sharing directors, should be applied with caution because, in line with arguments by Smith and Lipsky (1993), these practices might have a damaging impact on NFP boards' identity as an embodiment and representation of community interests. Moreover, the professionalization process has not come without challenges. Evidence shows that NFP boards have faced tensions and conflict due to this increased diversification in directors' motives for joining. Achieving the right balance in applying corporate governance mechanisms to a charity has proven to be a difficult task for many.

Conclusion

Understanding the pressure to improve governance is critical to understanding the changes occurring in the NFP sector. It is, therefore, not surprising that many authors have investigated the impact of contracting-out and related reforms on service providers. However, while there might be other filters in between the government policies and organizational performance, such as boards of directors, other funding providers and different layers of management, most of the studies have focused on the direct link between the government and the operational level of these organizations. The intermediary layers of management and directorship have been largely neglected. This research is one of the first studies into the impact of public policy reform in the employment services sector on NFP boards. Its findings are, therefore, expected to be meaningful on several fronts.

First, it provides policymakers with evidence of the impact of the reform upon NFPs at a level that has never been studied before, which means a more comprehensive evaluation of the reforms themselves is possible. Thus, such findings should be an additional input to be taken into account when policymakers are contemplating any further reform initiatives. Second, based on the findings of this study, directors of NFPs have a chance to reflect on what is happening at the board level in their own organizations. They might want to seriously reconsider the impacts of the managerial professionalization process on their identity as a governance group within the context of the broader NFP agency. Third, for those researchers who are interested in boards' roles in organizational change as a result of NPM reforms, this study could be used as the first step to making sense of the processes at work. Australia's advanced employment services privatization status means that the Australian experience can direct attention to factors likely to be important in other privatizing sectors.

However, this study is not exempt from several limitations which deserve further investigation. First, the sample of this study, while being representative of the sector, did not include all NFPs in the sector. Consequently, a deductive and quantitative approach to further confirm our conclusions with the data to be collected from the whole sector is definitely worth pursuing. Likewise, a larger sample might give even greater confidence in the findings. Second, by focusing on

NFP boards only, this study makes no comparison of a possible convergence in behaviours with FP providers which are also integral to the Australian employment services market. As Eardley *et al.* (2001) found, reforms have had an impact on FP providers as well. For example, some FPs have been found to become more concerned about clients and their needs, an attitude generally associated with the NFP sector. Therefore, a study which explores changes of FP boards under the same reform process would provide additional insight into the system overall.

Third, this research has not gone beyond the professionalization of NFP boards *per se* to explore its implications on the rest of the organization. Studies which investigate if and how board professionalization influences, for instance, CEO performance and other organizational activities, such as advocacy, are likely to be revealing. Lastly, the data used for the purpose of this research was collected on a non-longitudinal basis while reform in the employment services sector in Australia has undergone several stages. It, therefore, would be insightful if impacts of each reform stage on boards in general, and NFP boards in particular, could be separately studied on a longitudinal basis.

References

Abello, D. and Macdonald, H. (2002), Job Network: changing community sector values, *The Drawing Board: An Australian Review of Public Affairs*, 3: 51–63.

Aguilera, R. V. (2005), Corporate governance and director accountability: an institutional comparative perspective, *British Journal of Management*, 16: S39–S53.

Becker, H. S. (1970), *Sociological Work: Method and Substance*, Chicago, IL: Aldine Publishing.

Bezrukova, K., Jehn, K. A, Zanutto, E. L. and Thatcher, S. M. B. (2009), Do workgroup faultlines help or hurt? a moderated model of faultlines, team identification, and group performance, *Organization Science*, 20: 35–50.

Brown, R. J. J. (2006), Criticizing the critics: Sarbanes-Oxley and quack corporate governance, *Marquette Law Review*, 90: 309–35.

Considine, M. (1999), Markets, networks and the new welfare state: employment assistance reform in Australia, *Journal of Social Policy*, 28: 183–203.

Considine, M. (2001), *Enterprising States: The Public Management of Welfare-to-Work*, Cambridge: Cambridge University Press.

Considine, M. (2005), The reform that never ends: quasi-markets and employment services in Australia. In E. Sol and M. Westerveld (eds), *Contractualism in Employment Services: A New Form of Welfare State Governance*, The Hague: Kluwer Law International and Aspen Publishers, pp. 41–71.

Considine, M., Lewis, J. M. and O'Sullivan, S. (2011), Quasi-markets and service delivery flexibility following a decade of employment assistance reform in Australia, *Journal of Social Policy*, 40: 811–33.

Cooper, L. (2005), Conformance and performance: board directors' accountability to their not-for-profit organisations' constituents in the aged care sector – the Ach group experience, *Third Sector Review*, 11: 67–84.

Dalton, D. R., Daily, C. M., Ellstrand, A. E. and Johnson, J. L. (1998), Meta-analytic reviews of board composition, leadership structure, and financial performance, *Strategic Management Journal*, 19: 269–90.

Dey, A. (2008), Corporate governance and agency conflicts, *Journal of Accounting Research*, 46: 1143–81.

Eardley, T. (2002), Mutual obligation and the Job Network: the effect of competition on the role of non-profit employment services, *Australian Journal of Social Issues*, 37: 301–14.

Eardley, T., Abello, D. and Macdonald, H. (2001), *Is the Job Network benefiting disadvantaged job seekers? Preliminary evidence from a study of non-profit employment services*, SPRC Discussion Paper 111, Sydney: Social Policy Research Centre.

Fama, E. F. and Jensen, M. C. (1983), Separation of ownership and control, *Journal of Law and Economics*, 26: 301–25.

Forbes, D. P. and Milliken, F. J. (1999), Cognition and corporate governance: understanding boards of directors as strategic decision-making groups, *Academy of Management Review*, 24: 489–505.

Freidson, E. (1988), *Profession of Medicine: A Study of the Sociology of Applied Knowledge*, Chicago, IL: University of Chicago Press.

Garratt, B. (2003), The future for boards: professionalisation or incarceration? *Keeping Good Companies*: 526–31.

Golden, B. R. and Zajac, E. J. (2001), When will boards influence strategy? Inclination x power=strategic change, *Strategic Management Journal*, 22: 1087–111.

Guzzo, R. A. and Dickson, M. W. (1996), Teams in organizations: recent research on performance and effectiveness, *Annual Review of Psychology*, 47: 307–38.

Hansmann, H. (2010), The Economics of Nonprift Organizations. In K. J. Hopt and T. V. Hippel (eds), *Comparative Corporate Governance of Non-profit Organizations*. Cambridge: Cambridge University Press, pp. 60–72.

Hardwick, P., Adams, M. and Zou, H. (2011), Board characteristics and profit efficiency in the United Kingdom life insurance industry, *Journal of Business Finance & Accounting*, 38: 987–1015.

Hartarska, V. and Nadolnyak, D. (2012), Board size and diversity as governance mechanisms in community development loan funds in the USA, *Applied Economics*, 44: 4313–29.

Hermalin, B. E. and Weisbach, M. S. (1991), The effects of board composition and direct incentives on firm performance, *The Journal of the Financial Management*, Winter: 101–12.

Hillman, A. J. and Dalziel, T. (2003), Boards of director and firm performance: integrating agency and resource dependence perspectives, *The Academy of Management Review*, 28: 383–96.

Jackson, S. (1992), Team composition in organizational settings: issues in managing an increasingly diverse work force. In S. Worchel, W. Wood and J. A. Simpson (eds), *Group Process and Productivity*, Newburry Park, CA: Sage, pp. 138–73.

Jensen, M. C. and Meckling, W. H. (1976), Theory of the firm: managerial behavior, agency costs and ownership structure, *Journal of Financial Economics*, 3: 305–60.

Johnson, R. A., Hoskisson, R. E. and Hitt, M. A. (1993), Boards of directors involvement in restructuring: the effects of board versus managerial controls and characteristics, *Strategic Management Journal*, 14: 33–50.

Kaczmarek, S., Kimino, S. and Pye, A. (2012), Board task-related faultlines and firm performance: a decade of evidence, *Corporate Governance: An International Review*, 20: 337–51.

Keating, P. (1994), Ministerial statements: working nation, 4 May, http://parlinfo. aph.gov.au/parlInfo/search/display/display.w3p;query=Id%3A%22chamber %2Fhansardr%2F1994-05-04%2F0070%22 (accessed 3 December 2013).

Kimberlin, S. E. (2010), Advocacy by nonprofits: roles and practices of core advocacy organizations and direct service agencies, *Journal of Policy Practice*, 9: 164–82.

Laragy, C. (1999), *Justice versus accountability in employment and welfare services*, paper given at the National Social Policy Conference, University of New South Wales, Sydney, Australia, 22 July.

Larson, M. S. (1977), *The Rise of Professionalism: A Sociological Analysis*, Berkeley, CA: University of California Press.

Lau, D. C. and Murnighan, J. K. (2005), Interactions within groups and sub-groups: the effects of demographic faultlines, *Academy of Management Journal*, 48: 645–59.

Lyons, M. (2001), *Third Sector: The Contribution of Non Profit and Cooperative Enterprises in Australia*, Sydney: Allen & Unwin, pp. 93–105.

Lyons, M. and Chan, V. (1999), *The effect of competitive markets on nonprofit organisations – The case of employment services*, paper given at the National Social Policy Conference, University of New South Wales, Sydney, Australia, 22 July, pp. 1–12.

Medcof, J. W. (2001), Resource-based strategy and managerial power in net-works of internationally dispersed technology units, *Strategic Management Journal*, 22: 999–1012.

Mellahi, K. (2005), The dynamics of boards of directors in failing organiza-tions, *Long Range Planning*, 38, 216–79.

Mendes, P. (2009), View points: retrenching or renovating the Australian welfare state: the paradox of the Howard government's neo-liberalism, *International Journal of Social Welfare*: 102–10.

Mizruchi, M. S. (1983), Who controls whom? an examination of the relation between management and boards of directors in large American corpora-tions, *Academy of Management Review*, 8: 426–35.

Monks, R. A. G. and Ninow, N. (2011), *Corporate Governance*, Chichester: John Wiley & Sons.

Nicholson, G. J. and Kiel, G. C. (2004), A framework for diagnosing board effectiveness, *Corporate Governance*, 12: 442–60.

Petrovic, J. (2008), Unlocking the role of a board director: a review of the literature, *Management Decision*, 46: 1373–92.

Pfeffer, J. (1981), *Power in Organizations*, Marshfield, MA: Pitman Publishing.

Pfeffer, J. and Salancik, G. R. (1978), *The External Control of Organizations: A Resource Dependence Perspective*, New York, NY: Harper & Row.

Ramina, G. and Carney, T. (2003), New public management, the Job Network and non-profit strategy, *Australia Journal of Labour Economics*, 6: 253–75.

Rogers, C. (2007), The impact of the Australian government Job Network contracting on not-for-profit service providers, *Australian Journal of Public Administration*, 66: 395–405.

Ruigrok, W., Peck, S. and Tacheva, S. (2007), Nationality and gender diversity on Swiss corporate boards, *Corporate Governance: An International Review*, 15: 546–57.

Ryan, W. P. (1999), The new landscape for nonprofits, *Harvard Business Review*, 77: 127–36.

Shan, Y. G. and Xu, L. (2012), Do internal governance mechanisms impact on firm performance? Empirical evidence from the financial sector in China, *Journal of Asia-Pacific Business*, 13: 114–42.

Smith, S. R. and Lipsky, M. (1993), *Nonprofits for Hire: The Welfare State in the Age of Contracting*, Cambridge, MA: Havard University Press.

Tillquist, J., King, J. L. and Woo, C. (2002), A representational scheme for analyzing information technology and organizational dependency, *MIS Quarterly*, 26: 91–118.

Ulrich, D. and Barney, J. B. (1984), Perspectives in organizations: resource dependence, efficiency, and population, *Academy of Management Review*, 9: 471–81.

Van-Ness, R. K., Miesing, P. and Kang, J. (2010), Board of director composition and financial performance in a Sarbanes-Oxley world, *Journal of Academy of Business and Economics*, 10: 56–74.

Wageman, R. (1995), Interdependence and group effectiveness, *Administrative Science Quarterly*, 40: 145–80.

Walsh, J. P. and Seward, J. K. (1990), On the efficiency of internal and external corporate control mechanisms, *Academy of Management Review*, 15: 421–58.

Wang, Y.-H., Chuang, C.-C. and Lee, S.-Y. (2010), Impact of compositions and characteristics of board of directors and earnings management on fraud, *African Journal of Business Management*, 4: 496–511.

Watson, T. (2002), Professions and professionalism: should we jump off the band-wagon, better to study where it is going? *International Studies of Management & Organization*, 32: 93–105.

Williams, B., Onsman, A. and Brown, T. (2009), From stretcher-bearer to paramedic: the Australian paramedics' move towards professionalisation, *Journal of Emergency Primary Health Care*, 7, 4: 1–12.

Yee, H. (2001), *The concept of profession: a historical perspective based on the accounting profession in China*, paper given at the Accounting History International Conference, Osaka, Japan, 8–10 August.

4

Quasi-markets and the Delivery of Activation – A Frontline Perspective

Rik van Berkel

Introduction

Frontline workers in public organizations work in complex contexts. Vinzant and Crothers (1998: 11) argued that these workers are 'in the center of a matrix of influences' exercised, among others, by the law, the agency for which they work, their colleagues and other agencies. In understanding the ways in which workers operate in these complex contexts, the concept of discretion has become pivotal. In its most basic meaning, discretion implies that workers' agency plays a role in shaping how contextual influences determine the work they do and the decisions they make. Against this background, many researchers argue that the black box of frontline work needs to be investigated in order to fully understand how policies are implemented (Brodkin and Marston 2013; Hill 2003), how New Public Management (NPM) influences service provision processes (Brodkin 2011) and how policy target groups are treated (Schram *et al.* 2009).

This article follows the tradition of frontline work research and aims to contribute to our understanding of the practical functioning of quasi-markets for the provision of social services. Quasi-markets not only confront frontline workers with new agents and agencies but also with new roles in their interactions with these agents and agencies. The article looks at the marketized provision of employment, welfare-to-work or activation services,[1] that is, services provided to unemployed people in the context of welfare-to-work policies which aim to promote their employability and labour-market participation. The marketization of this type of services has received considerable scholarly attention (Considine 2001; Sol and Westerveld 2005; Struyven and Steurs 2005; van Berkel *et al.* 2012). Most studies adopted an institutional

Contracting-out Welfare Services: Comparing National Policy Designs for Unemployment Assistance,
First Edition. Edited by Mark Considine and Siobhan O'Sullivan.
© 2015 John Wiley & Sons, Ltd. Published 2015 by John Wiley & Sons, Ltd.

perspective, analyzing and comparing market characteristics and purchaser-provider relationships. Relatively few studies (e.g. Brodkin 2007; Johnson Dias and Maynard-Moody 2007; McDonald and Marston 2008; Soss *et al.* 2011) looked at how frontline workers operate in quasi-market contexts. This article analyzes two aspects of the functioning of quasi-markets which have been identified as threatening the effective functioning of quasi-markets and as potentially having perverse effects for social services and their users. The first concerns risk selection in quasi-market contexts: 'creaming', 'parking' and cherry-picking taking place in provider agencies jeopardize adequate service provision, especially for people most in need of support. Second, the monitoring of providers may lead to considerable administrative burdens and bureaucratic pressures in service provision processes which threatens the promise of quasi-markets to be cost-efficient, reduce service costs and improve service quality.

The article is structured as follows. The next section discusses how processes of risk selection and monitoring are analyzed in the literature on quasi-markets. The third section introduces the context of our empirical research of frontline workers in Dutch agencies involved in purchasing and providing activation services for social assistance recipients by providing a brief institutional analysis of the marketized provision of these services. The fourth section outlines our research methods, followed in the fifth section by a presentation of research findings on frontline processes of risk selection and monitoring in quasi-markets. The final section concludes.

The Marketized Provision of Activation Services

Quasi-markets for the provision of social services are without doubt among the most debated and contested NPM reforms. Le Grand (1991: 1260) characterized these markets as follows:

> not-for-profit organisations competing for public contracts, sometimes in competition with for-profit organisations; consumer purchasing power in the form of vouchers rather than cash; and, in some cases, the consumers represented in the market by agents instead of operating by themselves.

Although quasi-markets for the provision of activation services are diverse (Bredgaard and Larsen 2008; van Berkel *et al.* 2012), generally speaking these markets satisfy Le Grand's characteristics. Providers of activation services include either non-profit or for-profit organizations (or a mix); in some cases, target groups of activation programmes are given purchasing power in the form of vouchers or similar instruments (Hipp and Warner 2008; Sol and Westerveld 2005) although this seems to be the exception rather than the rule; and, as a consequence, 'consumers' – here: the target groups of activation policies – are often represented in the market by the agencies which administer their income benefits as these agencies often act as purchasers (van Berkel *et al.* 2011). Quasi-markets for activation services sometimes have two additional characteristics. First, the split of purchasers and providers that ideal-typically is an important element of markets is absent in many countries: buy or make decisions (Plantinga *et al.* 2011) of purchaser agencies often result in a mix of in-house produced and outsourced services. Second, outsourcing of services not always involves strong competition, such as in preferred-supplier models where the number of providers is limited (McDonald and Marston 2008).

Proponents of quasi-markets mentioned a range of potential benefits, such as cheaper services, service innovation, higher service quality and increased responsiveness to service users (Osborne and Gaebler 1992; cf. Finn 2009). However, many studies of quasi-markets point at factors which jeopardize the proponents' expectations, two of which are elaborated upon here: risk selection and the administrative burden related to monitoring.

Risk selection

In publications discussing the marketized provision of activation services, processes of risk selection through creaming, cherry-picking and parking in provider agencies are a recurring theme (Bredgaard and Larsen 2008; Sol and Westerveld 2005; Struyven and Steurs 2005). According to these publications, service providers paid according to performance will be inclined to focus their efforts on clients with whom they can easily realize performance targets, while 'difficult' clients are parked or referred back to the purchaser. Although there is little reason to question the validity of the theoretical argument that providers operating in a quasi-market are likely to engage into risk selection practices, empirically it may be more difficult to explain these practices and to attribute them unambiguously to quasi-market logics and service provider behaviour. In the context of social services which address complex problems, links between client characteristics, service characteristics and outcomes are hard to establish (Kirkpatrick 1999). Because of that, formulating realistic performance targets concerning what type of results should be realized with what groups of clients is far from simple. In addition, purchaser agencies are responsible for selecting clients who meet the client characteristics as stipulated in contracts for referrals to providers. This may be simple when, for example, client groups are defined in terms of age. But when client groups are defined in terms of more complex characteristics (labour-market distance, employability, motivation), client selection and referrals become less straight-forward. In these cases, the quality of profiling becomes a major concern (Mosley and Sol 2005), as does the mutual acceptance of profiling outcomes by purchasers and providers. In this context, Mosley's and Sol's (2005: 13) qualification of profiling as 'a standardised and validated instrument' may be too optimistic. Not only because standardized profiling instruments are not always used and their validity and objectivity may be contested (Behncke *et al.* 2007), but also because profiling may be insufficient to assess multi-problem client groups (cf. Struyven 2004). In other words: risk selection in provider agencies cannot be analyzed and interpreted in isolation from the definition of performance targets and the quality and adequacy of profiling and referral processes in purchaser agencies.

Furthermore, analyses of risk selection in provider agencies sometimes tend to ignore the fact that risk selection is a widespread phenomenon in service provision processes and is not a typical characteristic of quasi-markets. Lipsky's (1980) and other studies of street-level bureaucracies functioning in 'traditional' public administration contexts convincingly showed that risk selection is a routine strategy of workers coping with large caseloads and scarce resources. In addition, mechanisms for steering contracted provider agencies also play a role in steering public purchaser agencies (e.g. through financial incentives) and the workers in these agencies (e.g. through performance management). Thus it is very well possible that risk selection processes which are observed in provider agencies originate in risk selection processes taking place in purchaser agencies.

Monitoring

In quasi-markets, adequately monitoring service providers is considered vital. As Struyven (2004) argued, the (public) purchasers remain accountable for the efficient and effective use of public funds. Furthermore, monitoring is an important instrument to reduce information asymmetry between purchasers and providers (Corra and Plantinga 2009). However, purchasers may incur significant costs in setting up monitoring systems, and meeting monitoring requirements may be accompanied by considerable administrative costs for providers. Monitoring performance where social services address complex problems is difficult, and the administrative burden and costs involved in monitoring are affected by the intensity of monitoring as well. Monitoring may be limited to *post-hoc* monitoring of realized outcomes but may also be more detailed and take place throughout the contract period. In this context, Struyven (2004: 38) commented that:

> [T]he basic starting point of market competition is after all that the provider can decide independently how the services are provided so as to meet the needs of the jobseeker. Overly-detailed everyday management by the principal meets with resistance from the market and leads to detrimental effects.

Whereas Struyven warned against overly-detailed monitoring and interference on the part of purchasers, other authors argued that the absence of systematic and regular monitoring creates risks as well (Hardy and Wistow 1998).

The nature and intensity of monitoring is likely to reflect characteristics of purchaser-provider relationships. Hardy and Wistow (1998: 34) argued that a 'mature purchasing' framework should be characterized by 'long-term relationships; mutual trust; a mutual understanding of the needs and intentions of purchasers, on the one hand, together with the motivations and vulnerabilities of providers, on the other; and sufficient stability in purchasing patterns'. However, purchaser-provider relationships based on these characteristics are not self-evident. Greve (2000) distinguished between hard contracting and soft contracting, where soft contracting resembles the kind of purchasing framework which Hardy and Wistow (1998) recommended. Whereas soft contracting is characterized by trust and co-operation, distrust is at the basis of hard contracting: parties will cheat when they get the chance, contracts are detailed in order to cover any eventualities, and sanctions and rewards are in place as incentives to comply with contractual agreements (Greve 2000: 155). In purchaser-provider relationships where distrust dominates, monitoring processes will probably be more detailed and intensive, and involve higher costs and administrative burdens. This was confirmed in an analysis of contracted employment services in Australia: lack of trust on the part of the purchaser resulted in a considerable administrative workload for providers in meeting accountability requirements (McDonald and Marston 2008).

An issue less frequently discussed is that monitoring in the context of activation services not only focuses on provider but also on client behaviour (Struyven 2004). When activation services are outsourced but benefit administration remains the responsibility of the purchaser agency, monitoring clients referred to providers is necessary for the purchaser agency to enforce the conditionality of benefit entitlements. This requires information coordination between purchaser and provider because the former depends on client information provided by the latter. When provider agencies consider clients' behaviour as potentially sanction-worthy, they will have to inform the purchaser agency which can then start the procedure required to threaten with sanctions or to actually impose a sanction.

Research Context

The Netherlands was one of the first countries in Europe to outsource the provision of activation to private for-profit organizations, and because of this pioneering role, it received considerable international attention (Bredgaard and Larsen 2008; Considine 2001; Sol and Westerveld 2005). However, the reforms following this initially quite radical marketization process have received far less attention although they resulted in considerable modifications of the original quasi-market model. In the following, our discussion focuses on activation services for social assistance recipients and on the public local welfare agencies – operating under the responsibility of local government – that are responsible for the administration of social assistance benefits as well as for organizing the provision of activation services for assistance recipients.

Several years after the introduction in the Netherlands of marketization, a new Social Assistance Act was introduced (2004) which deregulated and decentralized decision making concerning activation considerably (van Berkel *et al.* 2011). This included decisions concerning service provision models: local welfare agencies were free to organize the provision of activation services in-house or through outsourcing and to make decisions concerning the nature and number of external service providers. This triggered a gradual decline of the role of private providers. Yearly monitor studies of the new Act reported that local welfare agencies spent 40 per cent of their budget for activation services on private providers in 2011, compared to 56 per cent in 2005. In 2011, 22 per cent of the budget was spent on in-house produced services and 30 per cent on services provided by other (semi-) public agencies (Divosa 2005, 2012a). Especially so-called sheltered employment companies, traditionally responsible for offering sheltered employment to people with severe mental, physical or intellectual disabilities,[2] saw their role in providing activation services for social assistance recipients increase (Divosa 2012a). These companies combine characteristics of public, private and non-profit organizations and have, therefore, been characterized as hybrid organizations (van der Torre *et al.* 2012). Summarizing, the second half of the 2000s saw a gradual de-marketization (more in-house service production; cf. Hefetz and Warner 2004) as well as a gradual de-privatization (a shift in outsourcing from private to public or hybrid providers). It is likely that these trends will continue in the near future. Significant cuts in budgets available for activation,[3] and Dutch government proposals to integrate into one act employment services aimed at social assistance recipients and at the target groups of sheltered employment companies are stimulating closer co-operation between, and sometimes mergers of, local welfare agencies and sheltered employment companies.

Apart from de-marketization and de-privatization processes, many local welfare agencies have strengthened the role of their frontline workers in selecting providers, determining the nature of services for individual clients and monitoring outsourced services (van Berkel *et al.* 2010). Attempts to strengthen local welfare agencies' control over outsourced services may be interpreted as a form of 'hard contracting'; many agencies were disappointed about the results private providers realized in the early years of marketization. A further development in service provision was that public workers in various local welfare agencies where a mix of in-house and outsourced services exists can, to a certain degree, make their own make or buy decisions by deciding whether individual clients are served in-house or referred to external providers.

Research Methods

The data presented in the next section comes from a research project into the frontline delivery of activation services for social assistance recipients remote from the labour market. The study looked at front-line workers in local welfare agencies and in contracted sheltered employment companies which are involved in providing services for this target group. The services provided by sheltered employment companies may be different in different local contexts but often include assessment services, internal or external work experience projects aimed at promoting unemployed people's employability, job placement support and services and post-placement services. Local welfare agencies and sheltered employment companies stand in a purchaser-provider relationship to each other, although local welfare agencies – as explained above – often act as purchaser and provider simultaneously. Our research project focused on social assistance recipients remote from the labour market because Dutch activation services are targeted at this group mainly: recipients close to the labour market are increasingly expected to find their own way to the labour market. The research project addressed several issues related to the functioning of quasi-markets: the roles of frontline workers in both types of agencies in the provision of activation services, the combination of purchaser/provider roles in local welfare agencies, and frontline interactions between workers in both types of organizations in client referrals, service coordination and monitoring.

The study involved two steps: a series of interviews with frontline workers in three local welfare agencies and three sheltered employment companies contracted by these agencies, followed by a survey in 14 local welfare agencies and six sheltered employment companies. This article mainly presents data from the interviews as these provided the most in-depth insights into processes of risk selection and monitoring. In the welfare agencies and sheltered employment companies where interviews were conducted, we interviewed 25 per cent of all workers who worked with social assistance recipients remote from the labour market. The interviewees were 19 local welfare agency workers and ten sheltered employment company workers. The interviews, which took 75 minutes on average each, were recorded and fully transcribed. For data analysis, NVivo (software for analysing qualitative data) was used.

In this article, survey data is presented where they can support the validity of our interview findings. For the survey, all frontline workers in 14 local welfare agencies and six sheltered employment companies who were involved in providing employment services to social recipients remote from the labour market were asked to participate. They were sent an email explaining the objective of the research project and received a personal link to a web-based questionnaire. The response rate was 52 per cent; no population data are available to compare the respondents with the population. In total, 163 frontline workers in local welfare agencies and 31 in sheltered employment companies completed the survey questionnaire. The survey data were analyzed using SPSS (a software package for statistical analysis). The local welfare agencies and sheltered employment companies involved in the interview study also participated in the survey.

Research Findings

Risk selection

A large majority (86 per cent) of local welfare agency respondents in the survey reported using a mix of services provided by themselves and by external providers. Most of them (90 per cent) were responsible for front-line buy or make decisions: they decided themselves in individual cases whether services are provided in-house or by external providers. The most important considerations in making these decisions are, first, workers' estimation of the adequacy of services provided by external providers given individual client characteristics; and, second, workers' appraisal of whether or not they themselves are able to activate clients successfully. Our interviews revealed that workers in local welfare agencies decided individually what client information they consider relevant in making buy or make decisions. There are no standardized criteria that guide referral decisions and workers do not use standardized profiling tools. Sometimes these decisions are made on the basis of administrative data and client files, in other cases workers make the decision after interviewing clients.

Before we look at risk selection, it should be mentioned that although performance management is usual in local welfare agencies and sheltered employment companies (75 per cent of respondents in our survey worked with performance targets), it is relatively mild. Half of the respondents with performance targets reported that not realizing targets had no consequences. Only 10 per cent of respondents working with performance targets reported that not meeting targets could have financial consequences.

Turning our attention now to risk selection in provider agencies, it is not hard to find quotes in the interviews with frontline workers in these agencies which seem to indicate processes of risk selection:[4]

'Nowadays we work with As, Bs and Cs. As are clients with good chances of finding a job. Bs are clients with a considerable labour-market distance and Cs are clients whose situation is hopeless. So we're not expected to pay attention to the Cs.' (SEC)

'I wasn't looking forward to have her in my caseload. She is a single mother, two kids, a debt of 30,000 euros. She can't apply for child care because each euro goes to her creditors. So I am not going to get her into a job. (…) I can see her four hours a day because she cannot come here before 9.30 AM and she has to leave early (…). The [local welfare agency worker] asked me to accept her anyway. But there is not much I'm going to do with her the next few months. I can complete her CV but I can't offer her training.' (SEC)

'Sometimes after interviewing a new client I just know: this isn't going to work. Local welfare agency workers are not happy when we tell them we can't accept this client, but usually we stand firm. Though sometimes we go along with the local welfare agency even though we know that we are not going to find this client a job.' (SEC)

'We had the impression that – apologies for the expression – [frontline workers in the local welfare agency] shoved the most difficult clients on to us. As if they thought: we tried, we fastened our teeth into this case, now it's up to you to give it a try.' (SEC)

At first sight, these quotes seem to be clear instances of service providers acting rationally under market conditions. Providers have to realize contractually specified service targets in terms of, among others, improving clients' employability or realizing job placements. This may stimulate them to focus on clients who are most easily activated, and to use the argument of 'inadequate referrals' by local welfare agency workers as an excuse for parking or referring back 'difficult' clients. But on closer inspection, other interpretations are also possible, and deciding which interpretation is correct is far from simple. First of all, the absence of standardized profiling tools makes it rather difficult to come to an agreement on the adequacy of referrals in the first place, as no more or less objective and shared criteria exist to solve disputes about the adequacy of referrals. In some cases, a solution for the problem of inadequate referrals was sought in organizing so-called 'warm' referrals, where workers at the local welfare agency and the provider agency have a meeting with a client at the start of the activation process, *'Some local welfare agency workers organize a meeting with me and the client. They ask me to make an assessment whether a referral is useful. But it depends on [the local welfare agency worker] whether or not a meeting takes place'* (SEC).

Second, local welfare agency workers make referral decisions under conditions which can influence the quality of these decisions. For example, high caseloads sometimes stimulate these workers to base referral decisions on administrative data rather than individual interviews with clients to save time. This increases the probability of inadequate referrals as administrative data often provides limited insight into clients' situations.

Third, sheltered employment company workers reported that market conditions were getting tighter: the clients referred to them were becoming more difficult, whereas the service trajectories which providers were expected to offer were getting shorter and more strictly focused on job placements rather than improving clients' employability. This reflects a more general shift of priorities in local activation policies and services, which have become more strictly focused on quick job placements rather than on longer activation trajectories aimed at a broader spectrum of possible outcomes. Against this background, the question arises whether risk selection in provider agencies is a strategy to avoid having to deal with difficult clients or a strategy to cope with unrealistic expectations and demands of purchasers:

> *'We always looked at job opportunities, but in the past we had the possibility to make intermediate steps. Now you are forced to say: if we can't do that [making intermediate steps] anymore, it isn't going to work. (…) Some people have many problems, and if [local welfare agency workers] ask you: "is this person going to find a job in a year's time?", you take the safe side. We never wanted that, and it's very awkward. For exactly those people need our support.'* (SEC)

Fourth, local welfare agency workers' make or buy decisions are not disinterested. For example, when local welfare agency workers make buy or make decisions based on an assessment of whether or not they can realize quick successes with clients themselves, risk selection takes place inadvertently, *'I can refer someone to [a provider] for training, job applications and things like that. But if I have the impression that a client can find a job shortly, then I will work with him myself, and start activities with him to find a job'* (LWA).

So when workers in provider agencies complain about clients that are too difficult, it may be hard to determine whether they are merely trying to select easy clients or have a point and are confronted with the consequences of risk selection by local welfare agency workers. It should be mentioned, however, that risk selection in local welfare agencies may also have the opposite effect for providers, and confront them with easy rather than difficult clients. Several local welfare agency workers reported that due to managerial or political pressures to make clients independent of social assistance, they select their most employable clients for activation. In these cases, risk selection already takes place before the buy or make and referral decisions are made, *'You simply can't choose to pay attention to everyone. That won't work. We take clients with opportunities, opportunities to become independent of social assistance quickly. And we focus on them'* (LWA).

Monitoring providers and clients

Monitoring activities involved monitoring providers as well as clients. The monitoring process included several components. Managers of local welfare agencies are responsible for evaluating the overall performance of providers. Apart from this *post-hoc* evaluation of performance, frontline workers have an explicit task in the day-to-day monitoring of providers for those clients in their caseloads which have been referred to providers. Part of this monitoring process is formalized: workers in provider agencies are obliged to submit periodical progress reports on individual clients to frontline workers in the local welfare agencies. The latter are expected to read the reports, take action when necessary and enter the reports into the information system which generates data that managers use in their evaluation of providers' performance. In addition, a kind of informal frontline agreement exists that workers in provider agencies report important information on clients' progress to local welfare agency workers as soon as possible, rather than waiting until the progress report is due.

In practice, frontline monitoring activities often combine the two functions of monitoring providers and monitoring clients: exchanging information (through progress reports or through informal contacts) may serve the purpose of giving account of providers' work with clients but may also serve the purpose of coordinating service provision. Service coordination is needed when workers at provider agencies need more time to realize service objectives with individual clients or consider adjustment of services in individual cases necessary. However, most cases where workers at provider agencies consider coordination necessary are cases involving problems with clients such as no-shows, lack of co-operation or motivation, or violent behaviour. In these cases, local welfare agency workers are informed with the purpose to organize a tripartite meeting with the client to discuss the situation. In fact, by invoking the help of local welfare agencies, workers in provider agencies mobilize the 'bad cop' role (Marston *et al.* 2005), for only local welfare agency workers are authorized to threaten with and actually impose sanctions.

This double function of monitoring helps to explain why workers at provider agencies adopt a somewhat ambiguous attitude towards it. In as far as it is functional in terms of the progress of service provision processes, they find it useful:

> *'Suppose you're working with a client and things don't run smoothly. If we wait with informing the local welfare agency until the progress report is due, we can't act quickly. But if you inform the local welfare agency right away, you can act immediately. The local welfare agency can tell the client that things need to change or that a sanction will be imposed otherwise.'* (SEC)

In general, workers accept the principle of giving account. But giving account is experienced as an 'administrative burden' when writing the periodical progress reports takes quite some time, when the reports are not considered useful because there is no progress to report about, or when workers feel that they need to report things they already reported informally:

> *'Horrific. It didn't use to be like this, but now the local welfare agency wants us to register more and more. (…) Every three months we need to submit a progress report. But when something special happens in between, they want us to report that as well. (…) Once every three months doesn't sound much. But when you have 32 clients, that makes 32 reports every three months, plus you report when something special happens. That's far too much.'* (SEC)

> *'I call them [local welfare agency workers] regularly and tell them how things are going. I'm talking with them for 15 minutes and then they tell me: put the information in the progress report. So then I have to type out the whole story that I just told them.'* (SEC)

The administrative nature of reporting is reinforced by the fact that according to several workers in provider agencies, workers at the local welfare agency do not have time to read the reports and just enter them into the system. However, workers at the local welfare agency did not confirm this.

For workers in local welfare agencies, the progress report procedure takes quite some time as well. The information in the reports needs to be entered into the information system which is also the reason why informally exchanged information needs to be included in the progress reports:

> 'Sometimes we already know it [the information in the report] but it has to be registered. We have to enter it into the system to make sure that money trans- actions run smoothly. (…) In most cases, the reports are submitted digitally (…) so then we copy and paste it into the diary of the client.' (LWA)

Our survey showed that the administrative workload of both type of workers is an issue indeed. Workers in local welfare agencies reported spending one-third of their working time on administrative work, work- ers in sheltered employment companies one-quarter. Ideally, both types of workers said they would like to spend about 15 per cent of working time on administration.

Generally speaking, local welfare agency workers do not adopt a very pro-active attitude in the monitoring process. The progress reports hardly ever trigger them to intervene into the services provided exter- nally, and they ask providers for information about the progress of ser- vices or clients only sporadically. Lack of time is mentioned as the most important reason preventing local welfare agency workers from moni- toring providers and clients actively, 'I got 80 clients, I can't monitor each of them actively' (LWA). Only few workers monitored more pro-actively, independent from the information they receive from the providers:

> 'I had a client who told me he wanted to be a garbage man or a bricklayer. During a conversation with [name provider] I asked: "what did you do to help him with a vacancy for garbage man or bricklayer?" That gave her a fright, she wasn't used to be monitored by a case manager. "I made a CV", she told me. "No", I said, "what job applications did you support him with?" ' (LWA)

Active monitoring sometimes remained limited to only a few clients in local welfare agency workers' caseloads, 'When I wonder why it takes so long for a client to find a job, I raise the alarm. (…) So I select my best clients and keep the provider well in hand concerning the progress of their job finding' (LWA).

In our survey, we asked respondents how they would like the service provision process to be organized, ideally, by presenting them with various statements and asking them for their opinion about these statements. Two statements referred to the relationships between purchaser and provider. Workers tend towards favouring closer frontline co-operation between purchasers and providers. Of all workers, 60 per cent (strongly) agreed with the statement that, ideally, monitoring takes place through regular dialogue rather than periodical progress reports; only 13 per cent (strongly) disagreed. The opinions of both groups of workers did not differ. They did, however, differ on the statement that, ideally, the content of externally provided services should be decided upon by local welfare agency workers and providers together. Local welfare agency workers were more positive about this: 60 per cent (strongly) agreed, compared to only 30 per cent of workers in provider agencies. Possibly, workers in provider agencies fear that this might threaten their autonomy in decision making about the content of activation services. Nevertheless, closer co-operation at frontline level between purchaser and provider agencies scored quite high when we asked respondents to rate a series of recommendations according to their urgency for improving service provision: both groups of workers placed it in fourth place (out of 17).

Conclusion and Discussion

This article discusses the functioning of quasi-markets in the provision of employment services from a frontline point of view. It specifically looks at two issues which the literature on quasi-markets considers as potentially problematic: risk selection in provider agencies and the monitoring of provider agencies by purchasers. Based on our findings, we make the following observations.

Identifying processes of risk selection in provider agencies is complex. Complaints of provider agencies about inadequate referrals may be a strategy to avoid having to serve difficult clients but may also be justified. The definition of service outcomes and the processes of profiling, selecting and referring clients are often far from unproblematic, especially when target group definitions are complex and when profiling instruments are contested or even absent, as was the case in our study. Furthermore, attributing observed risk selection to the marketization of service provision and the rational behaviour of providers may often be too simple. The problem of risk selection is present throughout service provision processes and not limited to providers nor to quasi-market conditions of service provision. Theoretically, this implies that when studying processes of risk selection, research needs to analyze the entire service provision chain and to look at decisions taken by providers and purchasers throughout the service provision process.

Monitoring in the agencies in our study was rather intensive and asked for significant efforts of frontline workers, both in provider and purchaser agencies. In as far as monitoring and the administrative tasks related to it facilitated the coordination of activities of workers in provider agencies and local welfare agencies, and was experienced as contributing to the service provision process, workers considered it as useful and experience it as unproblematic. However, the added value of the obligatory periodic progress reports was questioned, especially by workers in provider agencies. Writing the reports was experienced as mainly an administrative burden in those cases where workers were reporting information which local welfare agency workers already knew. Workers in local welfare agencies experienced the reports differently. For them, the administrative burden mainly consisted of entering the reports into the information systems. As they lack the time to monitor their clients more actively, the reports at least provide them with a periodic overview of how clients referred to provider agencies are doing. However, one can question whether the reports make a significant contribution to the service provision process. For as we see, local welfare agency workers only incidentally decide to take action on the basis of the information in the progress reports. This confirms experiences of workers in provider agencies that the reports mainly serve an administrative purpose rather than contribute to the quality of services provided: if the reports contain information which local welfare agency workers often know already and does not induce these workers to take action, on balance the only purpose of the reports is to comply with the contractual obligation to submit them.

Our survey results showed that frontline workers in both purchaser and provider agencies tend to prefer forms of soft contracting over hard contracting, in the sense that they favour closer frontline co-operation rather than the formalized forms of monitoring which currently exist. Against this background, it will be interesting to see how present developments in the Dutch activation market will affect purchaser-provider relationships. In many municipalities, closer forms of co-operation and in some cases even mergers between local welfare agencies and sheltered employment companies are being discussed and implemented. This may eventually result in a preferred supplier model for the provision of employment services, or even in the full abolishment of the quasi-market model. However, as we hope this article shows, we should be careful in expecting any immediate positive impacts of these shifts in service provision models on processes of risk selection and on the administrative burden workers experience.

Acknowledgements

The study reported in this article was funded by the Dutch foundation Stichting Kennis Ontwikkeling HBO, reference number PRO-2-012. The author would like to thank the anonymous reviewers for their constructive comments.

Notes

1. These terms are used as synonyms in this article.
2. We use the term 'sheltered employment companies' here even though the companies have diversified the types of work participation they offer their target groups which include, for example, supported employment.

3. According to Divosa 2012b, the national re-integration budget will be reduced from €1.7 billion in 2011 to €0.75 billion in 2015.
4. In interview quotes, 'LWA' refers to quotes from frontline workers in a local welfare agency; 'SEC' refers to quotes from workers in a sheltered employment company. Some quotes have been adjusted slightly to make them understandable for an international audience.

References

Behncke, S., Frölich, M. and Lechner, M. (2007), *Targeting Labour Market Programmes: Results from a Randomized Experiment*, Bonn: IZA.

Bredgaard, T. and Larsen, F. (2008), Quasi-markets in employment policy: do they deliver on promises? *Social Policy & Society*, 7, 3: 341–52.

Brodkin, E. (2007), Bureaucracy redux: management reformism and the welfare state, *Journal of Public Administration Research and Theory*, 17, 1: 1–17.

Brodkin, E. (2011), Policy work: Street-level organizations under new managerialism, *Journal of Public Administration Research and Theory*, 21, suppl2: i253–77.

Brodkin, E. and Marston, G. (eds) (2013), *Work and the Welfare State*, Washington, DC: Georgetown University Press.

Considine, M. (2001), *Enterprising States. The Public Management of Welfare-to-Work*, Cambridge: Cambridge University Press.

Corra, A. and Plantinga, M. (2009), New modes of governance in the Dutch reintegration market. Analyzing the process of contracting out, paper given at the ASPEN/ETUI-REHS conference, Brno, 20–21 March.

Divosa (2005), *WWB monitor. Een jaar Wet Werk en Bijstand*, Utrecht: Divosa.

Divosa (2012a), *Denken in kansen. Deel 1*, Utrecht: Divosa.

Divosa (2012b), *Factsheet gevolgen Miljoenennota 2013 voor participatiebudget*, http://www.divosa.nl/sites/default/files/20120921-Factsheet-gevolgen-Miljoenennota-2013-voor-Participatiebudget.pdf (accessed 20 April 2013).

Finn, D. (2009), The welfare market and the flexible New Deal: Lessons from other countries, *Local Economy: The Journal of the Local Economy Policy Unit*, 24, 1: 38–45.

Greve, C. (2000), Exploring contracts as reinvented institutions in the Danish public sector, *Public Administration*, 78, 1: 153–64.

Hardy, B. and Wistow, G. (1998), Securing quality through contracts? The development of quasi-markets for social care in Britain, *Australian Journal of Public Administration*, 57, 2: 25–35.

Hefetz, A. and Warner, M. (2004), Privatization and its reverse: explaining the dynamics of the government contracting process, *Journal of Public Administration Theory and Practice*, 14, 2: 171–90.

Hill, H. (2003), Understanding implementation: street-level bureaucrats resources for reform, *Journal of Public Administration Research and Theory*, 13, 3: 265–82.

Hipp, L. and Warner, M. (2008), Market forces for the unemployed? Training vouchers in Germany and the USA, *Social Policy & Administration*, 42, 1: 77–101.

Johnson Dias, J. and Maynard-Moody, S. (2007), For-profit welfare: contracts, conflicts, and the performance paradox, *Journal of Public Administration Research and Theory*, 17, 2: 189–211.

Kirkpatrick, I. (1999), Markets, bureaucracy and public management: The worst of both worlds? Public services without markets or bureaucracy, *Public Money & Management*, 19, 4: 7–14.

Le Grand, J. (1991), Quasi-markets and social policy, *The Economic Journal*, 101, 408: 1256–67.

Lipsky, M. (1980), *Street-level Bureaucracy. Dilemmas of the Individual in Public Services*, New York, NY: Russell Sage Foundation.

Marston, G., Larsen, J. and McDonald, D. (2005), The active subjects of welfare reform: a street-level comparison of employment services in Australia and Denmark, *Social Work & Society*, 3, 2: 141–57.

McDonald, C. and Marston, G. (2008), Re-visiting the quasi-market in employment services: Australia's Job Network, *The Asia Pacific Journal of Public Administration*, 30, 2: 101–17.

Mosley, H. and Sol, E. (2005), Contractualism in employment services: a socio-economic perspective. In E. Sol and M. Westerveld (eds), *Contractualism in Employment Services: A New Form of Welfare State Governance*, The Hague: Kluwer Law International and Aspen Publishers, pp. 1–21.

Osborne, D. and Gaebler, T. (1992), *Reinventing government. How the entrepreneurial spirit is transforming the public sector*, London and New York, NY: Penguin.

Plantinga, M., De Ridder, K. and Corra, A. (2011), Choosing whether to buy or make: the contracting out of employment reintegration services by Dutch municipalities, *Social Policy & Administration*, 45, 3: 245–63.

Schram, S., Soss, J., Fording, R. and Houser, L. (2009), Deciding to discipline: race, choice and punishment at the frontlines of welfare reforms, *American Sociological Review*, 74, 3: 398–422.

Sol, E. and Westerveld, M. (eds) (2005), *Contractualism in Employment Services: A New Form of Welfare State Governance*, The Hague: Kluwer Law International and Aspen Publishers.

Soss, J., Fording, R. and Schram, S. (2011), The organization of discipline: from performance management to perversity and punishment, *Journal of Public Administration Research and Theory*, 21, suppl. 2: 1203–32.

Struyven, L. (2004), *Design Choices in Market Competition for Employment Services for the Long-term Unemployed*, OECD social, employment and migration working papers No. 21, Paris: OECD.

Struyven, L. and Steurs, G. (2005), Design and redesign of a quasi-market for the reintegration of jobseekers: empirical evidence from Australia and the Netherlands, *Journal of European Social Policy*, 15, 3: 211–31.

van Berkel, R., van der Aa, P. and van Gestel, N. (2010), Professionals without a profession? Redesigning case management in Dutch local welfare agencies, *European Journal of Social Work*, 13, 4: 447–63.

van Berkel, R., De Graaf, W. and Sirovátka, T. (eds) (2011), *The Governance of Active Welfare States in Europe*, Basingstoke: Palgrave Macmillan.

van Berkel, R., Sager, F. and Ehrler, F. (2012), The diversity of activation markets in Europe, *International Journal of Sociology and Social Policy*, 32, 5/6: 273–85.

van der Torre, L., Fenger, M. and van Twist, M. (2012), Between state, market and commnnity. A study of the slogans of sheltered work companies, *Public Management Review*, 14, 4: 521–40.

Vinzant, J. and Crothers, L. (1998), *Street-level Leadership. Discretion & Legitimacy tn Front-line Public Service*, Washington, DC: Georgetown University Press.

5

Conditionality and the Financing of Employment Services – Implications for the Social Divisions of Work and Welfare

Isabel Shutes and Rebecca Taylor

Introduction

Increasing conditionality in access to welfare has been central to the reform of welfare states (Dean 2004; Dwyer 2004) and to the development of welfare-to-work policies and programmes (Peck 2001). In what has been described as a shift from a welfare to a 'workfare' state (Peck 2001), access to welfare benefits for those out of work has become increasingly conditional on undergoing activities towards (re-)entering employment. In contrast to the principles associated with the postwar welfare state regarding rights to welfare as unconditional and universal on the basis of social citizenship, in the restructured welfare state, rights to welfare have been replaced by conditional entitlements on the basis of individual responsibility to sell one's labour through the market (Dwyer 2004). At the same time, the principle of work-related conditionality has increasingly been extended to groups not in paid work due to disabilities or caring responsibilities, who would previously have been exempt from those conditions. There has thus been greater emphasis on and greater reach of work-related activities delivered by employment services as the condition under which welfare is provided.

This shift in the principles underlying the provision of welfare has been described as a move away from de-commodification to the re-commodification of labour (Offe 1984). While many welfare rights in the development of welfare states have always been conditional, it is the extent to which the principle of conditionality has replaced the

Contracting-out Welfare Services: Comparing National Policy Designs for Unemployment Assistance, First Edition. Edited by Mark Considine and Siobhan O'Sullivan. © 2015 John Wiley & Sons, Ltd. Published 2015 by John Wiley & Sons, Ltd.

principle of rights as central to the organization of welfare provision which is significant (Dwyer 2004). Within this context, there has been a shift towards the market in the organization of welfare and employment services. Across many advanced industrial countries, the joining together of the provision of welfare benefits with employment services has been followed by the contracting out of the delivery of employment services to private (for-profit) and non-profit providers (Considine 2000, 2001). In the development of quasi-markets in employment services, the principle of work-related conditionality has increasingly been extended to the public financing of those services. This form of conditionality involves the obligation of contracted providers to achieve employment outcomes as a condition of funding. In contrast to the financing of the public employment service, within a market of employment services, in which provision is contracted out to competing providers, this form of conditionality commodifies those out of work by attaching financial value to placing them in work.

These developments call into question the implications of work-related conditionality for the social divisions of work and welfare. Analyses of the social divisions of work and welfare focus attention not only on the effects of different welfare systems in terms of the outcomes of particular social groups, but also on how particular systems, and the principles underlying those systems, shape the delivery and experiences of provision for different social groups. This article examines, specifically, how work-related conditionality in the financing of a market of contracted employment services impacts on the provision of services to unemployed groups. The first section sets out the conceptual concerns of the article with regard to understanding the social divisions of work and welfare and how the restructuring of welfare – including, specifically, the financing of employment services – has implications for the provision of services for different social groups. The second section refers to the ways in which work-related conditionality has been extended to the public financing of contracted employment services. The third section then examines the effects of this form of conditionality on the provision of employment services to unemployed groups and more disadvantaged groups in particular, drawing on empirical research in different national contexts and specifically on the Work Programme in the UK. The analysis examines three interrelated dimensions of the effects of this form of conditionality on, first, the type of providers which are included and excluded within the market; second, the type of services which are provided; and, third, the targeting ('creaming' and 'parking') of different unemployed groups by providers. Based on these findings, the article concludes by considering the implications for the social divisions of work and welfare. Those implications concern the extent to which work-related conditionality in the financing of contracted employment services may limit the development of support which adequately addresses the needs of different social groups.

The Social Divisions of Work and Welfare

Welfare systems are shaped by social divisions of class, gender, 'race'/ ethnicity, nationality and disability, among others. At the same time, welfare systems shape those divisions and inequalities in different ways. Analyses of the social divisions of work and welfare seek to understand how different types of welfare and labour market regimes influence the experiences and position of different social groups in relation to paid and unpaid work and welfare.[1] With regard to the postwar welfare state, the 'false universalism' of the principles of welfare rights based on social citizenship was criticized for the exclusive rather than inclusive ways in which welfare rights were experienced by different social groups, including women, people with disabilities and minority ethnic groups (Williams 1989, 1995). Rather than simply conferring universal welfare rights to lessen the inequalities of modern capitalist societies, welfare states became the focus of critical analysis regarding the social divisions that influence both people's access to and experiences of social citizenship (e.g. Lewis, G. 2003; Lewis, J. 1992; Lister 2003; Williams 1989). Understanding the principles which underlie and structure the provision of welfare – which give rise to particular social relations and experiences of welfare for different social groups – is thus inter-related with understanding the different outcomes of those groups (Orloff 1993).

With the restructuring of welfare, it has been argued that social citizenship has increasingly been replaced by 'market citizenship', with a fundamental shift towards enabling market participation as underpinning the means and purposes of welfare provision (Jayasuriya 2006). This emphasis on market means and purposes is evident in the shift towards work-related conditionality in rights to welfare, on the one hand, and towards work-related conditionality in the public financing of contracted providers of employment services, on the other hand. As discussed in the following section, employment outcomes have increasingly been applied as a condition of funding in quasi-markets of employment services. Drawing on an understanding of the social divisions in which welfare systems are embedded, the concerns of this article are to examine the ways in which this form of work-related conditionality has shaped both the structure and the provision of contracted employment services, and the implications for addressing the needs and interests of particular social groups.

The Financing of Contracted Employment Services

In the context of the wider restructuring of welfare states, the provision of employment services has entailed changes in the roles and relations between the state and market as regards the financing and delivery of those services. In the UK, the financing and delivery of employment services was for much of the 20th century the responsibility of the state (Wright *et al.* 2011). In Australia, public employment services were likewise established as a commonwealth (federal) government responsibility in the postwar period (Carson and Kerr 2010). Since the 1990s, there has been a shift towards quasi-markets in employment services. Many countries, such as Australia in the late 1990s, separated the public financing of employment services (for which the state at national, regional or local levels retains responsibility) from the provision of those services. The delivery of employment services has been increasingly privatized in countries such as Australia, the Netherlands and the UK, with the contracting of private (for profit) and non-profit providers (Bredgaard and Larsen 2008; Considine 2001; van Berkel 2010).

In Australia, the Job Network, established in 1998,[2] introduced a system of private and non-profit providers of employment services, contracted by the federal government, with the statutory employment service (Centrelink) providing initial assessment of benefits claimants and referrals to the Job Network (Considine *et al.* 2011). In the UK, the statutory employment service, Jobcentre Plus, established in 2001, likewise provided initial assessment of benefits claimants as well as jobsearch and adviser support services through its local offices, whilst numerous employment-related programmes (such as the former New Deal programmes) were contracted out to local and national providers from the private and non-profit sectors, and other statutory providers. The introduction of the Work Programme in 2011 involved a further shift towards a supply-chain model of contracted provision for the unemployed[3] in which central government directly contracts large national and predominantly private sector 'prime providers', who both deliver services in-house and, in addition, sub-contract other providers (known as 'tier 1' and 'tier 2' providers). The provision of employment services in these and other Organisation for Economic Co-operation and Development countries, such as the Netherlands, Germany, Denmark and the USA, is thus now marked by supply chains of contracted providers funded publicly to deliver employment services (Sol and Westerveld 2005; van Berkel and van der Aa 2005; van Berkel 2010), though not necessarily contracted directly by the state.[4]

The allocation of public financing within these quasi-markets of contracted employment services has increasingly been oriented towards employment outcomes. Under this system, a proportion of funding paid to a contracted provider is conditional on a benefits claimant referred to the provider entering work. The ratio of funding linked to employment outcomes as opposed to inputs (referrals of benefits claimants to a provider) has varied across programmes. Under the former Jobs and Training Partnership Act (JTPA) system in the USA,[5] within some states, 30 per cent of payments for programme participants was attached to employment outcomes achieved within 13 weeks of programme completion (Felstead 1998). In the UK, under the former New Deal programmes (prior to 2008), 30 per cent of payments was likewise attached to employment outcomes achieved within 13 weeks of programme completion (DWP 2010). The balance in payments to providers has increasingly shifted from service fees towards employment outcomes. In addition, there has been a shift towards financially rewarding providers according to the duration in which a programme participant remains in work. In the Job Service Australia, in addition to an initial job placement payment, providers are paid for employment outcomes for participants at 13 and 26 weeks (Finn 2011). With the introduction of the Work Programme in the UK, the majority of funding paid to contracted providers is now conditional on employment outcomes.[6] While prime providers are required to specify minimum service standards in their contract with central government (Finn 2012), funding is not allocated to achieving those standards. Indeed, the small upfront 'attachment fee' paid to prime providers was phased out of the programme after the first year, in a move towards a funding model based entirely on 'payment by results'. In addition, employment outcomes are paid only for participants who remain in work for a minimum of between 13 and 26 weeks depending on the participant group, with further payments made the longer the participant remains in work (for up to two years) (DWP 2013). This shift significantly increases the financial risk to contracted providers, with funding depending entirely on employment outcomes obtained at the *end* of provision. It thus raises questions regarding which providers are able to take on that risk, and on what basis regarding the provision of services to particular unemployed groups.

Within these systems of funding contracted employment services, unemployed groups are differentiated in varying ways. In the UK, prior to the Work Programme, different 'customer groups' such as lone parents, disabled people, young people, and the long-term unemployed, were served by one of the New Deal programmes. Other types of programmes were also targeted to more disadvantaged groups (such as the Ethnic Minority Outreach programme[7]) or more disadvantaged areas (such as the Action Teams for Jobs programme[8]). Contracted providers of those programmes were thus required to achieve employment outcomes for these particular programme groups. The Work Programme has integrated provision into a single programme. Although participants referred to the programme are broadly differentiated according to which benefits group they are assigned to (which is used as a proxy for difficulties faced in entering employment [Finn 2011]), the programme operates on the proviso that providers will assess need and tailor services to a broad range of individuals, delivering end-to-end support to all participants regardless of category, levels or types of assistance needs. Both primes and tier 1 sub-contractors deliver this end-to-end support, with sub-contracting at the tier 2 level intended to allow for the purchasing of specialist support from providers that have experience of working with and addressing the needs of particular groups (e.g. people with disabilities or mental health needs, or particular minority ethnic groups). Although tier 2 specialist providers are not required to achieve employment outcomes for their services, their funding is dependent on prime providers (predominantly private, for-profit organizations) purchasing their services (Rees *et al.* 2013).

Unemployed groups may also be differentiated according to the payment levels attached to placing them in work, with higher payments being made for employment outcomes for groups considered harder to place in work. This is intended to limit the risk that providers will orient their services to those more likely to enter employment in order to receive outcome payments. The model is thus intended to limit the risk of providers creaming participants (selecting those who are easier to place in work) and parking participants (providing less assistance to those who are more difficult to place in work) – issues which are examined in the following section of this article. Under the Australian Job Network system, bonus payments were available to providers for placing long-term unemployed participants in jobs (Dockery and Stromback 2001). In the Work Programme, while providers are paid for assisting all unemployed groups, higher payments are made for employment outcomes for particular groups (DWP 2013). However, the distinction made between different groups is rather limited with respect to the range of different levels and types of needs among people who are not in paid work. Higher levels of payments overall are made for people with disabilities claiming Employment Support Allowance (ESA) or previously Incapacity Benefit (IB), and for an early entry group (which includes people considered to face particular disadvantage, e.g. refugees, who could previously have been referred to the New Deal programmes at an early stage [DWP 2013]).

The Effects of Conditionality of Funding in a Market of Employment Services

This section examines the effects of this form of conditionality in the financing of contracted employment services on the provision of those services to unemployed people, and to more disadvantaged groups in particular. The analysis draws on the findings of research in different national contexts where quasi-markets in employment services have been most developed (the UK, Australia, the USA and the Netherlands), including research carried out by the authors (Rees *et al.* 2013; Shutes 2011). The findings relate to different types of programmes under which contracted providers have been partly or almost entirely funded on the basis of employment outcomes. It focuses, in particular, on findings relating to the current Work Programme in the UK, which, as indicated previously, has aimed to implement a 'payment by results' model whereby the majority of funding is conditional on employment outcomes. The following three inter-related dimensions of the effects of conditionality on provision are examined: first, the effects on the type of providers which are included and excluded from the delivery of publicly funded contracted employment services; second, the effects on the type of services which are provided to unemployed groups; and third, the effects on the targeting (creaming and parking) of different unemployed groups by providers.

Type of providers

Increasing work-related conditionality in the funding and development of a market of employment services has implications for the type of providers which are willing and able to enter the market on those conditions. In the UK, the shift from the New Deal and various employment support programmes of the 1990s and 2000s to the current Work Programme has been accompanied by apparent shifts in the types of providers being contracted to deliver services. In particular, there has been considerable concern that small and non-profit organizations are being 'squeezed out' of the programme in favour of large corporate organizations (Crisp *et al.* 2011), although there is no way to effectively benchmark the involvement of these organizations on previous programmes (Rees *et al.* 2013).

In the Work Programme, the profile of provider types differs across the supply chain. Fifteen of the 18 prime contractors are private sector organizations, with one non-profit organization, one public sector organization and one mixed private/non-profit organization (Lane *et al.* 2013). Further down the chain, providers are contracted by prime contractors at the tier 1 and 2 levels. At tier 1, there is a fairly even split between private and non-profit providers (with a small number of public sector providers) in terms of contract numbers, although market share is harder to establish. However, size is important here as there are few small local providers (either private or non-profit) involved at this level. Most are large national or regional organizations with a welfare-to-work remit (Rees *et al.* 2013). However, under previous programmes, such as the Ethnic Minority Outreach programme, in which all providers were contracted directly by the public employment service (Jobcentre Plus), a wider range of non-profit organizations operating at the local level were contracted to deliver those programmes, albeit some smaller providers faced difficulties in managing the administrative burden of contractual relations with Jobcentre Plus (Barnes *et al.* 2005). With regard to the Job Network in Australia, the development of the network between 1999 and 2008 led to a substantial reduction in the number and diversity of providers delivering employment services, in terms of size and sector – from 223 to 113 providers, all of which were either private or non-profit, with the exclusion of any former statutory organizations (Considine *et al.* 2011).

The involvement or lack of involvement of particular organizations in part relates to the financial risk which this funding model entails. In the Work Programme, at the prime provider level there is no longer a place for providers which are not able to take on the significant financial risk of managing a back-ended 'payment by results' funding model. The risk to providers is that without upfront payment, they must subsidize initial services for participants. Where a participant is unsuccessful in finding or staying in a job within the two years of the programme, the provider will not receive payment. In order to be accepted onto the Work Programme bidding framework, potential primes needed to be able to demonstrate, amongst other things, a turnover of at least £20 million (Finn 2012). Indeed, it has long been of wider concern that competition for contract-based funding in quasi-markets privileges larger organizations at the expense of smaller voluntary and community organizations which are unable to accept the financial risk of entering into a contract-based relationship (Deakin 1996).

Increasing work-related conditionality also entails risk to the 'mission' of some non-profit organizations (Wright *et al.* 2011), with implications for their involvement in the market and their relationships with the groups with which they work. It has been argued more generally that too strong an adherence to contract principles in the provision of publicly funded services may put at risk the distinctive contribution of voluntary and community organizations to meeting the needs of more disadvantaged groups (Eikenberry and Kluver 2004). This highlights the potential tensions between the accountability of non-profit organizations to the funders of their services, and accountability to the groups with whom they work, by responding to the (potentially conflicting) needs and interests of those groups (Lewis 1996). Research on non-profit providers of employment services targeted at refugees in the UK (prior to the introduction of the Work Programme) found that some providers were reluctant to enter into contracts with the public employment service (Jobcentre Plus) because of the implications of this type of funding for their mission. Indeed, not entering into these contracts was one means of maintaining the focus of the organization on meeting the needs of refugees rather than on achieving employment outcomes (Shutes 2011). In the Work Programme, Rees *et al.* (2013) found that financial risks were not necessarily a deterrent to bidding for tier 1 contracts for large national charities with substantial resources and reserves, although they were for some. However, non-profit providers identified a considerable reputational risk in terms of the programme's work-related conditionality and the mandatory participation of unemployed groups, which they struggled to align with their organizational mission.

The above effects of employment outcomes as a condition of funding have implications for the extent to which specialist (mainly non-profit) providers which have developed in response to the needs of particular social groups are excluded from the market of publicly funded employment services. Under the Work Programme, in principle, specialist providers can be sub-contracted at the tier 2 level to deliver support for particular groups/individuals on the programme. Funding for this support is not conditional on the specialist provider obtaining employment outcomes. At the tier 2 level, which is predominantly made up of specialist providers, there are slightly more non-profit than private providers, and larger numbers of small local organizations, although at this level there is considerable diversity with large multi-nationals listed alongside the community-based providers (Rees *et al.* 2013). However, since many tier 2 providers in the Work Programme have spot purchase agreements specifying only that a service may be procured at a given price rather than contacts based on indicative flows, being a listed tier 2 provider does not imply that these organizations are actually *delivering* any services (Rees *et al.* 2013). This raises questions regarding the extent to which conditionality of funding limits rather than supports a diversity of providers – not only in terms of sector (e.g. the balance of private/non-profit) but also in terms of size, locality and orientation towards particular groups.

Type of services

Financing providers on the basis of employment outcomes has implications for the type of services provided to unemployed groups, and the extent to which those services address the needs and interests of particular groups. An emphasis on employment outcomes has been found to encourage providers to focus on types of provision which are more likely to enhance the attainment of these outcomes, involving a shift away from education and training, such as language courses, vocational training and work placements, towards job search provision (Dockery and Stromback 2001; Felstead 1998; Gray 2000). Within the former Action Teams for Jobs programme in the UK, funding on the basis of employment outcomes was perceived by private providers as incentivizing them to get a participant any job, regardless of whether or not it was the most suitable job in the medium to long term for the participant, or something in which he/she was interested (Casebourne *et al.* 2006). With regard to the former New Deal for Young People, contracted providers expressed concerns that linking more of their funding to achieving job entries would lead to young people being encouraged to take jobs which were not of interest to them, when they might benefit more from participating for longer in an option on the programme (such as training or work placements) (Finn 2003). The Australian Job Network system was similarly found to reduce investment in training by providers where financial viability and competitive position within the market depended on maximizing employment outcomes at minimal cost (Carson and Kerr 2010). Considine *et al.* (2011) found that, with the development of the Job Network system, there was a reduction in flexibility in the approaches of frontline staff within as well as between providers, with increasing standardization of service provision as a means of minimizing risk and ensuring organizational viability within the market (Considine *et al.* 2011).

The extent to which these funding systems limit the provision of particular types of support may partly depend on the extent to which providers have access to *alternative* sources of funding. An emphasis on employment outcomes in the funding of provision targeted at refugees in the UK was found to place pressures on some providers to orient their services towards 'easy to find' jobs rather than jobs that reflected the skills and interests of refugees (Shutes 2011). This included trying to place refugee participants in a narrow range of low-skilled jobs, such as factory work and work within local ethnic minority communities, which did not require them to develop their English language skills. However, this was particularly the case for providers which were more oriented to competing for welfare-to-work programme funding. Non-profit providers which had more mixed sources of funding, including other sources of public funding, were able to stream funding which was not dependent on employment outcomes to support those with more complex needs, while only using funding which was dependent on employment outcomes to fund provision for more 'job ready' refugees.

Pressures to contain the costs of services may also place limits on the extent to which provision addresses the needs of particular groups. In the Work Programme, a substantial increase in conditionality of funding has been exchanged for increasing provider autonomy in terms of what support they provide (Rees *et al.* 2013). Under previous programmes, central government (Department for Work and Pensions) dictated the type and the terms and conditions of services that contracted providers might deliver (e.g. number of weeks of job training). By contrast, the Work Programme contains only minimum service requirements and the provider decides how to work with a participant. However, recent research has found there to be limited use of specialist support to address particular needs (e.g. training) or the needs of particular groups (e.g. those with mental health conditions) within the supply chains of prime providers and sub-contracted provision (Newton *et al.* 2012; Rees *et al.* 2013). Where specialist providers were used, in many cases this involved providers seeking unpaid assistance from organizations outside the programme whose services were free of charge (funded by other sources) or at low cost, rather than the specialist tier 2 providers listed by primes (Newton *et al.* 2012; Rees *et al.* 2013). This was partly attributed (by providers) to a perceived under-resourcing of the programme due to prime providers under-cutting the attachment fee at the commissioning stage to successfully compete for funding. It was also considered to be due to the rise in unemployment during the first years of the programme's operation, making it harder to achieve job outcomes which might then pay for specialist support (Rees *et al.* 2013).

Targeting of unemployed groups

Financing contracted providers on the basis of employment outcomes has also been found to encourage the creaming and parking of unemployed people referred to their services. Research on the JTPA programme in the USA found substantial evidence of creaming of participants by providers at the enrolment stage of the programme (Heckman *et al.* 2002). Financial incentives attached to employment outcomes encouraged providers to select the more 'job ready' individuals. Providers were less likely to enrol those who were African American, with low levels of educational attainment, from lower income families and without recent employment experience. Evidence of creaming was also found amongst providers of Intensive Assistance programmes for the long-term unemployed under the Australian Job Network system. Providers were reluctant to attract Indigenous Australian participants, due to the perception that placing them in jobs would be difficult and, therefore, unlikely to produce a funded outcome (Dockery and Stromback 2001).

Where providers are not able to select referrals to their services, the provision of services may still be targeted towards more 'job ready' participants by parking those considered the hardest to help, i.e. providing them with minimal assistance. Under the Australian Job Network, evidence of the parking of participants was of particular concern, whereby providers made less effort to find work for those who were difficult to place in work because the chances of success were low (Considine *et al.* 2011; Struyven and Steurs 2005). In the context of the Netherlands, a national study of the experiences of purchasers and providers of employment services indicated that parking participants was a strategic response to the competitive pressures of a market financially oriented towards job outcomes (van Berkel and van der Aa 2005). In the context of the former Action Teams for Jobs programme in the UK, funding private provider-led teams on the basis of employment outcomes was perceived by providers as incentivizing a focus on 'easier to help' participants (Casebourne *et al.* 2006). There was considered to be little incentive to work with people with multiple barriers to work as no payment was made for 'distance travelled' in terms of a participant's progress and improved ability to access work.

Evidence on the creaming and parking of unemployed people by providers thus raises issues with regard to the ways in which work-related conditionality in the financing of employment services limits support for more disadvantaged groups and, moreover, contributes to inequalities in the provision of those services to unemployed groups. In order to direct provision to more disadvantaged groups, as noted previously, programmes may be targeted towards a particular group (such as the former New Deal for Lone Parents in the UK) or higher payments may be made for particular groups within a non-targeted, generalist programme, in order to incentivize and provide additional funding to providers for assisting those groups. With regard to the former, there is evidence to suggest that creaming and parking may still occur within provision targeted towards particular groups in response to pressures to achieve employment outcomes. In the Jobcentre Plus Ethnic Minority Outreach programme (EMO), targeted at minority ethnic groups, contracted providers were likewise found to target those 'easier to help' (Barnes *et al.* 2005). In the second year of the pilot, as a result of the increased emphasis by Jobcentre Plus on achieving job outcomes, projects began to prioritize working with clients considered to be more likely to access employment in the short term (i.e. those perceived as being more 'job ready'): around half of the participants had recent employment experience (having left their last job in the previous six months), while only 16 per cent had been out of work for two or more years (Barnes *et al.* 2005). The evaluation of Pathways to Work, a programme targeted at people with disabilities who were claiming IB (prior to the introduction of the Work Programme), similarly found 'a clear management steer' towards parking harder to help participants (Hudson 2010).

Research on employment provision targeted at refugees by non-profit providers in the UK found that the condition of employment outcomes attached to 30 per cent of payments for participants resulted in different strategies among the providers (Shutes 2011). These strategies included the parking of refugees who were 'harder to help', such as those with limited English language proficiency, and, as noted previously, a reliance on placing refugees in a narrow range of low-skilled, low paid and ethnically segmented jobs which did not require English language proficiency. In order to limit risk to providers, targeting this funding on 'easier to help' refugees was another strategy, as some providers were able to obtain other sources of funding which were not conditional on employment outcomes in order to provide assistance to those with English language and other more complex needs. Across these programmes, however, work-related conditionality in the funding of provision targeted to refugees, minority ethnic groups and people with disabilities has contributed to that funding being directed away from the most disadvantaged within that group.

As noted previously, differential payments have been introduced as a means of addressing issues of creaming and parking. Research on the Work Programme found that the system of differential payments was regarded by providers as a 'blunt instrument', and payment groups were not necessarily viewed as coterminous with a participant's 'distance from the labour market' (Rees *et al.* 2013). For example, those in the ESA participant group (people with disabilities for whom higher payments applied) were considered not necessarily the hardest to help because most wanted to work. By contrast, among participants in the Jobseekers' Allowance (JSA) group (long-term unemployed who received lower payments), there were some who had substantial barriers to work which were not apparent from the participant group to which they were allocated on the basis of type of benefits claim. In fact, prime providers and sub-contractors operated their own triage systems such as RAG (red, amber, green) to assess new participants' distance from the labour market. Often, those considered to be 'furthest from the labour market' (the reds) received less support than those who were closest. The implications are that the 'real' hard-to-help do not necessarily match the differentiated payment groups and the extra work involved in supporting these participants is not rewarded, thus limiting the extent to which assistance may fully address the needs of those participants considered to be the most disadvantaged within the programme.

Conclusion

Increasing work-related conditionality in the financing of employment services, and in entitlements to welfare, point to dual processes of conditionality in the governance of employment services. How those processes are experienced, both by providers and by those unemployed, raises significant issues for understanding the social divisions in which contemporary reforms to employment services are embedded.

While systems of financing contracted provision vary – both within and across different national contexts – the effects of work-related conditionality raise the following issues. First, a market system which pays contracted providers on the condition of placing people in work, and keeping them in a job, may limit rather than promote a mix of types of providers appropriate to meeting the different needs of particular groups. That mix concerns not only the balance between public, private and non-profit providers within the market, but the size, locality and orientation of those providers. Conditionality of funding on the basis of employment outcomes carries significant financial and mission-related risk, which may exclude smaller, local and specialist types of non-profit providers – organizations which are typically valued for their relationships with more disadvantaged groups. This, in turn, has implications for the extent to which these types of organizations which are oriented towards addressing the needs of particular groups (such as people with disabilities, particular minority ethnic groups, refugees, lone parents, among others) are supported. Given that local non-profit organizations in deprived areas are much more reliant on public funding than those in less deprived areas (Clifford 2011), public funding clearly plays an important role in supporting those organizations to address the needs of more disadvantaged groups. It is, therefore, important to consider not only the overall level of funding allocated to employment provision, but how that funding is distributed through a supply chain of providers. In the UK Work Programme, smaller, local, non-profit providers which deliver specialist services are increasingly dependent on large private sector organizations higher up the chain for their share of public funding in working with disadvantaged groups. In a context of reduced public expenditure, the availability of alternative sources of public funding to support the employment-related activities of smaller organizations working with particular groups may further limit the allocation of resources to those organizations.

Second, this system may limit the diversity of types of services provided to unemployed groups and the provision of specialist assistance to particular groups. The evidence on the effects of employment outcomes attached to funding suggests that providers are encouraged to avoid services which do not 'guarantee' an employment outcome, conflicting with aims to tailor provision to the needs of particular groups and individuals. However, the under-resourcing of a programme, and the increased difficulties of obtaining payments for employment outcomes in a stagnant labour market, may also limit the availability of resources to contracted providers to deliver or sub-contract a range of types of services, including specialist assistance.

Third, this system may contribute to inequalities in the provision of services to unemployed groups by encouraging providers to differentiate particular groups/individuals according to the financial value or lack of value involved in providing them with assistance. While attempts to address creaming and parking in employment services have been made through differential payments – rewarding providers for working with particular groups – those systems do not necessarily serve to correct for these behaviours, not least because government and providers vary on how they define and value working with 'harder to help' groups. Moreover, evidence from the Work Programme suggests that systematic under-resourcing of a programme may substantially limit the extent to which providers are able to address the needs of more disadvantaged groups by sub-contracting specialist provision, irrespective of differential payments for those groups.

There is a need for more in-depth, comparative research to examine variation in different funding systems and its effects with regard to these issues. A more complex system of differential payments operates in the Job Service Australia, which classifies a wider range of groups according to levels of assistance needs, allocating differential payments to those groups. In addition, a Job Seeker Account is used to ring-fence funding for types of provision which address particular barriers to work. Providers are also now paid for 'pathways' outcomes, which are intended to reward progress towards employment. These payments can be made for a young participant's enrolment in an education or training programme, for example (Finn 2011). The latter two components of the system in Australia raise questions regarding the ways in which sources of funding which are *not* attached to employment outcomes and are ring-fenced for certain types of provision might, potentially, serve to support a wider range of services and specialist assistance for particular groups. While the UK Work Programme contractually requires providers to specify minimum service standards, given that providers' funding is primarily conditional on employment outcomes, this contractual requirement may be of limited effect in ensuring that those services are indeed delivered, and that the needs of those who are harder and potentially more resource intensive to help are adequately addressed. Moreover, where funding for particular services is not ring-fenced, the distribution of resources may not extend to the provision of specialist services in a supply chain of contracted providers to address particular needs.

Financing contracted employment services on the basis of employment outcomes points to broader implications for the ways in which social divisions and inequalities are framed and experienced within this system. Underlying this system of allocating public resources to the provision of employment services are market principles which position unemployed people as individual units of (paid) labour which need to be financially incentivized to sell their labour, and service providers as market agents which need to be financially incentivized to place people in paid work. This reframing of welfare, as Jayasuriya (2006) indicates, 'reconstitutes the state', by which the provision of welfare becomes defined in terms of modes of contractual governance which tie citizenship to market participation. Divisions of class, gender, race/ethnicity and disability which shape people's experiences, needs and interests in relation to paid and unpaid work, and which form the basis of claims-making regarding redistribution and recognition (Fraser 1997), are obscured from this model of welfare. Where those divisions are recognized, this is in terms of the additional financial value to providers for placing into work those who are classified as being 'harder to help', such as people with disabilities.

In the current context of economic crisis, labour market stagnation and the growth in low-waged, insecure work, there have been calls for reassessing work-related conditionality: for reassessing the justification for placing paid work as an individual obligation by attaching work-related conditions to social protection (Paz-Fuchs 2011). It is beyond the scope of this article to adequately address these debates. However, as the research discussed in this article indicates, there appears to be empirical grounds for reassessing the justification for attaching work-related conditions to the public financing of employment services. As the research demonstrates, there remain significant issues as regards the extent to which financing employment services on the condition of placing people and keeping people in a job limits the development of support which adequately addresses the needs and interests of different social groups in relation to work.

Notes

1. The influential works of Richard Titmuss developed an understanding of the 'social division of welfare' with respect to the fiscal and occupational dimensions of welfare in addition to (state) social services (Titmuss 1976). In this article, we draw on a sociological understanding of the social divisions (of class, gender, race, etc.) (see Payne 2006) which shape welfare and work.
2. And re-named Job Services Australia in 2009.
3. Jobcentre Plus continues to provide initial support to benefits claimants, with most claimants referred to the Work Programme at three to 12 months of unemployment depending on the benefits group in which they are categorized.
4. The Work Programme, for example, involves contractual relations between private and non-profit providers.
5. Through which programmes to support benefit claimants into employment were federally funded and locally administered with the contracting of local service providers. The Workforce Investment Act repealed the Act in 1998.
6. Attachment fees and outcome payments are paid at different rates for different programme groups. For those aged 25 and over (claiming JSA), with a maximum payment per participant of £1,600 for the attachment fee and initial job entry payment, 75 per cent of the total payment is for job entry (DWP 2013).
7. A Jobcentre Plus pilot programme aimed at assisting unemployed ethnic minority groups into employment, delivered by contracted private and non-profit organizations (Barnes *et al.* 2005).
8. A non-mandatory programme which operated in areas with high levels of unemployment.

References

Barnes, H., Hudson, M., Parry, J., Sahin-Dikmen, M., Taylor, R. and Wilkinson, D. (2005), *Ethnic Minority Outreach: An Evaluation*, London: Department for Work and Pensions.

Bredgaard, T. and Larsen, F. (2008), Quasi-markets in employment policy: do they deliver on promises? *Social Policy and Society*, 7, 3: 341–52.

Carson, E. and Kerr, L. (2010), Contractualism and social inclusion: strands of policy emulation in UK and Australian local employment services, *Policy and Politics*, 38, 1: 41–55.

Casebourne, J., Davis, S. and Page, R. (2006), *Review of Action Teams for Jobs*, London: Department for Work and Pensions.

Clifford, D. (2011), *Voluntary sector organisations working at the neighbourhood level in England: patterns by local area deprivation*, Third Sector Research Centre Working Papers no. 65, Birmingham: Third Sector Research Centre, University of Birmingham.

Considine, M. (2000), Selling the unemployed: the performance of bureaucracies, firms and non-profits in the new Australian 'market' for unemployment assistance, *Social Policy & Administration*, 34, 3: 274–95.

Considine, M. (2001), *Enterprising States: The Public Management of Welfare-to-Work*, Cambridge: Cambridge University Press.

Considine, M., Lewis, J. and O'Sullivan, S. (2011), Quasi-markets and service delivery flexibility following a decade of employment assistance reform in Australia, *Journal of Social Policy*, 40, 4: 811–33.

Crisp, R., Roberts, E. and Simmonds, D. (2011), 'Do-gooders, pink or fluffy, social workers' need not apply? An exploration of the experiences of the third sector organisations in the European Social Fund and Work Programme, *People, Place and Policy*, 5, 2: 76–88.

Deakin, N. (1996), What does contracting do to users? In D. Billis and M. Harris (eds), *Voluntary Agencies: Challenges of Organisation and Management*, Basingstoke: Macmillan, pp. 113–29.

Dean, H. (2004), *The Ethics of Welfare: Human Rights, Dependency and Responsibility*, Bristol: *Policy Press*.

Department for Work and Pensions (DWP) (2010), *Provider Guidance. Version 18 V1.0 March 2010*, http://www.dwp.gov.uk/docs/pg-part-4.pdf (accessed 28 April 2013).

Department for Work and Pensions (DWP) (2013), *The Work Programme. Invitation to Tender. Specification and Supporting Information*, http://www.dwp.gov.uk/docs/work-prog-itt.pdf (accessed 28 April 2013).

Dockery, A. and Stromback, T. (2001), Devolving public employment services: pre-liminary assessment of the Australian experiment, *International Labour Review*, 140, 4: 429–51.

Dwyer, P. (2004), Creeping conditionality in the UK: from welfare rights to conditional entitlements? *Canadian Journal of Sociology*, 29, 2: 265–87.

Eikenberry, A. M. and Kluver, J. D. (2004), The marketization of the nonprofit sector: civil society at risk? *Public Administration Review*, 64, 2: 132–40.

Felstead, A. (1998), *Output-Related Funding in Vocational Education and Training: A Discussion Paper and Case Studies*, Thessaloniki: European Centre for the Development of Vocational Training.

Finn, D. (2003), The 'employment-first' welfare state: lessons from the New Deal for Young People, *Social Policy & Administration*, 37, 7: 709–24.

Finn, D. (2011), *Job Services Australia: Design and Implementation Lessons for the British Context*, London: Department for Work and Pensions.

Finn, D. (2012), *Subcontracting in Public Employment Services: the Design and Delivery of 'Outcome based' and 'Black Box' Contracts*, Brussels: European Commission.

Fraser, N. (1997), *Justice Interruptus: Critical Reflections on the 'Postsocialist' Condition*, New York, NY: Routledge.

Gray, A. (2000), The comparative effectiveness of different delivery frameworks for training of the unemployed, *Journal of Education and Work*, 13, 3: 307–25.

Heckman, J., Heinrich, C. and Smith, J. (2002), The performance of performance standards, *Journal of Human Resources*, 37, 4: 778–811.

Hudson, M., Phillips, J., Ray, K., Vegeris, S. and Davidson, R. (2010), *The Influence of Outcome-based Contracting on Provider-led Pathways to Work*, London: Department for Work and Pensions.

Jayasuriya, K. (2006), *Statecraft, Welfare and the Politics of Inclusion*, Basingstoke: Palgrave Macmillan.

Lane, P., Foster, R., Gardiner, L., Lanceley, L. and Purvis, A. (2013), *Work Programme Evaluation Procurement, Supply Chains and Implementation of the Commissioning Model*, London: Department for Work and Pensions.

Lewis, G. (2003), Difference and social policy. In N. Ellison and C. Pierson (eds), *Developments in British Social Policy* 2, Basingstoke: Palgrave.

Lewis, J. (1992), Gender and the development of welfare regimes, *Journal of European Social Policy*, 2, 3: 159–73.

Lewis, J. (1996), What does contracting do to voluntary agencies? In D. Billis and M. Harris (eds), *Voluntary Agencies: Challenges of Organisation and Management*, Basingstoke: Macmillan, pp. 98–112.

Lister, R. (2003), *Citizenship: Feminist Perspectives*, Basingstoke: Palgrave Macmillan.

Newton, B., Meager, N., Bertram, C., Corden, A., George, A., Lalani, M., Metcalf, H., Rolfe, H., Sainsbury, R. and Weston, K. (2012), *Work Programme Evaluation: Findings from the First Phase of Qualitative Research on Programme Delivery*, London: Department for Work and Pensions.

Offe, C. (1984), *Contradictions of the Welfare State*, Cambridge, MA: MIT Press.

Orloff, A. S. (1993), Gender and the social rights of citizenship: the comparative analysis of gender relations and welfare states, *American Sociological Review*, 58, 3: 303–28.

Payne, G. (ed.) (2006), *Social Divisions* (2nd edn), Basingstoke: Palgrave Macmillan.

Paz-Fuchs, A. (2011), *The Social Contract Revisited: The Modern Welfare State*, Oxford: The Foundation for Law, Justice and Society and the Centre for Socio-Legal Studies, University of Oxford.

Peck, J. (2001), *Workfare States*, New York, NY: Guildford Press.

Rees, J., Taylor, R. and Damm, C. (2013), *Does sector matter: the role of the third sector in the work programme*, Third Sector Research Centre Working Papers, no. 92, Birmingham: Third Sector Research Centre, University of Birmingham.

Shutes, I. (2011), Welfare-to-work and the responsiveness of employment providers to the needs of refugees, *Journal of Social Policy*, 40, 3: 557–74.

Sol, E. and Westerveld, M. (eds) (2005), *Contractualism in Employment Services: A New Form of Welfare State Governance*, The Hague: Kluwer Law International and Aspen Publishers.

Struyven, L. and Steurs, G. (2005), Design and redesign of a quasi-market for the reintegration of jobseekers: empirical evidence from Australia and the Netherlands, *Journal of European Social Policy*, 15, 3: 211–29.

Titmuss, R. (1976), *Essays on the 'Welfare State'* (3rd edn), London: Allen and Unwin. van Berkel, R. (2010), The provision of income protection and activation services for the unemployed in 'active' welfare states. An international comparison, *Journal of Social Policy*, 39, 1: 17–34.

van Berkel, R. and van der Aa, P. (2005), The marketization of activation services: a modern panacea? Some lessons from the Dutch experience, *Journal of European Social Policy*, 15, 4: 329–43.

Williams, F. (1989), *Social Policy: A Critical Introduction. Issues of Race, Gender and Class*, Cambridge: Polity Press.

Williams, F. (1995), Race/ethnicity, gender, and class in welfare states: a framework for comparative analysis, *Social Politics*, 2, 2: 127–59.

Wright, S., Marston, G. and McDonald, C. (2011), The role of non-profit organisations in the mixed economy of welfare-to-work in the UK and Australia, *Social Policy & Administration*, 45, 3: 299–318.

6

Support for All in the UK Work Programme? Differential Payments, Same Old Problem

James Rees, Adam Whitworth and Elle Carter

Introduction

In common with much of the advanced economies (Lødemel and Trickey 2001), since the arrival of New Labour in 1997 the UK has made a decisive shift from a 'passive' to an 'active' welfare system in which eligibility for out of work benefits is tied increasingly tightly and explicitly to the stated obligation to seek paid work. This policy shift has been justified philosophically through the reciprocal relationship between rights and responsibilities embedded within the Third Way (Blair and Schroder 1998; Giddens 2000; Powell 2000) and has resulted in considerable development of, and evolution in, 'activating' welfare-to-work programmes throughout the 2000s. With the implementation of the Work Programme from 2011 the UK has come closer to joining the ranks of other advanced economies in embracing outsourced provision, devolved decision-making around intervention design and payment by results.

This evolution in recent decades in welfare-to-work services across the advanced economies is a result of several interrelated trends and concerns. There have been significant shifts in the organization of services with the implementation of contracting out and the creation of quasi-markets to respond to the critiques of public choice theorists around claims of unresponsive 'bureaucratic' state institutions and, more recently, the desire to transfer risk away from government (Considine 2000; Bredgaard and Larsen 2008; Mythen *et al.* 2012). These organizational reforms have been closely associated with the turns towards new

Contracting-out Welfare Services: Comparing National Policy Designs for Unemployment Assistance,
First Edition. Edited by Mark Considine and Siobhan O'Sullivan.
© 2015 John Wiley & Sons, Ltd. Published 2015 by John Wiley & Sons, Ltd.

managerialim and contractualism as well as shifts to 'new' governance modes involving changed relationships between the state, citizens and disadvantaged groups (Ramia and Carney 2000; Considine 2001; Struyven and Steurs 2005). Lastly, the influence of paternalism (Mead 1986) on policy discourse, framing and making has strengthened consistently in the UK since the late 1990s such that the Third Way balance between rights and responsibilities at the level of the individual has shifted to place greater onus on individual obligations. Moreover, at policy level there has been a parallel shift in emphasis away from the 'carrots' of policy supports (e.g. childcare, 'making work pay') toward the 'sticks' of sanctions-backed conditionality in response to alleged behavioural 'defects' (cf. DWP 2010a). Taken together, the aim for policymakers has been to create more efficient and specialized provision that is also more flexible, responsive and personalized to the different needs of unemployed individuals, and against which the unemployed have limited options but to participate on the terms set out to them.

As discussed in detail below, the evolution of welfare-to-work programmes in the UK through to the current Work Programme is, in a variety of ways, clearly influenced by these trends. Of particular interest to the present article is the extent to which the specific design of the Work Programme is able to realize the key tenets underpinning international welfare-to-work reform over the past two decades – efficiency, effectiveness, personalization, value-for-money, innovation, flexibility – within a programme design which appears to create multiple tensions and vulnerabilities around achieving these objectives. Of particular focus here is the challenge for the Work Programme to calibrate the incentives for providers to work differently in terms of meeting specific support needs – what Lister (2003) might term a process of 'differentiated universalism'. In contrast to this aim, the international literature has consistently raised fears that in such outsourced, payment by results welfare-to-work schemes (particularly private) providers would respond to financial pressures and incentives by 'creaming' off easier to serve claimants whilst 'parking' harder to service clients (Struyven and Steurs 2005; Considine et al. 2011). These fears have been strongly aired in the UK context from the earliest days of the Work Programme (PAC 2012) and have escalated, both as the economic backdrop has become more challenging than anticipated during the design phase and as evidence has accumulated during the early months of the scheme expressing concerns of creaming and parking (Newton et al. 2012; Lane et al. 2013; PAC 2012, 2013; WPSC 2011, 2013; Rees et al. 2013). The argument from the Department for Work and Pension (DWP) is that the specific design of the Work Programme – the existence of minimum service guarantees and, in particular, the use of nine claimant groups with differential payments across each – would effectively mitigate incentives for prime providers to cream and park, and the public statements of the DWP remain consistent in arguing that there is no evidence to suggest that this is not working (PAC 2013). Within this context, the present article draws on analysis of recently published official Work

Programme data alongside qualitative research on providers' experiences (Rees *et al.* 2013) in order to explore early evidence around creaming and parking in relation to the structures and incentives of the Work Programme's design.

The remainder of the article proceeds as follows. In the following section the evolution of welfare-to-work policies in the UK since the late 1990s is outlined with an emphasis on drawing out the key principles and aims under-pinning that evolution. This is followed by a summary of the international evidence on creaming and parking, its risks for the Work Programme in light of the scheme's stated aim of delivering 'differentiated universalism' (Lister 2003) in welfare-to-work support and the ways in which the detail of the scheme's design seeks to mitigate those risks to achieve that aim. The quantitative and qualitative material is then used to analyze the evidence and experiences around creaming and parking while the last section discusses the findings and reflects on the implications for Work Programme design and for international learning.

The Path to the Work Programme: A Radical Departure from an Established Trend

On coming to power in 1997 after almost two decades in opposition, New Labour quickly embarked on a series of 'activating' New Deal welfare-to-work schemes. Various New Deals were created for different claimant groups with different levels of conditionality. New Deal for Young People, for example, was a mandatory scheme which famously offered 'no fifth option' for those refusing to participate whilst those considered to have more 'legitimate' reasons for not working – most notably disabled adults and single parents – were offered voluntary schemes. In common across all of the New Deals, however, was a clear emphasis on supply-side measures and a 'work first' strategy of propelling working-age welfare recipients back into the labour market as swiftly as possible (Peck and Theodore 2000). In shifting the policy focus clearly to the supply-side, demand-side issues around weak local labour markets and job availability were largely rejected as 'old Left' and not feasible in today's global economy (Blair and Schroder 1998). Unemployment was, therefore, recast largely as an individual problem of employability rather than a structural problem of insufficient employment availability in local areas, a shift which has been the focus of considerable critique (Theodore 2007; Wright 2011) but which is seen particularly strongly and explicitly in the influential Freud report (Freud 2007). Supplementing these New Deals were a raft of policies to 'make work pay', most notably the introduction of the national minimum wage, tax credits and benefit run-ons. These incentivizing policies were combined with greater attention than previously to the framework of policy supports needed, particularly improving the availability of affordable childcare through the UK's first ever National Childcare Strategy and associated policies, such as childcare subsidies for low-income workers, Sure Start and free childcare places for three and four year olds.

111

If the early New Labour years were marked by the rapid construction of this activating welfare-to-work architecture then much of the following decade can perhaps best be described as one of 'creeping conditionality' during which there was a consistent trend of ratcheting up work-related behavioural requirements as well as the extension of these work-related conditionality requirements to traditionally inactive groups, particularly single parents and the disabled (Dwyer 2004). A critical juncture in the evolution of UK welfare-to-work policy was the publication of the Freud report in 2007 which received cross-party support and which was heralded as setting out the principles for welfare-to-work policies in the forthcoming decade: outsourcing and competition; 'black box' delivery models in which the state allows providers complete freedom over intervention design; personalized support; and payment by results. Arguing that unemployment is now frictional rather than structural, Freud also argued that enhanced conditionality and sanctions were needed to tackle the alleged behavioural causes of worklessness and the existence of a 'dependency culture', despite compelling evidence to the contrary (DWP 2010b; Shildrick *et al.* 2012). In the face of the empirical fragility of some of its key claims, the Freud report has, nevertheless, been highly influential to subsequent policy formulation. Almost immediately it set the template for New Labour's subsequent reformulation in 2009 of the main New Deal programmes into one Flexible New Deal (FND) in which welfare-to-work support was outsourced from Jobcentre Plus (the public sector employment support agency covering the UK) to external providers after one year of Jobcentre Plus support (or six months for fast-tracked claimants). In FND, financial payments to providers flowed mainly from successful job outcomes.

The arrival of the Conservative-Liberal Democrat Coalition government following the 2010 general election heralded a change in policy from the FND to the Coalition's Work Programme but also a continuation – indeed, a radical extension and intensification – of the principles set out in the Freud report (2007) and on which FND was designed. Although reflecting continuation from FND in terms of underlying principles the Work Programme, introduced in June 2011, is in various ways a genuine revolution in employment support policy, most notably in terms of the extent of sub-contracting and payments weighted to job outcomes as well as the 'black box' model of delivery. Delivery of the Work Programme takes place through contracts between the DWP and large-scale, mainly private sector prime providers which can both deliver services themselves and/or sub-contract to organizations within large and (sometimes) complex supply chains sitting underneath each prime. In very broad terms sub-contractors are either 'tier 1', delivering end-to-end services to participants throughout their time on the Work Programme, or 'tier 2', which contract with primes or tier 1s to provide specific interventions to participants. The Work Programme is structured geographically in the sense that Great Britain is divided into 18 large 'regional'[1] Contract Package Areas (CPAs) with two or three primes in each CPA to whom claimants are randomly allocated from

Jobcentre Plus if they have not found work within an initial period of Jobcentre Plus provision, the duration of which depends largely on the type of out-of-work benefit received and the Work Programme claimant group in which they are therefore placed. Unlike FND, which contained mandatory service components, a 'black box' delivery model operates in the Work Programme so that providers have almost complete flexibility over their interventions, with only minimum service delivery guarantees (which are themselves of variable ambition, detail and potential enforceability) set out by each prime provider (Finn 2012). This flexibility is required given that, unlike the various group-specific New Deals, Work Programme has to cater for the needs of all different types of largely long-term unemployed claimants within a single employment scheme, in part reflecting planned changes to the benefits system in the form of the consolidation of most of the major benefits and tax credits within the single Universal Credit from 2013.

Creaming, Parking and Differential Payments in the Work Programme

Creaming and parking by providers have long been considered endemic problems within welfare delivery systems involving outsourced provision combined with outcomes-based payments (Finn 2011), and international experience of similar welfare-to-work models highlights the extent of these issues in practice (Heckman *et al.* 2002; Dockery and Stromback 2001; van Berkel and van der Aa 2005; Finn 2011). 'Creaming' refers to providers skimming off clients who are closest to the labour market and targeting services on them in the expectation that they are more likely to trigger an outcome payment. 'Parking' refers to the opposite process, where those individuals deemed to be unlikely to generate an outcome payment are de-prioritized, perhaps receiving the minimum service specified in the contract. The issue is closely related to the more general economic literature around the difficulties in effectively managing principal-agent relationships via contracts (Bredgaard and Larsen 2008), and is made more likely where regulatory control or organizational norms or incentives against it are low – most obviously where providers are private organizations attracted to participation in welfare provision due to a simple profit motive. Of the 40 contracts won within the Work Programme, 35 were won by private sector primes, three by third sector organizations and two by public sector organizations, and fears of creaming and parking were strong from the outset. These concerns intensified in the context of tighter than expected cost-pressures on primes due to a combination of a more difficult than expected economic environment which affected job outcome (and hence payment) levels, the prevalence – and apparent success of – discounting practices at the bidding stage, and lower than expected caseloads within some payment groups (Inclusion 2011a).

International evidence suggests that creaming and parking by providers is widely experienced across different countries (Considine 2000;

Struyven and Steurs 2005; van Berkel and van der Aa 2005; Bredgaard and Larsen 2008; van Berkel *et al.* 2012; de Graaf and Sirovatka 2012). The literature also makes clear, however, that the detail of programme design and payment structures can play a role in either mitigating or facilitating such provider behaviours (Considine 2000; Struyven and Steurs 2005; van Berkel and van der Aa 2005; Considine *et al.* 2011; Finn 2011, 2012). In bringing together such a diverse range of claimants into one single programme the DWP was aware from the outset that this was a challenge for the Work Programme and sought to mitigate these risks through the programme's design. This was attempted partly through the requirement for primes to set out minimum service guarantees but primarily through the placement of each individual into one of nine Work Programme claimant groups based on the type of benefit received as a proxy for the level of their perceived support needs. These claimant groups are important to providers because they carry with them different entry requirements and, crucially, different levels of financial reward for job outcome payments, scaled according to some notion of the average difficulty of transitions to employment for each claimant group (NAO 2012; Lane *et al.* 2013). To adopt Lister's terminology the issue is one of 'differentiated universalism' (Lister 2003) – seeking equality whilst (indeed, through) recognising difference – whereby policymakers seek to use the differentiated payments across claimant groups to incentivize Work Programme providers to treat different claimants *differently* dependent upon their distance to the labour market and barriers to work, in order that all claimants receive the amount and type of support so as to *equalize* opportunities to move into employment. Payments across these claimant groups vary from a maximum of £3,810 for Jobseekers' Allowance (JSA) claimants aged 18 to 25, to £13,720 potentially for an individual within the Employment Support Allowance (ESA) group for recent Incapacity Benefit (IB) claimants. As Robert Devereux, Permanent Secretary of the DWP, explained to the Committee of Public Accounts in February 2011, this is a step on from previous programme design in the UK in the field of welfare-to-work: 'This set of prices, as has just been said, begins to move us towards trying to reflect some of the average difficulty … Everything we have done here takes us really a long way forward compared with where we were' (PAC 2012).

The DWP's hope is that, if designed appropriately, differentiated payments across claimant groups would translate the policy rhetoric of differentiated universalism into policy reality, mitigating providers' incentives to cream and park. Compared to FND, however, and to most comparable international welfare-to-work schemes operating an outsourced payment-by-results financing model, the Work Programme weights a smaller share of the provider's potential payment to the initial attachment – or joining – fee and a far larger share to employment transitions and, in particular, sustained job outcomes (generally measured in the Work Programme as six months of sustained employment). Within FND the ratio between the initial joining fee, a successful transition into work and a sustained job outcome was roughly 40:30:30 (Vegeris *et al.* 2011:13) whilst in the Work Programme the ratio is closer to 10:25:65,[2] although it varies somewhat across the nine claimant groups. With performance outcomes, therefore, mattering to a far greater degree in Work Programme than in comparable previous schemes it becomes critical to successfully mitigating the economically rational incentives to cream and park amongst primes both that the level of financial payments *between* payment groups realistically reflects the relative difficulty of moving claimants within these groups into (sustained) employment *and* that these claimant groups are relatively homogeneous *internally* such that a single level of payment realistically reflects the needs of all claimants within each claimant group. If either of these assumptions is not satisfied then there should be a logical expectation that creaming and parking will take place if providers are assumed to be economically rational and if they are confident that creaming and parking will go undetected and/or unpunished. In the following section the overarching question which the discussion of the quantitative and qualitative material seeks to answer is a simple one: does it appear that the DWP has succeeded in designing a scheme which mitigates against providers' incentives to cream and park?

Data and Methods

The quantitative analysis draws on the Work Programme's official statistics published online by the DWP. These statistics show the numbers of unemployed people referred and attached to the Work Programme and numbers of job outcome payments made to providers as a result of participants achieving sustained employment (six months of employment or three months for members of 'harder to help' payment groups) (DWP 2013). We construct the DWP's preferred 'job outcome rate' measure (job outcomes/referrals) from the most recent official programme statistics, and this covers the period from programme launch in 2011 to the end of September 2013. The qualitative analysis draws on a research project which involved key informant interviews and case studies of delivery in two localities (Rees *et al.* 2013). The eight key informant interviews included respondents from third sector and employment services infrastructure organizations, private and third sector prime contractor organizations, and some large national third sector organizations delivering the Work Programme as sub-contractors. The case studies of delivery were located in two areas chosen to provide geographical and labour market diversity (inner-city vs. semi-rural, north vs. south England) and different supply chain models. In each area a brief 'mapping' exercise identified the role and type of organizations in the supply chains. This was followed by a phone survey of these sub-contractors (approximately 65 per cent contacted) which confirmed a number of their basic characteristics, their position and role in the supply chain and the nature of their provision. These issues were further explored in two focus groups with sub-contractors (one each for tier 1 and tier 2 providers) held in one of the localities. Lastly, interviews were conducted with four of the five private sector primes operating in the two sampled areas (the fifth declined to take part) and 14 of their sub-contracted providers.

Differential Payments but Still Differential Outcomes: Rhetoric vs. Reality in the Work Programme

As a first step in understanding claimants' differing needs, profiling tools have become increasingly commonplace within welfare-to-work programmes both in the UK and internationally. Within the Work Programme prime providers are adopting a whole range of approaches to profiling and using these analyses to guide (at least in the first instance) the intensity and type of interventions targeted at the individual (Newton *et al.* 2012: 47–9). Tellingly, however, rather than adopting the DWP's claimant groups as the structure for their activities, prime providers tend to develop their own streams of claimants and related intervention packages, suggesting that the differentiated payments embedded within the Work Programme's claimant groups may well not correspond to providers' view of claimants' distance to the labour market. Rather, commenting on the providers' use of these profiling tools one provider suggested that the RAG (red, amber, green) rating system[3] used by some primes and their end-to-end providers to 'triage' their caseloads was, in effect, a mechanism for creaming those rated 'green', focusing energies and resources on those easiest and most likely to move into work, whilst parking claimants rated 'red' who are considered to need more time and resource to support back into work. Asked if this was the case, one sub-contracted provider stated:

> *'That's done openly. [At the first customer assessment] you'd give an antic- ipated job start date and you categorise people on day one into red, amber and green categories ... So from day one you're categorised and if you're a green customer you've got an anticipated job start date, you've got an action plan to work towards that, and you have to be seen so that is once or twice a week. So you're pushed. If you're amber your job start date is obviously further away, and it's the expectation that you'll have activity at least once a fortnight. If you're red it could be a phone call once a month. So people are not using the word parking because it's politically incorrect, but it's happening.'* (tier 2 provider)

Indeed, Work Programme providers with long-standing experience of welfare-to-work provision argued that such practices were not just endemic but that they could also be seen as a rational response to the current payment by results model and its misalignment with the actual support needs of individual claimants across and within the claimant groups. Nevertheless, while interviewees expressed the view that most providers would cream if given the chance there were a number of ways in which potential mechanisms for creaming could be shut off. One was strict random allocation of jobseekers between a prime's 'in-house' delivery and delivery by their 'end-to-end' delivery partners. One prime claimed this was preferable in any case because it permitted proper comparison of performance between providers in the supply chain and, therefore, improved performance management, but it was impossible to verify whether this system could in reality be circumvented. The incentive for primes to cream skim could be removed entirely where they outsourced all delivery to their sub-contractors, as is the case with a number of primes in the Work Programme; but certainly this may in effect push the issue down to the sub-contractor level. Whilst feeling that creaming and parking were hard to avoid in the current design given the intense dual pressures around costs and targets, not all providers were comfortable with these practices. This provider, for example, was uncomfortable behaving in this way towards claimants but felt torn by the need to deliver the targets for the organization within the budget available:

'So we are going to have these numbers of customers that perhaps may never find employment in the two years. We'll never be paid for them either but we'll be paid for the other 50% that are likely to go on into work so there's a level of parking going on which we're not particularly comfortable with but we also need to achieve what we need to achieve and what the primes need to achieve so it's trying to get a balance really.' (tier 1 provider)

However, another provider argued that parking was a sensible way to manage the caseload and that the extent of parking would need to be assessed over the full length of the attachment period:

'I think from a provider perspective we are expected to prioritise customers that are coming through who are job ready and to move those through as quickly as we can, and I think from a financial perspective that's realistic because you've got to get the money in the system to keep it all flowing. I don't think you purposefully park people but it could seem like that from the outside because it's taking longer to get those people job ready or ... they're being referred onto, say, drug and alcohol services who will be working with them and until they have their condition managed then you can't work with them. So there might be a perception of parking because it's taking longer and efforts are, at this group, to move them through [the system].' (tier 2 provider)

To try to get a sense of the nature and scale of the issue, figure 1 summarizes the most recent official Work Programme job outcomes data published by the DWP in December 2013, which covers the first 27 months of the programme's operation. This is, admittedly, early data in the lifetime of the scheme but it does suggest problems in the extent to which the current differentiated payments design is effectively calibrating provider incentives *between* payment groups. At its simplest level, the differential payments across the claimant groups should at least be

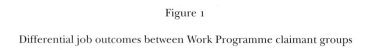

Figure 1

Differential job outcomes between Work Programme claimant groups

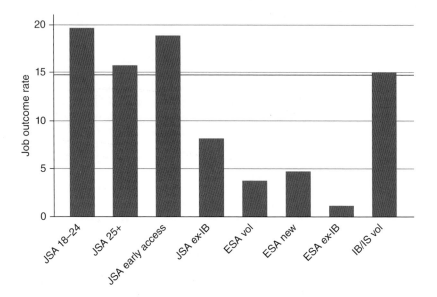

calibrated so as to equalize providers' incentives to work with (of course only notional) 'average claimants' *between* the separate claimant groups as Devereux's evidence to the Public Accounts Committee, cited above, focuses on. *If* the differentiated payment system is effectively calibrating providers' incentives *between* the Work Programme's claimant groups in terms of some idea of the 'average claimant' within each of these groups, then one would, on average, expect the job outcome rates to be relatively evenly balanced between the various claimant groups. Figure 1, however, shows in contrast that there are considerable imbalances in job outcome rates between the claimant groups, suggesting underlying imbalances in the extent to which the current payment levels are equalizing the balance between costs, risks and returns across these claimant groups. Whilst the overall job outcomes rate comes out at just under 15 per cent (the horizontal line) two groups are doing markedly better than this average, and a number of payment groups are doing markedly less well.

Part of the hesitance of providers in adopting the DWP's claimant groups as their own framework for targeting claimants reflects their recognition that the groups are relatively crude and with significant internal heterogeneity. This is well known both by policymakers and within the academic literature yet the persistence of the differentiated payments model attached to such broad and internally diverse claimant

118

groups has significant implications for claimants in terms of their increased exposure to systemic risks of creaming and parking. As a consequence, and in contrast to Robert Devereux's response to the Committee of Public Accounts, cited above, the appropriate question in terms of seeking to design out creaming and parking is not whether the current programme design is more subtle than previous welfare-to-work schemes but, rather, whether it is adequate to overcome creaming and parking. Although it remains early days for the Work Programme, the evidence accumulating here and elsewhere (Newton *et al.* 2012; Lane *et al.* 2013; PAC 2012, 2013; WPSC 2011, 2013; Rees *et al.* 2013) suggests not. The first phase of the DWP-commissioned qualitative evaluation of the Work Programme, for example, is surprisingly frank for an official evaluation: 'the available evidence to date suggests that providers are engaging in creaming and parking, despite the differential payments regime' (Newton *et al.* 2012: 124).

Cost pressures, combined with ambitious targets, were seen by many providers as a basic but central issue and there was a widespread perception that whatever process and design improvements might be made that the underlying reason for creaming, parking and poor performance against the DWP's minimum performance standards was under-resourcing of the programme. As one experienced operator in the welfare-to-work field commented:

> *'Regardless of what the government are saying … they haven't funded it properly to be able to get a good service. They wanted to move to an all encompassing service and they had an ideal opportunity to do that, and I for one thought it was brilliant that they did that … and they had a really good opportunity to make sure that that was funded properly so that we really could see improvement in people going back into work and it's just not happening, is it? Or it's not happening on the scale that they wanted it to.'*
> (tier 2 provider)

Within this pressurized context, primes were acutely aware that claimant groups were a blunt instrument oriented primarily around the prior benefit received and not necessarily coterminous with a customer's distance from the labour market. This could work in either direction, with some individuals placed in relatively 'job ready' groups attracting relatively low potential payments (e.g. JSA 18–24 or JSA 25+) actually being perceived by providers to face serious barriers to moving into paid work. Conversely, some individuals placed in relatively 'hard to place' claimant groups and thus attracting substantial financial payments for sustained job outcomes (e.g. ESA ex-IB[4] claimants) may actually be assessed by primes as needing relatively little support to move into paid work – the ideal client from a prime provider's perspective. This inevitably left providers reflecting on these frequent mismatches between their own evaluation of the individual's distance to the labour market and the Work Programme's evaluation as proxied by the level of financial payment attached to that individual's claimant group. As one third sector organization described, *'We've got a guy who carries around a mirror in his pocket to ward off evil spirits. Okay he might be on JSA but he's a long way from the job market isn't he?'* (tier 1 provider). Another provider in a different CPA noted the extent of undiagnosed mental health issues amongst JSA claimants:

> *'There have been a lot of undiagnosed mental health conditions, as secondary [pause] as secondary illnesses to what's actually going on ... some of these people have got extremely complex barriers before they even think about going into work ... And yet they're a JSA customer and they [pause] the number of times that I want to say, 'This person should not be on the Work Programme, they're probably a work [pause] if anything, they're a Work Choice*[5] *customer ... or they need to be left alone for at least six months and helped to sort out the other issues that they have.'* (tier 2 provider)

One interesting finding is that whilst the creaming and parking debate, both here and elsewhere, tends to be framed in the language of incentive structures and rational economic behaviour, there is evidence that some parking might arise inadvertently because of the inexperience or inadequate information held by providers and that there might be a learning curve to go through similar to that seen in the Job Network (Dockery and Stromback 2001). One end-to-end provider, for example, described how job advisers within a particular prime might lack the knowledge (and are bowed by pressure from high case loads) to refer jobseekers to appropriate sub-contractors, by implication leaving them to be parked. Additionally, the initial assessment is supposed to 'flag' customer needs but this was not, apparently, working effectively. They, therefore, decided to send their own staff to work alongside job advisers to 'drive' referrals to the sub-contractor:

> *'Our workers are backing [named prime] officers making sure that people remember to refer people to [named tier 1 provider], that actually if you've got somebody who's got a substance misuse or mental health issue you're better off referring them to [same tier 1 provider] than holding onto them and not being able to get them a job.'* (tier 1 provider)

Another provider commented similarly that whilst assessment tools may be widely used they are also far from comprehensively developed or utilized such that frontline advisers were sometimes ill-prepared to refer effectively:

> *'And actually, will those frontline advisors know what to do with that customer? Doubt it. Probably park them. But what I thought was, right, let me come up with something that takes the best of what Australia have got in terms of assessment, using health professionals, occupational therapists, develop that in the UK to make an assessment that's face to face, that actually gives direction for that customer so what happens is now [is progression to specific services].'* (tier 2 provider)

Whilst potentially emerging from informational as well as economic motivations, therefore, the quantitative material presented in figure 2 is also consistent with, and lends support to, the idea that the current Work Programme design does not adequately mitigate incentives to cream and park across different types of claimants *within* claimant groups in addition to simply *between* those groups. To explore this issue, figure 2 focuses on differences in job outcome rates between claimants with and without employment 'disadvantages' relating to disability and single parenthood across the three largest payment groups which together make up around 80 per cent of referrals to date. The rationale for these analyses is that single parents and the disabled might be expected to be 'harder to place' for providers and, as such, might rationally be expected to be more vulnerable to parking.

The trend in figure 2 for lower outcome rates amongst the relatively 'disadvantaged' payment group members is seen clearly and consistently across the three payment groups when comparing participants with a reported disability against those with no disability. Drawing on the social model of disability, where societal barriers operate to prevent disabled people from participating as equals in society (Barnes and Mercer 2003), there are additional barriers faced by disabled people seeking work (Patrick 2012), and the additional costs associated with

Figure 2

Differential job outcomes within Work Programme claimant groups

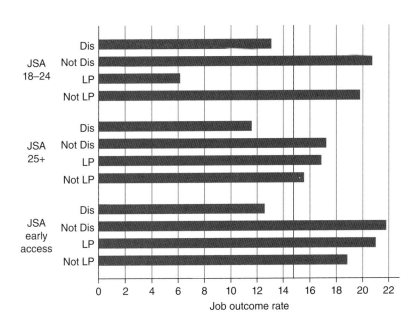

overcoming these barriers may be at play in lower outcome rates for this group. Clearly, these data do not prove that creaming and parking are taking place, but they are in line with that practice and at a minimum highlight that the current differential payments structure is not calibrated to individual variation.

The chronic scarcity of care compatible employment opportunities (Gingerbread 2010) and lack of affordable local childcare (Daycare Trust 2012) stimulate an expectation that lone parents may face particular difficulties in securing sustained work from the Work Programme. Figure 2, however, shows that the story from the Work Programme so far is a little more complex in that whilst younger lone parents fare consistently less well than younger non-lone parents in terms of their job outcome rates older lone parents fare consistently better than older non-lone parents. It is unclear why these findings should be seen, although it might be partly due to the fact that younger lone parents have younger children (Coleman and Lanceley 2011) and that, for the reasons outlined above, younger children present stronger obstacles to lone parent employment (Bryson *et al.* 1997). Older lone parents also tend to have stronger human capital and work histories than younger lone parents (Coleman and Lanceley 2011).

The JSA Early Access group comprises three separate types of claimants: mandatory entry of 18-year-olds not in education, employment or training (NEETs); mandatory entry of JSA 'repeaters' (those receiving JSA for 22 of the past 24 months); and voluntary early entry for pre-identified 'vulnerable' JSA claimants (DWP 2013). Whilst it is impossible to say categorically from the publicly available data, it seems most likely that lone parents have been recruited to this group as JSA repeaters and thus to have some recent labour market experience. When compared with lone parents in the JSA 18–24 payment group, lone parents in the JSA Early Access group are also likely to be generally older and to have older children. Moreover, whilst job outcomes are triggered only after six months of sustained work for the JSA payment groups, this occurs after three months for the JSA Early Entry group, which will certainly help to make the job outcome rates in this group seem relatively more impressive than the other two JSA groups.

To explore these issues further our analyses take advantage of the fact that the Work Programme is broken down into 40 separate contracts with primes across the 18 CPAs, with some primes delivering across several CPAs and so having several contracts. Figure 3 extends the quantitative analyses by focusing on the question of consistency in results, again making use of the ability within the official data to disaggregate job outcomes by disability and single parenthood. For each Work Programme contract, figure 3 shows the difference between the disabled and non-disabled job outcome rates (horizontal axis) and the difference between the single parent and non-single parent job outcome rates (vertical axis). For both axes, a difference of zero implies identical job outcome rates between the two groups, positive values mean that the non-disabled/non-single parent job outcome rate is higher than

Figure 3

Patterned inequalities in job outcomes across Work Programme contracts

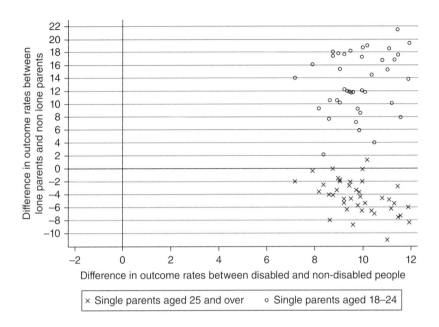

Difference in outcome rates between disabled and non-disabled people

| × Single parents aged 25 and over | o Single parents aged 18–24 |

the disabled/single parent job outcome rate, and negative values mean the opposite. Figure 3 is presented as a quadrant, and if the Work Programme's model of claimant groups and differential payments was successfully calibrating providers' incentives across claimants then one would expect any resulting differences in rate differences to be due to chance rather than anything systematic. In this case, the points would tend to centre around zero at the intersection of the two lines shown and to show a fairly random cloud of points around that intersection.

In contrast to this neutral picture, figure 3 highlights across the horizontal axis that disabled participants experience markedly lower job outcomes than non-disabled participants in every Work Programme contract. Looking along the vertical axis, there is also a consistent pattern in most (though not all) contracts that younger lone parents fare markedly less well than younger non-lone parents. In contrast, however, it is interesting to see that older lone parents tend to see somewhat better job outcome rates than older non-lone parents, the result perhaps of the combination of weaker needs for care-compatible work and childcare along with evidence showing that lone parents have a particularly strong motivation to work (Tu and Ginnis 2012). If differential job outcome rates between 'easier to help' and 'harder to help' claimants are accepted to be an indicator of potential parking then the

123

consistency in these findings across the 40 contracts lends weight to the notion that strategies, practices and cultures of prime providers in relation to creaming and parking may well be involved.

Conclusion

The Work Programme represents a radical extension of the incremental evolution of employment services witnessed in recent years in the UK. It implements for the first time, at a national level, a fully outsourced 'black box' model with payments based almost entirely on job outcome results. The programme aims to realize the key tenets underpinning international welfare-to-work reform over the past two decades but appears to be vulnerable to multiple tensions inherent within its design. This article focuses on the challenge for the all-encompassing Work Programme to calibrate the incentives for providers to work differently, but equally, in meeting the specific support needs of all jobseekers. The DWP sought to mitigate the identified risks around creaming and parking primarily through the placement of each individual into one of nine claimant groups, each with different levels of financial payments for job outcomes scaled according to a notion of the average difficulty of securing transitions to employment in each. The DWP's hope is that, if designed appropriately, differentiated payments across claimant groups would turn the rhetoric of 'differentiated universalism' into policy reality, mitigating providers' incentives to cream and park.

The combination of the quantitative and qualitative data presented above, however, suggests that this has not been achieved in practice and that creaming and parking may also be systemic in that they flow directly from the current design of the Work Programme. *If* the differentiated payment system was effectively calibrating providers' incentives *between* the Work Programme's claimant groups then one would, on average, expect the job outcomes rates to be relatively evenly balanced between the various claimant groups. This is not the case in practice, suggesting underlying imbalances in the extent to which the current payment levels are equalizing the balance between costs, risks and returns across these claimant groups. Disaggregating the data for 'harder to place' groups across the 40 Work Programme contracts displays an alarming degree of consistency in the findings that disabled people and young lone parents experience relatively lower job outcome rates than their 'non-disadvantaged' peers. Far from delivering 'differentiated universalism', the Work Programme at present seems instead to be reinforcing, exacerbating and making systemic the negative impacts of employment disadvantages.

Therefore, and in response to the question posed at the outset of the article, it is extremely difficult to argue on the basis of this evidence that the DWP has succeeded in designing the Work Programme payment groups and differential payments such that they mitigate providers' incentives to cream and park different individuals either across or within its broad payment groups, all in a context where providers are experiencing intense pressures around costs, cash flows and performance. Clearly, these quantitative data alone do not *prove* that parking is taking place – one needs to align the evidence on outcomes with the qualitative evidence around Work Programme processes for that – but the patterns seen are perfectly in line with what would be expected *if* parking were occurring. When taken together with the various emerging qualitative evidence discussed here, from the official Work Programme evaluation (Newton *et al.* 2012; Lane *et al.* 2013) and from government select committees (PAC 2012, 2013; WPSC 2011, 2013), then the notion that creaming and parking are serious problems within the Work Programme becomes compelling.

It will be of particular interest to an international audience that this evidence has been found despite the progression to what, at least superficially, appears a more complex and nuanced framework from the DWP in terms of payment groups and differential payments. Whilst value for money arguments from policymakers support a heavy weighting of payments onto job outcomes this strengthens the ever present challenge to mitigate providers' incentives to focus their energies and resources where it will pay. Value for money arguments such as these carry risks around parking, not just for claimants but also for ongoing social security budgets for those who fail to be supported into work. At present, it seems the Work Programme design may not have struck the right balance between value for money, incentives and claimant protections. With a challenging economic backdrop constraining job outcomes and with providers – and government select committees (WPSC 2013) – united in questioning the adequacy of resources within the programme to meet the support needs of more challenging claimants, such risks and weaknesses in the programme design are magnified. The challenge for UK and international policymakers seeking to embrace quasi-marketized welfare-to-work delivery is to drive forward the evolution of their programmes, such that they better balance their inevitable tensions between efficiency and equity.

Acknowledgements

The support of the Economic and Social Research Council (ESRC), the Office for Civil Society (OCS) and the Barrow Cadbury UK Trust is gratefully acknowledged. This work was part of the programme of the joint ESRC, OCS Barrow Cadbury Third Sector Research Centre.

Notes

1. The North East, North West, Scotland and Wales are all examples of the scale of CPAs.
2. Authors' calculations based on Inclusion 2011b.
3. The RAG rating uses a traffic light system to group individuals either as red (hard to move into work), amber (moderately difficult to move into work) or green (easy to move into work).

4. Incapacity Benefit (IB) is currently being replaced by the Employment and Support Allowance (ESA).
5. Work Choice is a separate employment programme offering support to individuals with disabilities and long-term health conditions.

References

Barnes, C. and Mercer, G. (2003), *Disability*, Cambridge: Polity Press.

Blair, T. and Schroder, G. (1998), *Europe: The Third Way/Die Neue Mitte*, Friedrich Ebert Foundation Working Document No. 2, http://library.fes.de/pdf-files/bueros/suedafrika/02828.pdf (accessed 29 November 2013).

Bredgaard, T. and Larsen, F. (2008), Quasi-markets in employment policy: do they deliver on promises? *Social Policy and Society*, 7, 3: 341–52.

Bryson, A., Ford, R. and White, M. (1997), *Making Work Pay: Lone mothers, employment and well-being*, Social Policy Research, 129, York: Joseph Rowntree Foundation.

Coleman, N. and Lanceley, L. (2011), *Lone Parent Obligations: Supporting the journey into work*, Research Report 736, Sheffield: Department for Work and Pensions.

Considine, M. (2000), Selling the unemployed: the performance of bureaucracies, firms and non-profits in the new Australian 'market' for unemployment assistance, *Social Policy & Administration*, 34, 3: 274–95.

Considine, M. (2001), *Enterprising states: The public management of welfare-to-work*, Cambridge: Cambridge University Press.

Considine, M., Lewis, J. and O'Sullivan, S. (2011), Quasi-markets and service delivery flexibility following a decade of employment assistance reform in Australia, *Journal of Social Policy*, 40, 4: 811–33.

Daycare Trust (2012), *Childcare costs in 2012*, London: Daycare Trust.

de Graaf, W. and Sirovatka, T. (2012), Governance reforms and their impacts on the effects of activation policies, *International Journal of Sociology and Social Policy*, 32, 5/6: 353–63.

Department for Work and Pensions (DWP) (2010a), *Universal Credit: Welfare that works*, Cm 7957, Norwich: HMSO.

Department for Work and Pensions (DWP) (2010b), *Ad-hoc analysis of households who have never worked*, London: DWP.

Department for Work and Pensions (DWP) (2013), *Work Programme Official Statistics: Background Information Note*, London: DWP.

Dockery, A. and Stromback, T. (2001), Devolving public employment services: preliminary assessment of the Australian experiment, *International Labour Review*, 140, 4: 429–51.

Dwyer, P. (2004), Creeping Conditionality in the UK: From welfare rights to conditional entitlements? *The Canadian Journal of Sociology*, 29, 2: 265–87.

Finn, D. (2011), *The Design of the Work Programme in International Context*, a report for the National Audit Office.

Finn, D. (2012), *Sub-contracting in Public Employment Services: The Design and Delivery of Outcome Based and Black Box Contracts*, European Commission: DG Employment, Social Affairs and Inclusion.

Freud, D. (2007), *Reducing Dependency, Increasing Opportunity: Options for the Future of Welfare to Work*, London: Department for Work and Pensions.

Giddens, A. (2000), *The Third Way and its Critics*, Cambridge: Polity Press.

Gingerbread (2010), *Changing the Workplace: The Missing Piece of the Jigsaw*, London: Gingerbread.

Heckman, J., Heinrich, C. and Smith, J. (2002), The performance of performance standards, *Journal of Human Resources*, 37, 4: 778–811.

Inclusion (2011a), *Work Programme Results: Perform or Bust*, http://www.cesi.org.uk/sites/default/files/response_downloads/perform_or_bust.pdf (accessed 29 November 2013).

Inclusion (2011b), *Can the Work Programme Succeed?*, http://www.cesi.org.uk/sites/default/files/response_downloads/work_programme_succeed.pdf (accessed 29 November 2013).

Lane, P., Foster, R., Gardiner, L., Lanceley, L. and Purvis, A. (2013), *Work Programme Evaluation: Procurement, Supply Chains and Implementation of the Commissioning Model*, London: Department for Work and Pensions.

Lister, R. (2003), *Citizenship: Feminist Perspectives*, New York, NY: NYU Press.

Lødemel, I. and Trickey, H. (eds) (2001), *An Offer You Can't Refuse: Workfare in International Perspective*, Bristol: Policy Press.

Mead, L. (1986) (ed.), *The New Paternalism: Supervisory Approaches to Poverty*, Washington, DC: The Brookings Institute.

Mythen, G., Walklate, S. and Kemshall, H. (2012), Decentralizing risk: The role of the voluntary and community sector in the management of offenders, *Criminology & Criminal Justice*, doi: 10.1177/1748895812458295.

National Audit Office (NAO) (2012), *The Introduction of the Work Programme*, London: The Stationery Office, http://www.nao.org.uk/wp-content/uploads/2012/01/10121701.pdf (accessed 29 November 2013).

Newton, B., Meager, N., Bertram, C., Corden, A., George, A., Lalani, M., Metcalf, H., Rolfe, H., Sainsbury, R. and Weston, K. (2012), *Work Programme Evaluation: Findings from the First Phase of Qualitative Research on Programme Delivery*, London: Department for Work and Pensions.

Patrick, R. (2012), All in it together? Disabled people, the coalition and welfare to work, *Journal of Poverty and Social Justice*, 20, 3: 307–22.

Peck, J. and Theodore, N. (2000), 'Work first': workfare and the regulation of contingent labour markets, *Cambridge Journal of Economics*, 24: 119–38.

Powell, M. (2000), New Labour and the third way in the British welfare state: a new and distinctive approach? *Critical Social Policy*, 20, 1: 39–60.

Public Accounts Committee (PAC) (2012), *Department for Work and Pensions: The Introduction of the Work Programme*, Eighty-fifth report of session 2010–12, London: The Stationery Office.

Public Accounts Committee (PAC) (2013), *Department for Work and Pensions: Work Programme Outcome Statistics*, Thirty-third report of session 2012–13, London: The Stationery Office.

Ramia, G. and Carney, T. (2000), Contractualism, managerialism and welfare: The Australian experiment with a marketised employment services network, *Policy & Politics*, 29, 1: 59–83.

Rees, J., Taylor, R. and Damm, C. (2013), *Does sector matter: the role of the third sector in the work programme*, Third Sector Research Centre Working Papers, no. 92, Birmingham: Third Sector Research Centre, University of Birmingham.

Shildrick, T., MacDonald, R., Furlong, A., Roden, J. and Crow, R. (2012), *Are 'Cultures of Worklessness' Passed Down the Generations?* York: Joseph Rowntree Foundation.

Struyven, L. and Steurs, G. (2005), Design and redesign of a quasi-market for the reintegration of jobseekers: empirical evidence from Australia and the Netherlands, *Journal of European Social Policy*, 15, 3: 211–29.

Theodore, N. (2007), New Labour at work: long-term unemployment and the geography of opportunity, *Cambridge Journal of Economics*, 31: 927–39.

Tu, T. and Ginnis, S. (2012), *Work and the Welfare System: A Survey of Benefits and Tax Credits Recipients*, London: Department for Work and Pensions.

van Berkel, R. and van der Aa, P. (2005), The marketization of activation services: a modern panacea? Some lessons from the Dutch experience, *Journal of European Social Policy*, 15, 4: 329–43.

van Berkel, R., Sagar, F. and Ehler, F. (2012), The diversity of activation markets in Europe, *International Journal of Sociology and Social Policy*, 32, 5/6: 273–85.

Vegeris, S., Adams, L., Oldfield, K., Bertram, K., Davidson, R., Durante, L., Riley, C. and Vowden, K. (2011), *Flexible New Deal Evaluation: Customer Survey and Qualitative Research Findings*, London: Department for Work and Pensions.

Work and Pensions Select Committee (WPSC) (2011), *Work Programme: Providers and Contracting Arrangements*, Fourth Report of Session 2010–12, House of Commons, London: The Stationery Office.

Work and Pensions Select Committee (WPSC) (2013), *Can the Work Programme Work for All User Groups?* First Report of Session 2013–14, House of Commons, London: The Stationery Office.

Wright, S. (2011), Can Welfare Reform Work, *Poverty*, 139: 5–8.

7

Broken Hierarchies, Quasi-markets and Supported Networks – A Governance Experiment in the Second Tier of Germany's Public Employment Service

Matthias Knuth

Introduction

Reforms of labour market policies in the 2000s have increasingly striven to exploit market mechanisms as alternatives to 'bureaucratic' steering (Considine 2001; Sol and Westerveld 2005). Services previously delivered by public welfare bureaucracies have been outsourced to private providers, and their remuneration has been increasingly switched from input- to outcome-based payments. Rationales for such choices may have been to overcome resistance to change within the Public Employment Service (PES) and to purchase services at lower costs. A less apparent rationale may have been to shift the blame for the often unsatisfactory effects of active labour market policies from the public to the private sector, thus transforming 'state failure' into 'market failure'.

A closer look reveals that a difference should be made between *privatization* and *marketization*. Privatization means the outsourcing of services which were formerly produced by the PES itself to external non-public providers, whereas marketization applies to changes of the mode of transaction between the public authority and such external providers, for example from earmarked grants to competitive tendering and subsequent contracting.

The German reforms of 2003–05 (the so-called *Hartz* reforms) combined 'third-order changes' (according to Peter Hall's classification: Hall 1993) in both the 'substantial' and the 'procedural' dimension of activation policies (Graaf and Sirovátka 2012). Refuting formerly widespread assertions of reform inertia in 'Bismarckian' welfare states, these reforms were exceptionally radical or 'path-shifting' in international

Contracting-out Welfare Services: Comparing National Policy Designs for Unemployment Assistance, First Edition. Edited by Mark Considine and Siobhan O'Sullivan.
© 2015 John Wiley & Sons, Ltd. Published 2015 by John Wiley & Sons, Ltd.

comparison (Knuth 2009; Dingeldey 2011). Nevertheless, their effects in the dimension of privatization were modest. The German PES never had a tradition of producing services which would require daily and long-lasting interactions with clients, such as training courses or job search training. Therefore, as far as German labour market policies have traditionally been 'active',[1] services to be provided have always been delegated to external providers of various kinds. Changes triggered by the reforms should, therefore, rather be characterized as *marketization*. The modes of transaction between the PES and external providers have changed from grants or 'negotiated procedure without publication' (as the direct picking of contractors is called in European legislation) to competitive tendering or issuing vouchers to jobseekers, thus creating quasi-markets (Le Grand and Bartlett 1993; Bredgaard and Larsen 2008), with alleged 'consumer choice' in the case of vouchers. In Germany, outcome-based payments are still rarely used in contracted services, whereas payments in return for placement vouchers are entirely outcome-based.

Very soon after the reforms had been implemented, the German Federal government announced a special programme for jobseekers aged 50 plus and receiving the new type of universal minimum income benefits which had just been introduced. This programme, in whose evaluation the author was involved, deviates from the general tendency of marketization in employment services in three respects:

1. A considerable part of the extra funding made available for 'active' measures was used for hiring additional jobcentre staff rather than engaging external providers: '*insourcing*' instead of privatization.
2. Part of the transactions with third parties was made in the form of *grants*.
3. *Networks* were deliberately created as modes of steering, and some financial resources were dedicated to their support.

This 'soft market, strong network' way of running a labour market programme produced outcomes superior to those in 'standard operations',[2] which motivates us to explore why this is so and how it contradicts conventional wisdom.

The unique type of governance which came into effect in this programme was not intentionally designed as an experiment. Rather, the makers of the programme responded to an institutional dilemma of 'broken hierarchies', which is briefly explained in the next section. In the third section, the special programme 'Perspective 50plus', on which this article is focused, is described and put into a broader policy perspective. Section four summarizes some findings from the evaluation of the programme, leading to the question of how it could be more successful than standard operations, which is explored in section five. Based on this explanation, section six proposes some conceptual clarifications in the academic discourse on bureaucracies, markets and networks.

Broken Hierarchies: The Structure and Governance of the German Public Employment Service before and after the Hartz Reforms

We assume that the unique governance of the federal special programme Perspective 50plus was adopted as an expedient from the fundamental governance dilemma which evolved as an unintended outcome of the German labour market policy reforms. Therefore, this dilemma has to be briefly explained at the outset.

The Federal Employment Agency

From the beginnings of unemployment insurance in 1927, Germany has followed the principle later proclaimed by the Organisation for Economic Co-operation and Development (OECD 2001) that the functions of benefit administration, job brokering and referral to 'active' measures should be integrated in one single organization. Following the model of 'Bismarckian' social insurance previously established for pensions and healthcare, the Federal Employment Agency which combines these functions is set up as a body of public law, separate from government as such, and steered, at least in theory,[3] through self-management of the social partners under the framework of national legislation. The government has no direct managerial control over the Agency. In order to prescribe specific instruments of active labour market policy, the government needs legislative justification. This, in conjunction with Germany's legalistic tradition in general, explains why single 'active' instruments are meticulously defined in law. For example, hiring subsidies are legally defined in terms of a maximum percentage of the employer's gross wage costs to be paid over a maximum number of months, with more generous variants for disabled jobseekers.

Traditional exceptions from the rule of steering labour market policies through legislation are *special programmes of limited duration* with which the government, on its own authority, may entrust the Federal Employment Agency on the basis of an administrative agreement. However, after the Hartz reforms, this mechanism is confined to the regime of unemployment insurance (recipients of contribution-based benefits), but it is no longer applicable in the 'second tier' of the PES which serves jobseekers receiving minimum income benefits, now a majority of almost 70 per cent of registered unemployed.

Hartz reforms stage IV: the contested role of the municipalities

The most significant change introduced in the 'substantial' dimension of the Hartz reforms (named after the chairman of the reform commission) was the abolition of unemployment assistance, the traditional follow-on benefit which jobseekers would receive after their entitlements for unemployment insurance benefits were exhausted. Unemployment assistance was 'merged' with social assistance into a new and universal tax-funded, means-tested and flat-rate minimum income benefit, somewhat misleadingly called 'unemployment benefit II'.[4] Since social assistance had been a function of the municipalities from its beginnings and fore-runners, no political consensus could be reached to transfer responsi-bility for the new benefit and associated services completely to the Federal Employment Agency (Knuth 2009). Contrary to the govern-ment's intentions, the Hartz reforms resulted in fragmenting rather than streamlining the PES, thus triggering 'third-order change' also in the 'procedural' dimension of the reforms.

A second tier of Public Employment Services with a complex governance structure

After a cumbersome hassle which even continued while the reform was already being implemented, and which involved a ruling by the Federal Constitutional Court in 2007, minimum income benefits and 'active' policies for recipients of these are now (as of 2012) administered as follows:

- In one-quarter of the roughly 440 territories at the level of counties or independent cities, minimum income benefits are administered by the municipal administrations alone, notwithstanding that the larger part of the financial resources is provided from the federal budget. These 110 municipalities were selected according to their application for assuming such responsibility. Following from the constitutional principle of municipal self-government, neither the federal government nor the states – let alone the Federal Employment Agency – have any direct *managerial* control over municipalities' operations. This makes for very singular relations when municipali-ties administer benefits and services which are in the primary responsibility of the federal government.
- In the other three-quarters of territorial units, the municipal admin-istration and the regional branch of the Federal Employment Agency are obliged to establish a 'joint facility' (*Gemeinsame Einrichtung*) with unified management and integrated processes but separate staff and responsibilities.[5] Whereas these hybrid organizations are made up of two separate employers on the inside, they are legally constituted on the outside as a unitary authority issuing single administrative acts, and clients will not be aware of dealing with two categories of frontline staff. In terms of administrative integration, this goes beyond the Dutch *werkplein* (which is simply co-location), the Flemish 'networked' jobcentres (Struyven and van Hemel 2009) or the Norwegian local welfare offices (Fimreite and Lægreid 2009). The governance super-structure for these 'joint facilities', including mechanisms for resolving disputes, is extremely complex because it involves so many stake-holders at three levels, federal, regional states and local. 'Joint facili-ties' are linked to the Federal Employment Agency's management line and information technology systems but the municipal partner is not under the Federal Employment Agency's control.

The Anglicism 'jobcentre' has been adopted through legislation as the generic term for both types of organizations, municipal jobcentres and 'joint facilities'. In effect, the jobcentres now form a second tier of Germany's PES, organizationally (and, in most locations, also physically) separate from the employment agencies which serve the 'insured' job-seekers. The hierarchy previously extending from Federal Employment Agency headquarters to local service units is broken as far as the second tier of the PES, the jobcentres, is concerned. With redundant, overlapping and potentially conflicting responsibilities on one side, and with 'black holes' of certain responsibilities and powers not given to any of the actors on the other, this system epitomizes what is now commonly called 'multi-level governance' (Kazepov 2010). 'Fragmentation' appears to better characterize this governance structure than 'decentralization' since local discretion varies between the two types of jobcentres and since decentralization was not the intention of the reform.

Implications of the second-tier governance structure

Although it has never officially been declared as a strategy, we assume that the governance and design chosen for the special programme Perspective 50plus was developed in response to the lack of straightforward and universal hierarchical relations within the second tier of the PES. Whereas in the past (and still in the first tier of the PES administering unemployment insurance), the government would be in a position to obligate the Federal Employment Agency to implement a special programme country-wide, such centralism is no longer possible in the second tier in which the municipalities are involved. As far as 'standard operations' are concerned, the municipalities are bound by law; beyond the law, no obligation can be imposed on them. Therefore, in order to implement the special federal programme for older recipients of minimum income benefits, participation in the programme was made voluntary for the jobcentres. What would have been an additional obligation and burden in the former hierarchical system was reframed as an honour and achievement (plus financial incentive) in order to win local participation in the programme. The government created a 'quasi-market' of grants for which jobcentres could apply, under procedures which are described later in the next paragraph. First, however, the political context of the programme must be briefly characterized.

The Federal Programme Perspective 50plus in the Context of Labour Market and Pension Reforms

Perspective 50plus in the context of organizational development in the new jobcentres

The Federal programme Perspective 50plus was announced in 2005, only six months after the new benefit system and the new jobcentres had started operating. Because of the new system's encompassing definition of 'being able to work',[6] and also since hitherto inactive spouses were now considered as clients in their own right, the national unemployment count surged, and even more so the number of individuals supposed to be served.[7] Jobcentres were struggling to deliver benefits on time but in the beginning could not do much more than that. Therefore, whether intentionally or not, one of the 'hidden agendas' of the programme was re-orienting the jobcentres towards activation and job brokering and engaging jobcentres of the two types side by side, irrespective of the still continuing political battle over the role of the municipalities in the new system.

Perspective 50plus in the context of demographic change and pension reform

The programme was specifically targeted at older (50 plus) recipients of minimum income benefits. The explicit and official context of the programme was the 'working longer' agenda intended to gradually eliminate Germany's deeply entrenched early retirement culture.[8] Adaptation to structural change of the economy and to the massive job loss in the wake of the German unification had been facilitated from the early 1980s to the late 1990s through a combination of extended unemployment benefit duration, exemptions from job search requirements for older workers, and immunity of employers' redundancy compensations from means-testing for benefits. By making entry into a premature pension from 60 conditional on long-term benefit recipiency, older workers and their employers had been literally incentivized to utilize unemployment benefits for building pathways into early retirement (Knuth and Kalina 2002; Wübbeke 2011). The reversal of these policies began in 1996 with pension and benefit reforms gradually taking effect. The stricter means-testing in the new minimum income benefit regime finalized this policy change from 2005 (Dlugosz et al. 2009). Legislation finally passed in 2008, which would gradually elevate the statutory retirement age from 65 to 67 between 2012 and 2029, was already more or less in the pipeline in 2005. In this context of 'restrictive' reforms, a bundle of 'positive' government initiatives was launched in order to demonstrate that working longer is possible, in order to raise employers' awareness of the challenges of demographic change and to prove that even the elderly long-term unemployed can find jobs. Perspective 50plus was the most conspicuous part of this bundle of initiatives.

The gradual roll-out of the programme

The programme's first phase lasted from late 2005 to 2007, the second phase from 2008 to 2010, and (as of writing this article) the programme is in its third phase from 2011 to 2015. In the beginning, only 93 out of 438 jobcentres were participating. By the end of 2012, the programme involved 421 jobcentres, so that the programme had become implemented almost country-wide.

Table 1

Key figures of programme development

		2008	2009	2010	2011
1	unemployed 50+ total (annual averages)	860,671	914,380	931,048	923,108
2	of these: receiving minimum income benefits (the target group of the programme – annual averages)	538,736	539,536	532,896	560,939
3	number of participants in programme (entrants)	73,873	124,701	188,891	192,254
3/2	coverage of target group	14%	23%	35%	34%
4	job take-ups in programme	19,490	31,133	56,208	68,083
4/3	job take-up rate in programme	26%	25%	30%	35%
5	total spending (million euros)	139.5	219.8	361.5	434.9
5/4	spending per job take-up (euros)	7,158	7,061	6,432	6,387

Source: Programme Monitoring Database.

Table 1 gives some overview of the development of the programme during its second phase and the first year of its third phase. While the numbers of unemployed people in the respective age and benefit category remained fairly stable,[9] the numbers of participants in the programme more than doubled, finally covering more than one-third of the theoretical target group. Job take-ups within the programme grew even faster, showing hardly any reaction to the economic slump of 2009 and finally reaching a gross success rate of more than one-third. Spending in the programme grew accordingly, but the ratio of spending per successful outcome declined slightly, indicating improvements in cost efficiency.

Funding mechanisms and negotiated targeting

The programme was initiated in 2005 with a call for proposals. Jobcentres were called to apply for funding additional to what was allocated to them for their standard operations. Actually, hardly any proposal was rejected; some jobcentres, however, were asked to make amendments before they were admitted.[10] Even with this minimal degree of real competition, the requirement to obtain funding on the basis of an explicit strategy and in the course of a strategic dialogue created a different sense of ownership as compared to standard operations. The difference amounts to the alternatives of 'money for the magnitude of your problems' (the standard mechanism of allocating funds) versus 'additional money for the ambitiousness of your strategy'.[11] Even though the additional funding provided in the framework of the programme was technically a grant, it was linked to projected results in terms of numbers of people to get re-employed and numbers of jobs to last longer than six months, and it was framed by an

Table 2

Structure of programme spending in 2011

additional jobcentre staff		44.0%
involvement of third parties ...		36.7%
... via grants	10.2%	
... via contracts	26.5%	
material costs and incidental expenses		7.4%
subsidies to employers		8.8%
subsidies to participants		3.1%
Total		**100.0%**

Source: Programme Monitoring Database.

agreement on objectives. Underperforming the agreed targets in one fiscal year by more than 10 per cent would result in the acceptance of only slightly lower targets in the next fiscal year and, consequently, in smaller grants for the jobcentres concerned. Through these rather soft mechanisms, a *public-public quasi-contractual relationship* was established between the federal ministry (not the Federal Employment Agency) and the jobcentres, even though this was not strictly a 'payment by result' scheme.

Participating jobcentres were free to use programme funding for additional staff of their own (whom, given the temporary nature of the programme, they would usually employ on fixed-term contracts); for engaging external service providers; or for any mixture of these two strategies. To a small extent, financial resources would go directly to participants (e.g. travel costs for job interviews, start-up grants) or to employers (hiring subsidies). Table 2 gives an impression of the spending structures in 2011 (unfortunately only available for this year). The largest part of the financial resources was used for additional jobcentre staff, followed by payments for external providers. The remarkable feature here is that more than one-third of payments to providers was made by extending to them part of the grant received, so that only slightly more than one-quarter of total spending was transacted through contract market mechanisms. This low degree of marketization is also remarkable in the German context where the general tendency of reforms in employment policies has been towards competitive tendering and vouchers, with little room left for grants.

Networking at local and regional level

The programme's subtitle was 'Employment Pacts in the Regions'. In the first phase of the programme, 'pacts' meant that participating jobcentres were supposed to liaise with employers, employers' organizations, labour unions, regional media and other multipliers in order to raise awareness for employing older workers. In the second phase, jobcentres wanting to join the programme had to partner with a jobcentre or group of jobcentres which were already in the programme. Thus the 'pacts' gradually grew into sometimes very large compounds of up to 25 (usually geographically adjacent) jobcentres. Many pacts comprised jobcentres of the two organizational types, fully municipalized jobcentres as well as 'joint facilities' formed between employment agencies and municipalities. Each such pact was equipped with a coordination unit which, in some of the pacts, also served as the clearing agent for managing the programme grants. In some pacts, this central coordinating function was outsourced to an external provider; in others, one of the jobcentres making up the pact would get resources to set up a coordination unit internally. Thus, already at the regional level, some programme resources were allocated to the creation and support of network relations. Also, public relations and internet presence were usually managed by the regional pact coordination unit. Quantitative targets were monitored only at the level of the pact, not the individual jobcentre, thus conducing to joint efforts of pact members for meeting the targets. The main rationales for proceeding in this way were knowledge transfer and avoiding coordination overload at the central level.

Programme management

As already explained, special federal labour market programmes in the minimum income benefit regime cannot be managed by the Federal Employment Agency since it has no responsibility over the fully municipalized jobcentres.[12] Alternatively, the Federal Ministry of Employment and Social Affairs could have formed its own management taskforce, which is, however, usually avoided.[13] Therefore, the government, through an open tendering procedure, commissioned a private non-profit organization to act as the Programme Management Agency (PMA), as this actor is called in the remainder of this article.

All in all, the PMA was entrusted with quite an impressive bundle of tasks:

- reviewing the proposals and follow-on concepts submitted by the jobcentres and making recommendations to the ministry;
- professional counselling of the participating jobcentres, their frontline staff involved in implementing the programme and their external partners;
- public relations activities for the programme at the national level, in addition to what jobcentres did at their regional levels, including running the programme's website and honouring, in annual conferences, 'employers of vision' who have integrated older unemployed in their operations;
- organizing knowledge transfer activities among the actors within the programme through annual regional conferences, an annual national conference, thematic workshops, facilitating peer exchanges between jobcentres, and running an internal knowledge database of 'good practice';

- running the programme monitoring database used for statistical reporting and, at the time of the evaluation, as the starting point for generating individual participants' datasets (see the next section);
- coordinating and mediating the dialogue between the jobcentres, the federal ministry, the Federal Employment Agency and the public;
- financial auditing of the programme, which was concentrated in a separate team in order to avoid trust-endangering interference with the professional advisory role of programme counsellors.

By reviewing the proposals submitted by jobcentres, and by auditing the proper use of the grants, the PMA acted as a sort of supervisor in the grant market created by the government. However, the PMA as the 'focal intermediary' of the programme was neither in a *hierarchical* relationship with the actors on the ground, nor was it in a *contractual* relationship with any of them, as would be the case for the prime contractors in Britain's Work Programme (Greer *et al.* 2012). The PMA rather acted as the 'spider in the web', in a central and therefore privileged role for the network, but with few statutory powers. 'Facilitative management' is the term coined by Hudson (2004) for this kind of coordination.

Before further exploring the governance of the programme, we first summarize some of its effects.

Perspective 50plus as a Relatively Successful Programme: Some Stylized Results from the Evaluation

Data

Scientific evaluation of the programme was commissioned, through open tendering, to a consortium of two independent research institutes, one of which is part of a university. Only in phase II was it possible to generate the kind of data needed for quantitative evaluation.[14] Outcome measurement was focused on participants during the year 2010, since data availability could not be secured earlier.[15] A database on participants and their activation treatment was created by the PMA and fed online by the jobcentres through protected access. Using sophisticated encryption techniques in accordance with legal data protection requirements, participants' client identification numbers were then transmitted to central statistical services of the Federal Employment Agency in order to link data stored there. Identifying participants in the central databases on employment and benefits served three purposes:

1. sampling for a telephone survey and transmitting contact data to the telephone survey studio commissioned;
2. compiling employment and benefit histories of participants for descriptive and evaluative purposes;

3. matching non-participants to participants for estimating net effects of the programme. The quantitative evaluation as a whole basically draws on three data sources:
   a. the database of participants created in the course of administering the programme;
   b. a two-wave CATI (computer aided telephone interview) panel survey of a representative sample of participants;
   c. historical registers of employment, benefits and previous labour market programme participation of participants and matched non-participants.

Programme participants' characteristics

In the course of 2010, around 190,000 people participated in programme activities of at least 25 hours. Participants' average age was 54; only few were aged above 60, though formally participation was open up to the statutory retirement age of, at that time, 65. The majority of participants had only completed the lowest level of school education (nine years), and significantly more than one-third had no certified vocational qualification. Not only those with migrant backgrounds admitted difficulties in writing a letter in German, and more than one-third had no experience with computers and online communication. Around 13 per cent had not been employed at all during the ten years before entering the programme, and for the remainder, the average period of time elapsed since the last employment spell was more than two years, even with 'mini-jobs' earning less than €400 per month included.[16] Consequently, experiences of unemployment over the last ten years accumulated to a median of five years.[17] Around one-quarter suffered from health conditions restricting their working ability. The high percentage of participants living in single households (significantly higher than for the same age group in the population at large), together with survey responses with regard to social networks, perceptions of loneliness and experience of depressive moods, point to a widespread syndrome of social marginalization among the target group. With regard to chances of taking up employment, calendrical age seems not to be the only problem of this target group, and probably not even the principal one.

Subjective responses of participants to the programme

Some survey items previously used in the context of the general evaluation of the new minimum income benefit regime (Bundesregierung 2008) were replicated in the telephone survey of programme participants, thus allowing comparisons of client satisfaction in 'standard operations' and in the special programme.[18] Among those who admitted having certain personal problems (physical or mental health problems, alcohol or drug abuse, over-indebtedness), significantly higher percentages of programme participants reported to have received specific support in tackling these problems than was the case outside the programme. Overall satisfaction with services as well as satisfaction with specific aspects, such as the time frontline staff had available for them, accessibility and friendliness of staff or their professional competence, was significantly higher among programme participants. Furthermore, around 45 per cent of them agreed with the statement, 'Before participation in this programme, nobody at the jobcentre really paid attention to me'. Overall, there is sound evidence that the programme had an added value in the subjective perception of its participants.

Employment and benefit outcomes

During the observation period from January 2010 to March 2011, one-third of those who had actively participated in the programme at some time in 2010 took up employment reaching the programme's minimum target quality: employment fully covered by social insurance lasting at least 32 days, or self-employment.[19] The programme's extended target of 'stable' employment lasting at least six months[20] was met by almost 70 per cent of those taking up work or 23 per cent of the total participants. This may not seem a lot; however, the roughly comparable indicator[21] for standard active labour market programmes for the same age and benefit group is only 19 per cent. Econometric evaluation[22] using alternative matching techniques[23] and testing several model specifications corroborated the programme's winning margin over standard treatment. A comparison of Kaplan-Meyer estimates of programme participants with new hires in the labour market at large showed that former participants' survival chances in employment were actually higher.[24] In terms of quitting benefit recipiency, however, outcomes were much more modest: only 27 per cent of those who took up work actually quit the benefit. This has to do with the design of the German minimum income benefit system which also provides universal in-work benefits fulfilling the function earned income tax credits have in some other countries. Because of participants' low earnings capacity and due to the frequent necessity of part-time arrangements for moderating weak health conditions, most participants could not fully support themselves even after taking up employment. Obviously, increasing wage dispersion (Card *et al.* 2012) and the growth of the low-wage sector in Germany (Bosch 2009) have contributed to this outcome.

The content of activation

Since jobcentres were free to use programme funds as they saw fit, treatments given to participants were very heterogeneous within and even more across local jobcentre districts. Therefore, a detailed analysis is beyond the scope of this article. Suffice it to say that the programme, though intended as an experimental one, did not result in finding a specific 'Columbus egg' for re-employing older and marginalized workers. Little was done that had been unheard of before, and most interventions and services are not necessarily age-specific but could be used for other groups as well. Rather, the relative success of the programme appears to rest on the *intensity of the treatment* (frequent interactions, taking the time each client actually needs) and the *flexible combination of measures* (which is difficult or even impossible in standard operations with legally defined and discrete 'instruments'). Furthermore, there is a *marked difference in the aggregate composition of measures* as compared to standard operations: more personal and personalized services (counselling and coaching) as opposed to monetary support, such as hiring subsidies; more human capital investment (short-term training) as opposed to fully subsidized 'make-jobs'; more start-up support.[25] The programme pioneered various approaches towards improving participants' subjective health conditions, their personal management of health problems and their health-related life styles. Some regional pacts in rural areas with poor public transport services sought for unorthodox solutions for clients' job-related transport problems, like support in re-qualifying for a driver's licence which had been previously withdrawn, or interest-free loans from the jobcentre for buying a second-hand car. However, the main success factor of the programme seems to have been simply lower caseloads achieved by engaging more frontline staff, either within the jobcentres or employed by external providers. Unfortunately, since the evaluation was focused on identifying new instruments and procedures, no provision was made for obtaining data on caseloads.

Cost-efficiency

When comparing spending in the programme Perspective 50plus with spending in standard operations broken down to the same age group and benefit category, it turns out that programme spending in 2010 was lower both per participant and per durable employment take-up. Two related factors seem to account for the advantage of the programme: higher success rates in terms of re-employment, and less use of costly hiring subsidies or make-work grants. It appears then that intensive person-to-person services, costly as they are, are actually more *cost-efficient* than the large-scale referral of clients to standardized programmes where they are cranked through profiling and activation routines similar to what the jobcentres have already done with them.

Explaining the Success of the Programme through the Features of its Governance

As already pointed out, the superiority of the programme in comparison to standard operations of jobcentres cannot be explained by any fabulous instrument which would have 'done the trick' for older workers in particular. In addition to making more staff available at the frontline, the programme's relative success seems to rest on fundamental differences in the governance of the programme as compared to standard operations.

Voluntary participation of jobcentres and bottom-up targeting

In their *standard operations*, jobcentres primarily follow rules. As a concession to New Public Management, there are also annually agreed objectives, and outcomes are monitored by indicators. It is a mixture of procedural and corporate governance,[26] with the latter being mostly of a window-dressing character. Agreements on objectives start at government level and are then transmitted down the hierarchy. Objectives and indicators are of a rather general nature like 'reducing long-term benefit recipiency' or 'increasing job take-ups'. They are not linked to any specific strategy or action, there is no procedure for determining why and how targets have been missed or met, and there are no incentives or sanctions.

The philosophy of Perspective 50plus was totally different. Jobcentres were invited to offer locally specific strategies and to commit themselves to quantified outcome targets in order to be rewarded with additional resources. Participation in the programme was voluntary for jobcentres (and, in most places, also for clients). Targets were straightforward and clearly defined with regard to employment outcomes and their quality and duration. As already explained, sanctions in case of missing the targets were very soft, but under-performing did have consequences. All this created a sense of ownership different from standard operations compared to which the procedure was more bottom-up, more specifically targeted, and tied to locally specific action plans.

Free choice and combination of treatments

Traditionally, and for reasons denoted above, labour market policy instruments in Germany are meticulously defined by legislation. In the programme Perspective 50plus, by contrast, actors on the ground were free to design and modify their interventions as they saw fit. With regard to incentivizing employers to hire from the caseload, for example, it was found that small employers preferred defined lump sums paid up front on the occasion of hiring and again after passing the six-month threshold. Even though in this way employers would receive less, they appreciated low bureaucratic effort and clear price tags. Creating this kind of incentive was possible within the programme but would not be allowed in standard operations. In effect, the freedom of choice amounted to a 'black box' approach similar to Britain's contracting in the current Work Programme – however, here this approach applied to the relationship between the government and *public jobcentres*, not private 'prime contractors' like in Britain.

Free choice of using finance internally or externally

Jobcentres were free to use the financial resources allocated through Perspective 50plus for buying services from external providers or for employing additional staff in order to produce services themselves. In the first phase of the programme, there was a tendency towards outsourcing because jobcentres were still overloaded with reorganization following the Hartz reforms. In the second phase, this tendency was reversed so that actually over time the programme triggered insourcing rather than outsourcing and privatization. In 2011, 44 per cent of programme spending was used for additional own staff (see table 2). Job take-up rates improved while this insourcing was developing (see table 1). We are not inferring a causal relationship here since growing experience and favourable labour market conditions have played their roles; however, at any rate insourcing did not downgrade performance. This supports Davies' (2008) observation that the PES, 'if allowed the same flexibilities and funding as private sector companies or charitable organizations', will match or even surpass the performance of contractors.

Jobcentres wanted to acquire their own experience with the target group rather than letting knowledge accumulate exclusively outside. Many jobcentres formed dedicated '50plus' teams. Co-operation between these teams and the frontline staff of external providers was much closer than in standard operations because they had a common reference base of actually working with clients. Some jobcentres formed joint '50plus' teams of internal and external staff. By and large, dealings of jobcentres with external providers were much more on an equal footing, characterized by a mutual professional culture and based on shared targets, whereas in standard operations it is often a matter of 'delegating clients away' to providers. In some cases (10 per cent of total spending in 2011, see table 2), the prevalence of a network rather than a market-type relationship between jobcentres and external providers was highlighted by using grants instead of contracts as the mode of transaction.

Role of the project management agency

The PMA had a crucial role in facilitating the whole process. For the Federal Ministry of Employment, they served as a temporary auxiliary management and auditing unit. For the jobcentres and their external partners, they created and operated the infrastructure for knowledge transfer and the physical and virtual platforms for professional competition. In order to be able to fulfil these varied and potentially conflicting roles simultaneously, it was probably crucial for the PMA to remain in a non-hierarchical, formally 'powerless' role vis-à-vis the jobcentres. The government retained its ultimate 'bureaucratic' power only to use it as rarely as possible. The jobcentres retained for themselves a theoretical exit option: participating voluntarily, they could have quit the programme any time, which, however, none of them did.

Network Steering

In the governance of the programme, we can identify use of the contract market (for commissioning the PMA at the central level and for engaging providers at the local level) and the creation of a quasi-market for public-to-public grants (awarded by the ministry to the jobcentres), which in some cases were forwarded to local providers instead of contracting them. Steering elements built into these market mechanisms were relatively weak; payment by results in a strict sense was nowhere applied. Instead, steering of the programme was primarily effected through network-type relationships. Networks at regional level, the

143

regional 'pacts' comprised of several jobcentres, served to exchange knowledge and experience and to join efforts for achieving common goals. The PMA's primary task was to link these regional networks. Through counselling of jobcentres and through annual conferences at the level of greater regions[27] and at national level, typical problems and successful approaches were made topical. Staff of external providers participated in these conferences on an equal footing with jobcentre staff – the PMA created professional platforms in which organizational affiliation and rank were secondary. Thus, 'networking' was not only something the jobcentres participating in the programme and the staff involved in it were supposed to do on their own and in addition to their day-to-day tasks. Resources were actually dedicated to the building and maintaining of these networks, and there was a strategy to do this – which differs markedly from the kind of politically requested 'pretend partnerships' analyzed by Entwistle *et al.* (2007).

Discussion

Markets, hierarchies (bureaucracies) and networks have commonly been discussed as alternative (Powell 1990; Thompson 1994; Hudson 2004), complementary, substitutional or rival modes of governance (Entwistle *et al.* 2007). In all these cases, they have been treated in a common perspective as forms of *coordination*. However, the network concept, though well developed in the context of social capital theory (Lin *et al.* 2001) and as a methodology (and even software) for analyzing configurations of individual as well as organizational actors (Scott 1991), has remained a rather vague metaphor in the governance context nearly 20 years after Dowding's critique (1995).

There may be certain fields of human activity which can be properly organized purely according to market, hierarchy or network paradigms, respectively. However, in the 'real world' of employment services (and other social services as well), these three elements are not alternatives; they are all essential. If there are several layers of public authority, and if there are organizations employing people, there will be hierarchy. If there are financial transfers based on selective case-by-case decisions involving some expectation of reciprocity between inputs and outcomes, these can be organized and analyzed as markets. And if frontline staff are supposed to fulfil professional roles in co-operation with other professionals, finding individual solutions for clients beyond what can be anticipated in the rulebooks produced by the hierarchy as well as beyond the indicators of payment-by-result schemes contracted through the market, these professionals must be supported in developing their networks. The problem of balance is that over-steering through hierarchical or market mechanisms can easily stifle network-type elements of governance. The potential predominance of hierarchies or markets over networks seems to be rooted in that the former deliver the 'hard' supplies, such as financial or personnel resources, whereas networks deliver 'only soft' supplies, such as information, knowledge, experience, shared practices and orientations, reputation, and access to certain communities. Putting it simply, markets and hierarchies transmit money in exchange for goods or services, whereas networks may merely transmit information about possible contracts or job openings but never the payment itself. Reversing the superiority of hierarchies or markets over networks is considered illegitimate in democratic societies under the rule of law. Where networks conquer hierarchies, this is called corruption or nepotism; where networks rule markets, this is called a cartel or organized crime. This consideration leads to another reason for the preponderance of markets and hierarchies over networks: the former can produce legitimacy of decisions and proceedings, which the latter cannot in societies that are no longer primarily based on kinship and custom. Thus, the three mechanisms under discussion cannot be adequately conceptualized by reducing them to 'coordination' as their common denominator.

So if we accept that in order to allocate material resources and to ensure legitimacy there must be some rule of hierarchy within the PES (and also within external providers as organizations), and if we accept that there must be some sort of market transaction between the PES and external providers, then the practical question is how should hierarchical rules and market transactions be designed as to allow network relations to flourish and bear fruit? However, before pursuing this question it should be spelled out what the fruit of network-type relations could be and why it is indispensible for effective employment (or other) services.

What ultimately obligates an employee to abide by hierarchical rule is her or his employment contract. Likewise, what obligates a service provider to produce the kind of service expected by the purchaser (and to transmit this orientation to his employees again by hierarchical rule) is a service contract. Employment and service contracts are both incomplete by nature. At the time of concluding the contract, the principal (employer or purchaser) may not know exactly what he wants, or what he will want at some later point in time during the fulfilment of the contract. Assuming, however, that the exact content of the desired service, possibly conditional on varying circumstances, is known, the spelling out of this will cause huge transaction costs, result in information overload through texts too long and complex to really guide people's behaviour, and give rise to opportunistic interpretation of the clauses of the contract (see Finn 2010 for examples). In employment services, it seems practically impossible to define outcomes in such ways as to definitely preclude 'creaming and parking'.

Given the incompleteness of contracts, network-type relations in employment services produced jointly by public and private staff can increase the probabilities that frontline workers will do the 'right thing' even where it is not exactly known from the outset what the 'right thing' is. In order to achieve this, networks must allow open discussions about goals, the sharing of experience about what works and frankness about what does not work. Economic and exclusionary competition on who

145

gets a contract must be superseded, during the periods between contracting rounds, by professional and non-exclusionary competition for good ideas and practice examples and by mutual support for achieving common goals. There is no guarantee that this will happen in networks, but it is possible.

In order to provide the space in which network-type governance can unfold its potential, hierarchical as well as contractual mechanisms must be curbed. Explicit rules resulting from them should be confined to general objectives to be pursued by the parties concerned and to procedures in dealing with one another. By contrast, such rules should refrain from exactly prescribing out-comes and operations. Investments in rule specificity, performance monitoring and contract management can be scaled down for the benefit of investment in the development of network-type relations. There is no question that for the sake of efficiency as well as legitimacy, recurrent renewal of contracts through open competition is indispensable. However, in order for network-type relations to flourish during the intervening periods, contracts should normally have longer effective durations of three to five years, possibly through clauses for extension of an initial period provided certain parameters are met, possibly with opting-out clauses from a long contract period if certain parameters are not complied with. At any rate, the pattern of contracting should reflect the orientation of the contracting authority towards establishing lasting collaborative relations rather than buying a standardized service at minimum price.

Conclusion

The example of Perspective 50plus informs us that in the market dimension, as far as the 'principal' of the transaction is a governmental actor, we may actually distinguish between two modes of transaction:

1. public procurement via competitive tendering resulting in the concluding of contracts; and
2. public allocation of funds via earmarked grants, for which the governmental actor can create a 'quasi-market' by calling for proposals and selecting among them.

We may thus speak of a 'contract market' and a 'grant market'. In our case, both market mechanisms were mainly used for the *selection of actors* into participating in the programme. Steering elements designed into these transactions were very soft; steering and coordination was largely left to network mechanisms. The result was superior to standard operations, which rely on law, hierarchical allocation of funds based on rules rather than targets, and on a contract market with tenders prescribing services or outcomes in ultimate detail. The superiority of the programme once again corroborates 'the strength of weak ties' (Granovetter 1973). However, where a large number of organizational actors are involved, effective networks do not grow spontaneously but must be intentionally created and supported, with resources allocated to this purpose.

Acknowledgements

This article would not have been possible without the co-operation of Dieter Simon, the project manager of Perspective 50plus in the organization referred to as the PMA throughout this article. He provided statistics and institutional backgrounds not covered in our evaluation, which was focused on implementation on the ground and on outcomes, not on the governance of the programme.

I am also indebted to an anonymous reviewer and to Ian Greer, who both shaped the final version of this article by insightful and helpful comments.

Notes

1. Even before the reforms, the German ratio of active/passive spending was moderate in international comparison, but higher than in countries of the 'liberal' welfare regime type (OECD 2003: 193).
2. Legally prescribed procedures and instruments and the routines apart from special programmes are referred to in this article as 'standard operations'.
3. The influence of social partners on the management of the Federal Employment Agency was severely reduced through the Hartz reforms (Klenk *et al.* 2009).
4. For details on the benefit reform, see Clasen 2007; Brussig and Knuth 2010; Barbier and Knuth 2011.
5. Within the 'joint facilities', the local employment agencies are responsible for benefits and employment assistance, whereas the municipal administration is responsible for housing allowances and psycho-social services not directly linked to employment (including childcare provision, debt counselling, etc.)
6. The definition is 'being able to work three hours per day under normal conditions of the labour market or being only temporarily unable to work that much'.
7. The majority of recipients of 'unemployment benefit II' are not counted as unemployed because they are temporarily not available for work (sickness, lone parents with small children, pupils from the age of 15) or because they are actually working but not earning enough to support themselves and their families.
8. At its 2001 Stockholm summit, the Council of the European Union had proclaimed a 50 per cent employment target for those aged 55 to 64 years old in the member states, and Germany seemed to be far off this target in 2005.
9. The considerable reduction in unemployment figures which Germany has experienced since 2005 has predominantly occurred among the 'insured' (the short-term) unemployed. By contrast, the numbers of older unemployed in general have slightly grown because of demographic change, blocking of outflows into early pensions, and extending job search requirements to older unemployed. The latter results in their inclusion in the administrative unemployment count.

10. Submission of updated and revised concepts and dialogue about these concepts was renewed at the beginning of the second and third phases of the programme; again, none of the applicants was actually rejected.

11. There are agreed outcome targets in standard operations as well, but these are not tied to the allocation of financial resources or to any other incentive or sanction.

12. It cannot be expected, for the time being, that such leadership would be accepted after municipalities, and their national umbrella organizations have struggled so hard to be recognized as providers of public employment services alternative to the Federal Employment Agency.

13. German government organizations are still dominated by juridical expertise, whereas management competencies are rare.

14. Previous evaluation was mainly based on case studies in jobcentres.

15. In Germany, permission to use social administration data for research purposes must be applied for in a formal procedure prescribed by legislation on data privacy. At the time when the project was commissioned, this entailed separate permissions by each of the 16 state governments.

16. The 'mini-job' (marginal part-time) is a special type of atypical employment with a flat-rate income tax paid by the employer and exemptions from social insurance contributions for the employee. Mini-jobs are mostly worked by mothers, married women, students and pensioners.

17. Because inactivity is still widespread among 'housewives' of this generation in West Germany, there is no exact correspondence between non-employment and unemployment.

18. It must be acknowledged that the two surveys were conducted at different points in time so that the quality of services in 'standard operations' may have improved since.

19. In the German institutional context, this excludes 'mini-jobs' (see note 16) as well as 'make-jobs' created through labour market programmes. Self-employment was accepted without any qualification of durability because there is no administrative database which would allow the monitoring of self-employment trajectories.

20. This was operationalized allowing for changes of employer as long as these did not result in interruptions of more than 31 days.

21. The target definition used in monitoring standard instruments is to be in employment six months after leaving a programme, possibly only on the valuation date. In our evaluation, this obviously less ambitious operationalization could not be replicated because, in a considerable number of cases, participation in the programme continued after taking up employment, taking the form of troubleshooting or coaching during the period of organizational integration.

22. Econometric evaluation was done by our project partner, the Institut für Angewandte Wirtschaftsforschung at Tübingen, led by Bernhard Boockmann.

23. The gradual accession of jobcentres to the programme was used for comparing employment chances of the target group in jobcentres within and outside the programme through difference-in-difference estimations; alternatively, individual propensity score matching of participants with non-participants was used. Both approaches established significant net effects of the programme compared to standard operations.

24. It has to be taken into account, of course, that this may actually reflect the weakness of participants who have little chance of improving through

job-hopping. Employment registers used for the comparison do not contain information why (or on whose initiative) a job has ended.

25. Since the durability of start-ups is nowhere captured in the administrative data, these had to be left outside the evaluation. Consequently, as far as start-ups were successful, success of the programme is underestimated.

26. See Considine and Lewis (1999, 2003) for the four governance types: procedural, corporate, market and network.

27. Each year, there were four regional conferences (North, South, East, West) and a national conference.

References

Barbier, J.-C. and Knuth, M. (2011), Activating social protection against unemployment, *Sozialer Fortschritt*, 60, 1–2: 15–24.

Bosch, G. (2009), Low-wage work in five European countries and the United States, *International Labour Review*, 148, 4: 337–56.

Bredgaard, T. and Larsen, F. (2008), Quasi-markets in employment policy: Do they deliver on promises? *Social Policy and Society*, 7, 3: 341–52.

Brussig, M. and Knuth, M. (2010), Rise up and work! *Social Policy and Society*, 9, 3: 311–23.

Bundesregierung (2008), *Bericht zur Evaluation der Experimentierklausel nach § 6c des Zweiten Buches Sozialgesetzbuch*, Unterrichtung durch die Bundesregierung, Bundestagsdrucksache, 16/11488, Berlin.

Card, D., Heining, J. and Kline, P. (2012), Workplace heterogeneity and the rise of West German wage inequality, *IAB Discussion Paper*, 26, Nuremberg: Institute for Employment Research of the German Federal Employment Agency.

Clasen, J. (2007), *Reforming European Welfare States, Germany and the United Kingdom Compared*, Oxford: Oxford University Press.

Considine, M. (2001), *Enterprising States, The Public Management of Welfare-to-Work*, Cambridge: Cambridge University Press.

Considine, M. and Lewis, J. M. (1999), Governance at ground level: The front-line bureaucrat in the age of markets and networks, *Public Administration Review*, 59, 6: 467–80.

Considine, M. and Lewis, J. M. (2003), Bureaucracy, network, or enterprise? *Public Administration Review*, 63, 2: 131–40.

Davies, S. (2008), Contracting out employment services to the third and private sectors, *Critical Social Policy*, 28, 2: 136.

Dingeldey, I. (2011), Germany: moving towards integration whilst maintaining segmentation. In J. Clasen and D. Clegg (eds), *Regulating the Risk of Unemployment, National Adaptations to Post-industrial Labour Markets in Europe*, Oxford: Oxford University Press, pp. 55–74.

Dlugosz, S., Stephan, G. and Wilke, R. A. (2009), Fixing the leak: Unemployment incidence before and after the 2006 reform of unemployment benefits in Germany, *IAB Discussion Paper*, 25, Nuremberg: Institute for Employment Research of the German Federal Employment Agency.

Dowding, K. (1995), Model or metaphor? *Political Studies*, 45, 1: 136–58.

Entwistle, T., Bristow, G., Hines, F., Donaldson, S. and Martin, S. (2007), The dysfunctions of markets, hierarchies and networks in the meta-governance of partnerships, *Urban Studies*, 44, 1: 63–79.

Fimreite, A. L. and Lægreid, P. (2009), Reorganizing the welfare state administration, *Public Management Review*, 11, 3: 281–97.

Finn, D. (2010), Outsourcing employment programmes: Contract design and differential prices, *European Journal of Social Security*, 12, 4: 289–302.

Graaf, W. D. and Sirovátka, T. (2012), Governance reforms and their impacts on the effects of activation policies, *International Journal of Sociology and Social Policy*, 32, 5/6: 353–63.

Granovetter, M. (1973), The strength of weak ties, *American Journal of Sociology*, 73, 6: 1360–80.

Greer, I., Stuart, M. and Greenwood, I. (2012), Marktorientierung und Beschäftigungsverhältnisse in der Aktivierungsindustrie: Eine Fallstudie zu Großbritannien und Deutschland. In K. Scherschel, P. Streckeisen and M. Krenn (eds), *Neue Prekarität, Die Folgen aktivierender Arbeitsmarktpolitik – europäische Länder im Vergleich*, Frankfurt am Main: Campus, pp. 291–310.

Hall, P. A. (1993), Policy paradigms, social learning and the state, *Comparative Politics*, 25, 3: 275–96.

Hudson, B. (2004), Analysing network partnerships, *Public Management Review*, 6, 1: 75–94.

Kazepov, Y. (ed.) (2010), *Rescaling Social Policies: Towards Multilevel Governance in Europe*, Farnham: Ashgate Publishing Group.

Klenk, T., Nullmeier, F., Weyrauch, P. and Haarmann, A. (2009), Das Ende einer Bismarck-Tradition, *Sozialer Fortschritt*, 5: 85–92.

Knuth, M. (2009), Path shifting and path dependence: Labour market policy reforms under German federalism, *International Journal of Public Administration*, 32, 12: 1048–69.

Knuth, M. and Kalina, T. (2002), Early exit from the labour force between exclusion and privilege: unemployment as a transition from employment to retirement in West Germany, *European Societies*, 4, 4: 393–418.

Le Grand, J. and Bartlett, W. (eds) (1993), *Quasi-markets and social policy*, Basingstoke: Macmillan Press.

Lin, N., Cook, K. S. and Burt, R. S. (eds) (2001), *Social Capital, Theory and Research*, New York, NY: Aldine de Gruyter.

Organisation for Economic Co-operation and Development (OECD) (2001), *Labour Market Policies and the Public Employment Service*, OECD Proceedings, Paris: OECD.

Organisation for Economic Co-operation and Development (OECD) (ed.) (2003), *Employment Outlook, Towards More and Better Jobs*, Paris: OECD.

Powell, W. W. (1990), Neither market nor hierarchy: Network forms of organization, *Research in Organizational Behavior*, 12: 295–336.

Scott, J. (1991), *Social Network Analysis: A Handbook*, London: Sage.

Sol, E. and Westerveld, M. (eds) (2005), *Contractualism in Employment Services, A New Form of Welfare State Governance*, The Hague: Kluwer Law International and Aspen Publishers.

Struyven, L. and van Hemel, L. (2009), The local integration of employment services: Assessing network effectiveness of local job centres in Flanders, *Environment and planning C: Government and Policy*: 1055–71.

Thompson, G. (ed.) (1994), *Markets, Hierarchies and Networks, The Coordination of Social Life*, London: Sage.

Wübbeke, C. (2011), The limitations of activation policies: unemployment at the end of working life, *Ageing and Society*, 31, 6: 977–1002.

8

The Public Accountability of Privatized Activation – The Case of Israel

Avishai Benish

Introduction

Accountability and democratic governance have always been central concerns in the study of social policy and administration (e.g. Brodkin 1997; Day and Klein 1987; Handler 1979). However, these issues have moved somewhat to the margins of scholarly interest with the introduction of the new forms of welfare governance over the last two decades. The development of quasi-markets and the management of performance-based contracts have captured most of the attention of activation scholars, while questions of accountability – including the public accountability of private activation contractors – have been usually dealt with indirectly or sporadically. As van Berkel and Borghi note, the publicness of activation and contractors' accountability have rarely been examined as issues in their own right (van Berkel and Borghi 2008: 393–4).

Nonetheless, the transformations in welfare governance raise major issues of accountability (Diller 2000; Donnelly 2011; Mulgan 2006; Reiss 2009; Sol 2003). The new institutional logic of welfare and employment programmes, which often come with stringent and complex eligibility criteria, more discretionary powers to street-level organizations and harsher sanctions, ultimately increases the risks of discretion to the public at large and to individual welfare recipients (Benish 2010; Brodkin 2007; Lens 2005). These concerns become even more prominent as services are increasingly privatized, sometimes relocating powers and discretion to private contractors, who are not subject to the public accountability norms and mechanisms (de Ridder 2010). These changes in welfare governance radically alter the traditional systems of accountability. On the one hand, accountability deficits are created as existing means of holding public agencies to account become less relevant; on

Contracting-out Welfare Services: Comparing National Policy Designs for Unemployment Assistance,
First Edition. Edited by Mark Considine and Siobhan O'Sullivan.
© 2015 John Wiley & Sons, Ltd. Published 2015 by John Wiley & Sons, Ltd.

the other hand, new forms of accountability emerge (Benish and Levi-Faur 2012; Mulgan 2003; Scott 2000).

In order to better understand the accountability implications of the privatized and marketized forms of welfare governance, the study examines the accountability of private activation contractors to the public though the case of activation in Israel. The Israeli case, still understudied in activation scholarship, offers an excellent context for studying transformation in public accountability, as it is an example of a far-reaching privatized and outcome-driven model of welfare governance (Benish 2008; Gal 2005; Maron 2012). As a radical case of privatization, in which significant discretionary powers were devolved to for-profit street-level activation agencies (including the power to sanction participants from receiving income support payments), it may help us to understand and critically evaluate how accountability changes under privatized service delivery systems.

This article proceeds as follows: the second and third sections present the destabilizing effect of privatisation on the traditional concept of public accountability, and develop a modular framework for analyzing accountability in privatised forms of governance. The fourth section discusses the Israeli activation programme, and the fifth elaborates the research methodology. The study's findings on the application of public accountability mechanisms and values to the Israeli activation contractors are presented in the sixth section. The seventh and the concluding sections analyze the reconstruction of accountability in the context of privatized activation and the tensions and instabilities produced by the interactions between privatization, devolution of discretion and accountability.

Public Accountability and Privatization

Traditionally, public and private actors have operated under distinctive regimes of accountability, in line with the long-standing public/private and state/market conceptual distinctions in western democracies (Clarke and Newman 2007).

Accountability in the public sphere is associated with democratic conceptions of citizenship. Public workers are accountable to citizens for their actions through various systems of accountability. These accountability systems make civil servants accountable to ministers and Parliament (political accountability); to their superiors in public bureaucracy (bureaucratic accountability); to administrative tribunals and courts (legal accountability); and to external comptrollers and ombudsmen (administrative accountability).[1] Thus, managers in the public sector operate under tight systems of control. Discretion is traditionally regarded as a problem, especially in welfare bureaucracies (Brodkin 2007), due to concerns over abuse of power and other inappropriate behaviours, such as corruption, nepotism and so on (Bovens 2005). Such concerns express public expectations of due process and fairness in the use of public power and taxpayer resources; they inspire continuing demands for accountability in how government operates.

Therefore, in the public sector, inputs and procedures are closely monitored; and efficiency, though important, is often subordinated to broader democratic concerns, such as due process, fairness, integrity and transparency (de Ridder 2010).

In contrast, accountability in the private sphere is associated with efficient markets and responsiveness to customers' preferences. In a market accountability regime, producers are primarily accountable to their stockholders for maximizing their profits, but they are also 'accountable' (or more precisely, have to be responsive[2]) to consumers for their products' quality and prices through the mechanisms of market competition (Mashaw 2006) and market regulation (Levi-Faur 2011). The producers are dependent on the customers' willingness to buy services at the offered price and on their capacity to remain viable in the market. In the market, the commanding values are efficiency and customer satisfaction. Managers in the private sector operate under a 'tightloose' system of control (Mulgan 2003: 166), whereby outcomes (or profits) are tightly controlled, but wide discretion is given in how to achieve these outcomes.

Privatization of public services destabilizes these traditionally distinctive concepts of accountability (Mashaw 2006: 135). Contractors fulfil public functions, but they are privately owned and they operate in a market-like setting. This public-private mix, which blurs the boundaries between the sectors, has intriguing implications on public accountability. On the one hand, privatization creates significant accountability deficits. Private street-level organizations are usually detached from traditional public accountability systems: they are not subject to the same degree of government control over their day-to-day practices as government departments; legislative committees cannot interrogate them in the same way as they can interrogate public servants; by default, they are out of the reach of the administrative jurisdiction of courts and administrative tribunals; freedom of information legislation normally does not apply to them; and they are beyond the jurisdiction of specialized public accountability agencies, such as government auditors and Ombudsmen (see e.g. Bovens 2005; Bovens *et al.* 2008; Mulgan 2003, 2005; Rosenbloom and Piotrowski 2005). As contracting has quickly moved from functions such as cleaning, gardening and refuse collection to much more complex and politically contested services, these accountability deficits led to increasing public concern over the potential abuse of discretionary powers by a range of non-state bodies which are disengaged from the accountability processes which apply in public organizations (Vincent-Jones 2005).

On the other hand, privatization introduces opportunities for new forms of accountability. Notably, the shift to performance and outcome-based management, embodied in New Public Management (NPM) and privatization, may have significant positive effects on accountability as it makes policy objectives and their achievement (or the failure to achieve) more transparent. Moreover, the use of performance-based management techniques may increase goal alignment between policymakers and street-level organizations. Lastly, the market-like setting may create 'downwards accountability' and empower service users when they have an option to move to another service provider (Scott 2000).

Thus, NPM reforms can be seen as an attempt to reconfigure public sector accountability along business lines (Mulgan 2003). Whereas in the 'old public administration' accountability was mainly input- and process-oriented based on *ex ante* control systems, NPM reforms emphasize accountability for achieved performance, efficiency and responsiveness to customers (Verhoest and Mattei 2010: 167).

However, the question whether these new accountability mechanisms actually counter-balance the accountability deficits created in the new structure remains open. Some argue that in the long run, given a well-functioning market for public services, competition will make most traditional public accountability systems unnecessary (Trebilcock and Iacobucci, as cited in Bovens 2005: 201). Others point out the limits of performance accountability to serve as appropriate accountability mechanisms. Goal alignment in complex services is frustrated due to the limited ability to formulate policy goals with clear and measurable objectives (Brodkin 2011); and new outcome-related-risks, such as 'creaming' and 'parking' arise.

In this context, some public law and administration scholars stress the need to extend traditional public accountability mechanisms and norms to the private actors enrolled in the delivery of public functions (see e.g. Diller 2000; Freeman 2003; Rosenbloom and Piotrowski 2005); and there is some empirical evidence of such extension, including in the context of activation (Benish and Levi-Faur 2012; Mulgan 2005, 2006). However, by and large, current studies find the extent of accountability imposed on contractors falls well short of that still expected from publicly owned agencies; and while public opinion continues to place a high premium on values such as fairness and due process in public agencies, non-government organizations are expected to be held accountable for results and the public is less interested in the means by which these results are achieved (Mulgan 2003: 169).

Capturing Public Accountability in Privatized Forms of Service Delivery

The previous section clarifies that conventional accountability narratives are unable to adequately capture public accountability in governance structures involving diffuse actors and methods (Scott 2006). To examine the public accountability of the private activation contractors, we need to 'unpack' the concepts of public and market accountability, right down to their building blocks (Mashaw 2006), and to reconstruct a modular analytical framework of public accountability which goes beyond the traditional public-private divide. Such a framework should allow us to capture both traditional and new avenues of accountability contributing to the contractors' accountability to citizens, which might otherwise be missed in traditional conceptions of public accountability.

Mulgan's (2003: 22–30) analytical framework of the dimensions of accountability (namely, who is accountable? to whom? for what? how?) is useful for articulating the various combinations of public and market accountability features in mixed models of service delivery. For the current study, the *who* comprise the private activation contractors and their workers. The *to whom* is ultimately the citizens, but as mentioned above, it includes accountability to the interested minister and ministry, and accountability to other public agencies, such as parliamentary committees, courts and administrative tribunals and the state comptroller.

The *for what* dimension is more complicated. Two relevant aspects focus on apparent differences between market and public accountability regimes. One aspect is whether the contractors are held accountable solely for efficiency and customer satisfaction, as in market governance, or whether they are also accountable for such public service values as due process, transparency and integrity (de Ridder 2010). The second and related aspect is whether and to what extent the contractors are called to account for their results, as in market regimes of accountability, or if their means are also scrutinized in terms of inputs and procedures, as traditionally done in public regimes of accountability.

The analysis which follows provides a comprehensive look at private activation agencies' accountability to citizens in these central dimensions of accountability in the context of the Israeli activation programme.

The Case Study: Activation in Israel

Activation in Israel, which is understudied in international activation scholarship, is an interesting case study for questions of public accountability in privatized activation services, largely because of its far-reaching privatization model (Benish 2008; Gal 2005; Maron 2012). The Israeli activation programme was enacted in December 2004 and became operational in August 2005. Driven by enduring dissatisfaction with the Israeli Public Employment Service and inspired by the global trend toward activation, the programme radically transformed welfare policy and governance in Israel. The programme emphasized the reduction of welfare dependency by a strong 'workfirst' approach for quick labour market integration of long-term unemployed people dependent on tax-funded income support benefits. The programme started as a policy experiment for two years in four regions; after some significant policy and administrative reforms, it was extended for an additional period under new contracts. The programme ended in April 2010 when Parliament, due to public criticism, refused to extend it. Recently, however, the newly elected Netanyahu government declared that the programme will be re-enacted.

At an organizational level, the Israeli activation programme – the focus of this study – introduced a strong NPM-driven approach relying on a public-private partnership model between government and private for-profit activation contractors. In the new setting, the state retained purchasing and regulatory functions in a special department at the Ministry of Industry, Trade and Labor ('the department'). The operation of the job centres, including the exercise of the 'employment test' for income support eligibility (previously carried out by the Public Employment Service), was entirely contracted out to four private for-profit firms.

The scope of privatization was considerable as the programme devolved significant discretionary powers to the contractors and their workers. For instance, the contractors' case managers were entrusted with the power to sanction participants who refused to take a job or did not comply with a personal 'employment plan' or other programme requirements. Moreover, the contractors and case managers initially had wide operational discretion in the services they provided. The main steering mechanism was a performance-based payment model, according to which the contractors were paid based on reductions in income support expenditures in their region; an additional bonus was paid for saving money on work support services. The contractors were expected to use innovative and personally tailored methods of activation in order to meet their targets (Maron 2012). However, choice among contractors was not available to the programme participants.

Research Methodology

The study is based on an in-depth analysis of the regulatory documents and other secondary materials on the Israeli activation programme. The regulatory materials include: the activation legislation and its amendments, secondary legislation, programme administrative regulations and manuals, and the contracts between the government and the contractors. The study is also based on an examination of all the protocols of parliamentary committees which discussed the programme, judicial and administrative tribunal decisions, reports of the state comptroller and other audit agencies' evaluations of the programme, and reports by public committees and advocacy groups.

Based on the modular analytical framework of accountability, presented above, these documents were analyzed in order to grasp the following accountability dimensions of the activation contractors:

1. their accountability relations with political, administrative, judicial and other public agencies;
2. the extent to which they are accountable for traditional public service norms; and
3. the extent to which they are held to account for their inputs and procedures rather than for their results.

Analyzing Contractors' Public Accountability

Contractors' accountability to public agencies

Accountability to the Ministry. The most intense accountability relations of the contractors were obviously with the department, which was responsible for selecting the contractors through competitive bidding and for regulating them. As the programme regulator, the department had the power to set standards for service provision through administrative and contractual provisions. Moreover, the terms of the contract enabled the department to request any information relevant to the programme (MITL 2005: §8.3.1), enter and inspect any part of the job centres, and access the contractors' records (MITL 2005: §8.2). The contractors also had various reporting and record keeping obligations (MITL 2005: §4.7.6). Lastly, the contract created an explicit 'forum' for accountability, as it stated that representatives of the contractor must regularly meet the department to review problems, issues, plans and other matters concerning the programme (MITL 2005: §8.6.1).

Although, formally, this accountability structure was almost unchanged, in practice, the accountability relations between the contractors and the ministry changed considerably over time. At first, in the spirit of NPM, the department afforded the contractors considerable discretion in how they carried out their tasks and focused almost entirely on their outcome indicators. However, as elaborated below, public concerns regarding contractors' trustworthiness and the department's close relationship with them led the department – as part of its own obligation to account to the public – to increase its formal control over the contractors though more extensive regulations and tighter enforcement.

Accountability to Parliament. The contractors were not formally obliged to account directly to the Israeli Parliament (the Knesset). As the programme attracted more public attention, however, a considerable number of parliamentary committee sessions were devoted to it, and these sessions became a central channel for complaints and controversies. The analysis of the records of these sessions shows that the contractors' representatives (usually job centre managers) participated in all sessions side by side with the department's staff. The records show that not only was the department called to account, but the contractors' representatives were also asked to account for accusations of disrespectful treatment of clients, unfair sanctioning practices and so on. This, of course, closely resembles how lower street-level public agencies are asked to account to the Parliament; and, indeed, it seems that the Parliament members did not perceive the contractors as positioned out of their reach as a result of their private status.

Thus, in practice, contractors were *indirectly* accountable to Parliament for their actions as part of the department's own accountability to Parliament. However, their accountability fell short of the requirements of public agencies, since they had no *formal obligation* to account to these committees.

Accountability to courts and administrative tribunals. From the start, the contractors were directly subject to a judicial review system which is similar to the one applied to public agencies. The enabling law gave each participant the right to appeal any decision of the contractors' case managers, first to an administrative tribunal and then to labour courts (in the Israeli system, these courts hear welfare appeals). Moreover, the contract established that contractors could be financially sanctioned if a high number of appeals was found justified. Lastly, in an important decision of an appeal brought forward by an advocacy group, the National Labour Court held that:

> Despite the 'privateness' of the contractors, due to the fact that they are fulfilling a public function according to law, their workers are also – and maybe especially – subject to all the rules of public and administrative law ... they are obligated to act only in the boundaries of the powers vested to them by law, according to relevant considerations; they have to act according to standards of equality, fairness, reasonableness and pro-portionality, transparency, and all the other standards that apply to government agencies. (*Lugasy v. The Ministry of Industry, Trade and Labour*, 30 May 2007, National Labour Court)

Thus, the contractors were subject to significant legal accountability constraints, very similar to these imposed on public agencies; and these legal mechanisms were strengthened with the extension of participants' rights to publicly funded lawyers, as discussed below.

Accountability to the state comptroller and to public committees.   The enabling law subjected the contractors to audits by the state comptroller as if they were public agencies. As audited agencies, the contractors had to submit an annual report to the comptroller on their income and expenditure; they were also obligated to submit any document required in the audit process. Following complaints about inappropriate treatment by the contractors, a parliamentary committee requested that the comptroller conduct a comprehensive audit of the programme implementation a year after it started. The audit included the department and the contractors, as well as other relevant government departments.

In addition, several *ad hoc* public committees were appointed during the programme implementation. The most significant of which was the Ye'ari committee (after the name of its chair), a special committee of the Israel Academy of Science and Humanities. The Ye'ari committee was appointed by the government shortly after the programme started and was composed of academics and government officials. It was asked to evaluate the programme implementation and provide the minister advice on its operation. Formally an advisory committee, it actually served as a central forum for public debate of the programme, and although they were not formally obligated to do so, the contractors appeared before the committee and testified. Eventually, the committee not only served as an accountability forum, but its report induced the department to strengthen its control over the contractors to safeguard participants' individual rights and the larger public interest (Ye'ari committee 2007).

Accountability for public service values

It is hard to imagine a more explicit and comprehensive application of public service values to the contractors than the National Labour Court's decision cited above, whereby the contractors were obligated to follow administrative law norms as they apply to public agencies. Yet a careful and detailed examination reveals a more complicated picture. While some norms were applied to the contractors as if they were public agencies, and even beyond, others were applied partly and indirectly.

Transparency. When advocacy groups applied for copies of the tender and contracts documents, the department was initially reluctant to disclose them, partly because the contractors argued they were commercially confidential. After more than six months of discussions, the government disclosed the documents but omitted – as 'commercial secrets' – several parts, including information about the contractors' shareholders, the bids, and the contractors' philosophy and strategies. When the programme was extended for an additional period, the second contract was uploaded to the department's website, again with some parts omitted, and the department started to use its website also to publish information on contractors' performance and summaries of inspections. In other words, while the transparency of the activation contractors increased over time, it still fell short of the transparency requirements of public agencies. At the level of the individual, the programme participants had a right to access any document in their personal records held by the contractor, except for internal consultations (MITL 2009: 142); this is very similar to the obligations of public agencies under the Israeli freedom of information legislation.

Integrity. The enabling law applied penal provisions to the contractors' workers, such as prohibition of bribery and other civil service laws forbidding conflicts of interest; these are usually applicable only to public servants.

Due process. As mentioned, from the initiation of the programme, the contractors were subject to due process constraints and were required to account to administrative tribunals and courts on the legal merits of their decision-making. The application of this norm was intensified, given increasing public concern over the fairness of the contractors to programme participants. Concerns were enumerated by advocacy groups in the media, in parliamentary sessions and in hearings of the public committees. Eventually, the state comptroller and the Ye'ari committee reports pinpointed the need to secure the rights of the programme participants; they recommended strengthening due process requirements on case managers' decisions and making public legal representation available to the participants at the administrative tribunal level (The State Comptroller 2007: 44; Ye'ari committee 2007: 147). These recommendations were adopted by the department and the

Ministry of Justice, leading to a standard of due process which exceeds that of public employment agencies, where no public legal aid is available in administrative tribunals.

Accountability for results or for inputs and procedures?

As mentioned, at first the department almost did not use its formal authority over the contractors. The department focused almost entirely on outcome-oriented indicators while leaving wide discretion for the contractors to self-regulate almost all aspects regarding how to achieve them. The programme started with no governmental guidelines on operation, and contractors were expected to develop their own manuals. Occasionally, the department issued directions and recommendations. Initially, many of these regulations were suggestive, articulated as soft-law and 'best practice' rather than mandatory rules.[3]

However, over time the department increased its rule-based control of the contractors. The most striking fact is that on January 2009, it published a comprehensive programme manual with about 170 pages of detailed and mostly mandatory regulations. A review of this manual reveals a consistent trend towards structuring and narrowing the contractors' discretion in benefit termination, support services allocation and many other detailed day-to-day aspects of the job centres' operation. This emphasis on *how* things are done was one of the main responses of the department to public concerns over the fairness of the contractors' decision making processes and their trustworthiness. A central concern repeatedly mentioned in parliamentary and other public discussions was that contractors abuse their wide discretion to seek profits while undermining public interests and values. Critics framed this problem as a *structural conflict of interest* between the contractors' commitment to the public and their commitment to their shareholders. This concern was intensified by the profit maximizing nature of all contractors in the case studied and by the incentives created by the payment model to cut welfare rolls and save on work support services. Although the responsibility of designing such incentives was the department's, it undermined the legitimacy of contractors' actions and fuelled the demand to subject them to greater control and scrutiny to make sure that discretion is used for proper public purposes. Critics also argued that the close partnership of the department and the contractors rendered the former prone to 'regulatory capture' and undermined its capacity to maintain a regulatory role.

These criticisms trickled into the Ye'ari committee report (2007: 146) calling for greater oversight of contractors and for relaxing the contractors' economic incentives in order to reduce the risk that they might achieve the results in unethical ways (Ye'ari committee 2007: 93). And, indeed, as a response, the department increased its regulation and monitoring of the contractors. In addition, the payment structure was revised in the second contract to focus on placements and retention, and the bonus for saving money in work support services was revoked.

Accountability Reconstructed: The Public Accountability of Private Activation

The analysis of activation in Israel shows that public accountability was sustained not only by holding the minister and the government publicly accountable, but also by applying significant public accountability requirements to the private activation contractors. Contractors' accountability was institutionalized through both public and market accountability mechanisms, creating what can be described as a hybrid accountability model, which leaps over the traditional distinctions between public and private accountability. This strengthens the empirical evidence of the convergence of accountability regimes in privatized activation programmes, as also found in Australia (Mulgan 2005, 2006) and the state of Wisconsin (Benish 2010; Benish and Levi-Faur 2012).

At the relational level of accountability, the programme regulations spanned a network of accountability relations between the private agencies and public bodies. The contractors were directly accountable to the ministry, the state comptroller, and administrative tribunals and courts; they were also called to account, albeit informally, to parliamentary committees and other *ad hoc* public committees. Such accountability relations go beyond 'ordinary' regulatory relations between public regulators and market players, and they strongly resemble the accountability relations which traditionally apply to public agencies.

At the level of the content of accountability, the National Labour Court's decision conveys a clear expectation that contractors should act according to democratic values (although in practice some public service norms, such as transparency, were applied to the contractors to a lesser extent). Moreover, contrary to the assumption that market-like performance-based mechanisms would serve as alternative accountability mechanisms, in practice, there was a strong and consistent trend towards regulating the contractors' activities and proceduralizing their decision-making, changing priorities to accountability for inputs and procedures. Outcome-based payments even *increased* accountability concerns since they were perceived as potentially encouraging discretionary practices that put the rights of welfare recipients at risk.

Thus, paradoxically, the efforts to focus on results ultimately led to a need for the kind of process orientation which the policymakers were originally trying to avoid. Since performance-based steering mechanisms are limited in their ability to control discretion in complex and hard-to-define tasks, and since the performance indicators themselves might sometimes create perverse incentives for the contractors (Benish 2010), the need to use process-based control mechanisms becomes inevitable, especially in the absence of choice among providers. This strengthens Sharon Wright's observation that these seemingly contradictory steering logics are sometimes actually mutually reinforcing (Wright 2011: 93). It also reminds us that in many public services, 'process is the product' (Mashaw 1996: 412).

161

Moreover, it is interesting to note that swings towards greater rule-based central control is also documented in activation programmes in other countries, such as Australia (Considine *et al.* 2011; Mulgan 2005), the UK (Wright 2011) and the Netherlands (Sol 2010). This might indicate that the apparently inexorable swing to central control is embedded in the *nature* of activation itself. It seems that various public concerns about activation policy, mainly the vulnerability of the 'customers', their limited ability to assert their rights, and their dependency on the activation agencies for a minimum income essential for satisfying the most basic necessities of life have led to public demand for greater accountability of the actors implementing this policy.

Therefore, accountability was reconstructed, or 're-assembled', on new, more functional, lines. This suggests that public expectations do not arrange themselves only according to the formal status of the actors but according to the essence of their powers. The case indicates that when sensitive discretionary powers are involved, especially when choice among providers is not available,[4] values such as fairness and due process and the means by which results are achieved carry considerable weight, even when non-government organizations are concerned. Decades of public sector welfare delivery, it seems, have created certain public expectations of how discretionary powers should be operated and how they should be accounted for, and these expectations remain when the functions are privatized.

However, while the hybrid accountability model described above clearly extends the reach of public accountability, it is also fraught with tensions and contradictions. Most apparent is the tension between the contractors' increased accountability requirements and the highly discretionary and decentralized nature of activation, in which flexibility, personalized care and innovative labour integration practices are key principles (see e.g. van Berkel *et al.* 2011; Considine 2001; Mosley and Sol 2005). Strong accountability requirements might lead to rigidity and undermine the programmatic (as well as the economic) rationale that led to contracting out in the first place. This tension between accountability and flexibility is well known in public administration (Behn 2001; Sol 2003), but it seems that the challenge of balancing them becomes more complicated in privatized activation where increasing contractors' discretion (to achieve personalized service and make efficiency gains) and controlling their discretion (in the name of accountability and fairness) are both strongly advocated. This resembles pushing the accelerator and the brake pedals simultaneously; it may inspire impressive steering performance, but it may also lead to instabilities and burnouts. The case studied suggests that sometimes rather than adding layers of accountability to counter-balance growing accountability concerns, the more sensible solution may be to reduce the accountability deficits created by privatization in the first place. In this vein, for instance, the Ye'ari committee recommended limiting the sort of discretionary powers which are devolved to the activation contractors (Ye'ari committee 2007: 104), designing performance incentives more cautiously (Ye'ari committee 2007: 88, 100), and relying more on non-profits (Ye'ari committee 2007: 82).

Moreover, the dual normative framework applied to the contractors might be hard to reconcile, given the different logics of the public and the private spheres (Clarke and Newman 2007; de Ridder 2010). This is reflected, for instance, in the fact that the profit motive of the contractors, which is legitimate and even desirable in market settings, was often framed as a conflict of interest problem undermining the legitimacy of contractors' decision making. Similarly, despite the sweeping declaration of the Israeli National Labour Court, in practice, the public norm of transparency was eroded in the name of 'commercial secrets'.

In addition, on the practical level, it remains unclear whether private activation agencies truly internalized public service values. Some scholars doubt whether 'public service values' were ever a reality, even in the public sector. But it seems that the commitments of for-profit firms to their stockholders and their bottom-line culture are intensifying concerns about ritual compliance (Braithwaite *et al.* 2007; see also Dias and Maynard-Moody 2007). This is especially relevant in the context of welfare, where street-level organizations can quite easily use informal practices to control the ability of participants to assert their rights (Brodkin 2011: 69; Lens 2005).

Conclusions

The study discusses the complicated implications of the new forms of welfare governance for accountability, especially with the trend towards privatization. In the case of Israel, activation contractors' accountability became a central issue in public debates of the programme. Eventually, despite their 'privateness', significant public accountability mechanisms were applied to the activation contractors, thereby extending the traditional concept of public accountability. This extension of public accountability requirements to the private contractors evolved due to the limited capacity of result-based accountability to legitimize contractors' discretion in such a complex and politically contested programme. Not only were performance-based accountability measures perceived insufficient to replace traditional accountability mechanisms, but privatization and the performance-based payment model also created new accountability concerns (i.e. potential conflicts between contractors' commitment to the public and to their owners) and intensified old ones (i.e. the tension between efficacy and fairness).

Subjecting the contractors to accountability requirements that resemble public agencies' accountability commitments mitigates some of these concerns but, at the same time, it contradicts the striving for flexibility embedded in activation policy. These contradictory dynamics and the complex interaction between privatization, discretion and accountability make the task of designing a balanced accountability regime for privatized activation extremely difficult.

The study stresses the need for research of activation accountability regimes and their dynamics in additional activation programmes with

163

different public-private mixes. This may further our understanding of the broader implications of activation reforms and the complex public expectations in which they operate. Street-level research of accountability is of particular importance, as one of the most intriguing questions in cases of convergence of public and private accountability is whether contractors, especially for-profits, truly internalize public service norms, given their sometimes conflicting ethos and interests.

Acknowledgements

The research was supported by a grant from The Israel Foundations Trustees (Research Grant #19 for the years 2011–13). I am grateful to Merav Zohari and Efrat Rotem, who served as research assistants. I also wish to thank the editors of this issue and to the anonymous reviewers for their tremendously helpful comments.

Notes

1. Accountability scholars suggest different typologies to capture the various types of accountability in public administrations (see e.g. Bovens 2005; Mulgan 2003: 30–5; Verhoest and Mattei 2010). The typology presented here for public accountability goes beyond the core sense of public accountability as political accountability, but for simplification it does not include managerial and market accountability systems which were adopted as part of NPM reforms within public administrations. Moreover, professional accountability, which is a central accountability mechanism in some areas of public administration, was not included in the analysis due to space limitations. In any event, it was not central in employment services in Israel even before privatization.
2. The use of the concept of accountability to describe providers' responsiveness to customers is a matter of dispute. As Mulgan notes: '[i]n the private commercial sector, accountability applies more to owners and shareholders, who can call the company's managers to account for the company's performance, than to customers whose main right is to exit by refusing to purchase' (Mulgan 2003: 21).
3. The most evident exceptions were strict regulations as to the minimum hours that the participants must be present at the centres (Maron 2012).
4. Choice for participants was never seriously considered in the Israeli programme. The absence of choice among providers seems not to be coincidental in the context of welfare. Although there are exceptions, such as in Australia and the Netherlands, it seems that in general policymakers are reluctant to offer choice to welfare receivers, thinking that benefit recipients will 'use "choice" to work against their responsibilities' (Elliott *et al.* 2005: 51).

References

Behn, R. D. (2001), *Rethinking Democratic Accountability*, Washington, DC: Brookings Institution Press.

Benish, A. (2008), Contracting out from public law perspective: Privatized welfare-to-work programs and the limits of oversight, *Hebrew University Law Review (Mishpatim)*, 38: 283–349 (Hebrew).

Benish, A. (2010), Re-bureaucratizing welfare administration, *Social Service Review*, 84, 1: 77–101.

Benish, A. and Levi-Faur, D. (2012), New forms of administrative law in the age of third-party government, *Public Administration*, 90, 4: 886–900.

Bovens, M. (2005), Public accountability. In E. Ferlie, L. E. Lynn Jr. and C. Pollitt (eds), *The Oxford Handbook of Public Management*, Oxford: Oxford University Press, pp. 182–208.

Bovens, M., Schillemans, T. and Hart, P. T. (2008), Does public accountability work? An assessment tool, *Public Administration*, 86, 1: 225–42.

Braithwaite, J., Makkai, T. and Braithwaite, V. A. (2007), *Regulating Aged Care: Ritualism and the New Pyramid*, Cheltenham: Edward Elgar Publishing.

Brodkin, E. Z. (1997), Inside the welfare contract: Discretion and accountability in state welfare administration, *Social Service Review*, 71, 1: 1–33.

Brodkin, E. Z. (2007), Bureaucracy redux: Management reformism and the welfare state, *Journal of Public Administration Research and Theory*, 17, 1: 1–17.

Brodkin, E. Z. (2011), Policy work: Street-level organizations under new managerialism, *Journal of Public Administration Research and Theory*, 21, 2: 253–77.

Clarke, J. and Newman, J. (2007), *Creating Citizen-Consumers Changing Publics & Changing Public Services*, London and Thousand Oaks, CA: Sage.

Considine, M. (2001), *Enterprising States: The Public Management of Welfare-To-Work*, Cambridge: Cambridge University Press.

Considine, M., Lewis, J. M. and O'Sullivan, S. (2011), Quasi-markets and service delivery flexibility following a decade of employment assistance reform in Australia, *Journal of Social Policy*, 40, 4: 811–33.

Day, P. and Klein, R. (1987), *Accountabilities: Five Public Services*, USA: Taylor & Francis.

de Ridder, K. (2010), Safeguarding public values in social security: A public administration perspective. In G. Vonk and A. Tollenaar (eds), *Social Security as a Public Interest: A Multidisciplinary Inquiry into the Foundations of the Regulatory Welfare State*, Antwerp: Intersentia.

Dias, J. J. and Maynard-Moody, S. (2007), For-profit welfare: contracts, conflicts, and the performance paradox, *Journal of Public Administration Research and Theory*, 17, 2: 189–322.

Diller, M. (2000), The revolution in welfare administration: Rules, discretion, and entrepreneurial government, *New York University Law Review*, 75, 5: 1121–220.

Donnelly, C. (2011), Privatization and welfare: A comparative perspective, *Law & Ethics of Human Rights*, 5, 2: 219–423.

Elliott, C., Morrell, H. and Branosky, N. (2005), *The Use of Contestability and Flexibility in The Delivery of Welfare Services in Australia and the Netherlands*, Leeds: Corporate Document Services.

Freeman, J. (2003), Extending public law norms through privatization, *Harvard Law Review*, 116, 5: 1285–352.

Gal, J. (2005), From welfare without work to work with welfare, *Social Security*, 69: 5–10 (Hebrew).

Handler, J. F. (1979), *Protecting the Social Service Client: Legal and Structural Controls on Official Discretion*, New York, NY: Academic Press.

Lens, V. (2005), Bureaucratic disentitlement after welfare reform: Are fair hearing the cure? *Georgetown Journal on Poverty Law and Policy*, 12: 13–54.

Levi-Faur, D. (2011), *Handbook on the Politics of Regulation*, Cheltenham: Edward Elgar Publishing.

Maron, A. (2012), Activation via intensive intimacies in the Israeli welfare-to-work program: Applying a constructivist approach to the governance of institutions and individuals, *Administration & Society*, doi: 10.1177/0095399712451896.

Mashaw, J. (2006), Accountability and institutional design: Some thoughts on the grammar of governance. In M. W. Dowdle (ed.), *Public Accountability, Designs, Dilemmas and Experiences*, Cambridge: Cambridge University Press, pp. 115–56.

Mashaw, J. L. (1996), Reinventing government and regulatory reform: Studies in the neglect and abuse of administrative law, *U. Pitt. L. Rev.*, 57: 405–41.

Ministry of Industry, Trade and Labour (MITL) (2005), *Tender for the Participation in the Welfare-to-Work Program – Restated Program Contract*, Jerusalem: MITL.

Ministry of Industry, Trade and Labour (MITL) (2009), Activation Manual – Release 01, Jerusalem: MITL.

Mosley, H. and Sol, E. (2005), Contractualism in employment services: A socio-economic perspective. In H. Sol and M. Westerveld (eds), *Contractualism in Employment Services: A New Form of Welfare State Governance*, The Hague: Kluwer Law International and Aspen Publishers, pp. 1–20.

Mulgan, R. (2003), *Holding Power to Account: Accountability in Modern Democracies*, New York, NY: Palgrave Macmillan. Mulgan, R. (2005), Outsourcing and public service values: The Australian experience, *International Review of Administrative Sciences*, 71, 1: 55.

Mulgan, R. (2006), Government accountability for outsourced services, *Australian Journal of Public Administration*, 65, 2: 48.

Reiss, D. R. (2009), Agency accountability strategies after liberalization: universal service in the United Kingdom, France, and Sweden, *Law & Policy*, 31, 1: 111–41.

Rosenbloom, D. H. and Piotrowski, S. J. (2005), Outsourcing the constitution and administrative law norms, *American Review of Public Administration*, 35, 2: 103–21.

Scott, C. (2000), Accountability in the regulatory state, *Journal of Law and Society*, 27, 1: 38–60.

Scott, C. (2006), Spontaneous accountability. In M. W. Dowdle (ed.), *Public Accountability, Designs, Dilemmas and Experiences*, Cambridge: Cambridge University Press, pp. 174–91.

Sol, E. (2003), The Netherlands: Tackling the trade-off between efficiency and accountability. In *Managing Decentralisation: A New Role for Labour Market Policy*, Paris: Organisation for Economic Co-operation and Development, pp. 203–17.

Sol, E. (2010), Public-private partnerships for the unemployed, *European Journal of Social Security*, 12, 1: 41–59.

The State Comptroller (2007), *Report on Certain Aspects of the 'Wisconsin Plan'*, Jerusalem (Hebrew).

van Berkel, R. and Borghi, V. (2008), Review article: The governance of activation, *Social Policy and Society*, 7, 3: 393–402.

van Berkel, R., de Graaf, W. and Sirovátka, T. (eds) (2011), *The Governance of Active Welfare States in Europe*, Basingstoke: Palgrave Macmillan.

Verhoest, K. and Mattei, P. (2010), Welfare governance reforms and effects in the post-golden age, *Public Management Review*, 12, 2: 163–71.

Vincent-Jones, P. (2005), Citizen redress in public contracting for human services, *Modern Law Review*, 68, 6: 887–924.

Wright, S. (2011), Steering with sticks, rowing for rewards: The new governance of activation in the UK. In R. van Berkel, W. de Graaf and T. Sirovátka (eds), *The Governance of Active Welfare States in Europe*, Basingstoke: Palgrave Macmillan, pp. 85–109.

Ye'ari committee (2007), *Recommendations Regarding the Future of Israel's Welfare to Work Program*, Jerusalem (Hebrew).

INDEX

Page numbers in *italics* refer to figures, those in **bold** refer to tables.

Contracting-out Welfare Services: Comparing National Policy Designs for Unemployment Assistance,
First Edition. Edited by Mark Considine and Siobhan O'Sullivan.
© 2015 John Wiley & Sons, Ltd. Published 2015 by John Wiley & Sons, Ltd.